THE OTHER SIDE OF THE FENCE

The Other Side of the Fence

AMERICAN MIGRANTS IN MEXICO

Sheila Croucher

UNIVERSITY OF TEXAS PRESS
Austin

Requests for permission to reproduce material from this work
should be sent to:
    Permissions
    University of Texas Press
    P.O. Box 7819
    Austin, TX 78713-7819
    www.utexas.edu/utpress/about/bpermission.html

♾ The paper used in this book meets the minimum requirements
of ANSI/NISO Z39.48-1992 (R1997) (Permanence of Paper).

LIBRARY OF CONGRESS CATALOGING-IN-PUBLICATION DATA
Croucher, Sheila L.
The other side of the fence : American migrants in Mexico / Sheila
Croucher. — 1st ed.
        p.   cm.
Includes bibliographical references and index.
ISBN 978-0-292-71975-0 (cloth : alk. paper)
1. Americans—Mexico—Case studies. 2. Immigrants—Mexico—
Case studies. 3. Mexico—Emigration and immigration—Case
studies. 4. United States—Emigration and immigration—Case
studies. 5. Transnationalism—Case studies. I. Title.
F1392.A5C76 2009
304.8′72073—dc22

                                            2008051317

CONTENTS

PREFACE

I made my first trip to Guanajuato, the capital city of the state of Guanajuato, Mexico, in the summer of 2005. I was working with the Wilks Leadership Institute at Miami University to enhance student civic engagement, and one of our areas of focus was the growing Latino community in southwest Ohio. We had learned that a large proportion of our new Latino neighbors were Mexicans from the state of Guanajuato. I decided to take a brief trip to Guanajuato to explore the possibility of introducing our students to both sides of the migration chain. That trip opened my eyes to a dimension of North American migration that I never anticipated.

One Saturday in June, while in the city of Guanajuato, I signed up for a day trip to a nearby town called San Miguel de Allende, described as a "picturesque colonial gem." A bus would take us on the hour-and-a-half trip and leave us for the day to explore the town. It is impossible to learn much about a town in six hours, but more than being impressed by San Miguel's architecture I became intrigued by its inhabitants. Not in the mood for shopping (a primary activity of visitors to the town), I decided to purchase a newspaper and position myself on a shaded bench in what appeared to be the town's central garden plaza. Of the four newspapers for sale by a Mexican vendor in this geographically remote town, one was in English. As I lounged on the bench I was also struck by the familiar sound of English coming from various directions: an argument about President Bush and Iraq coming from my left, a gleeful celebration (in distinctly Texan accents) of shopping successes coming from the right.

I assumed that my tour bus must have arrived in San Miguel at the same time as several other buses; and eventually I asked an English-speaking and seemingly American woman and her son seated next to me, "Where are you all from?" "We live here," she replied. They were horse ranchers, originally from Texas, and for nine years had been living just outside of town.

I regaled them with questions about why they had decided to move, what it was like living in Mexico, whether they had health insurance, whether they were able to drink the water, and what the Mexicans think of these American residents. Her response to this last question planted in my mind the seed that eventually germinated into this book. She said: "They love us here!"

The next summer I returned to San Miguel with the explicit purpose of studying the town's sizable and, I had learned, rapidly growing American population. I used that information to apply for a Ford Foundation-funded fellowship with the Center for Inter-American Studies and Programs (CEPI) at the Instituto Tecnológico Autónomo de Mexico (ITAM) in Mexico City. That financial support allowed me to spend six more months in Mexico in 2007, including in the Lake Chapala area — another American enclave in the state of Jalisco.

So many people, Americans and Mexicans, were incredibly warm to me and generous with their time, their homes, and their thoughts. Confidentiality precludes my mentioning anyone by name, but I am grateful to all of you and inspired by many of you. I hope that none of you feels that I have done any injustice to you, your communities, or your fascinating life stories in my attempt to offer an academic analysis of the transnational lives you live.

In addition to being indebted to all the kind people I met who are living in Ajijic, San Miguel, and Mexico City, I am grateful to CEPI for research funding, to Andrea Calderon for research assistance, and to my fellow CEPI fellows for their support and friendship: Leticia Arroyo Abad, Alejandra Armesto, and Katherine Reilly. Charles Wood at the University of Florida, and Peggy Shaffer, Steven Delue, Adeed Dawisha, and Jeanne Hey at Miami University, offered me valuable assistance and guidance. Dean Karen Schilling of Miami University's College of Arts and Sciences was enthusiastic in providing the additional financial support I needed to accept the fellowship. Mary Cayton and Terry Perlin supplied helpful comments on an early essay version of this research published in *Dissent* (Croucher 2007). Theresa May at the University of Texas Press skillfully shepherded the manuscript through the publication process.

The interest that various family members and friends took in this project also provided a needed source of encouragement. My mother, Mary Croucher, asked thoughtful questions. Elizabeth Silas's analytical and editing skills rank second only to her inspiring yoga instruction; and I am grateful to Martha Schoolman for calling my attention to Linda Kerber's discussion of "state*full*ness" and its relevance to the argument I was developing in this book. Finally, I am indebted, beyond words, to Carolyn Haynes, who tirelessly assists and supports me whatever the endeavor; and Frida, who although not usually helpful, is always a joyful reminder of the softer things in life.

It is my sincere hope that this project might in some small way help all of us, Americans and Mexicans, politicians, citizens, dual citizens, and non-citizens, immigrants and "natives," tourists and refugees, to recognize that whatever memberships we hold, or identities we claim and have claimed for us, we share a common humanity and will benefit from respecting each other accordingly.

THE OTHER SIDE OF THE FENCE

Introduction REVERSING THE LENS

Had people with such exotic customs, such irrational beliefs, such complex social organizations, and such tremendous power, been of any other skin colour they would have been studied in great depth and detail. Unfortunately, however, most of the world's anthropologists are white, and it is a rare anthropologist indeed who studies somebody of his own colour.
— RON CROCOMBE, LETTER TO EDITOR OF
THE *AUSTRALIAN AND NEW ZEALAND JOURNAL OF SOCIOLOGY*

Not only at the borders, but also in cities and towns throughout this North American country's heartland, immigrants are arriving in increasing numbers. Few speak the language of their adopted land, and most reside and socialize within an isolated cultural enclave. They continue to practice their own cultural traditions and celebrate their national holidays. The grocery stores are stocked with locally unfamiliar products that hail from the immigrants' homeland. These settlers maintain close political, economic, and social ties with their country of origin, and establish local organizations designed to promote its values. They vote in foreign elections, raise money for candidates running for office abroad, and meet with political party representatives from their country of origin while residing in the new land. Meanwhile, these immigrants also make political demands on the host country where they reside, although few choose to pursue formal citizenship there. Some live and work in the new country without proper documentation (read: "illegally"), and have even been involved in the unauthorized transport of drugs across state borders. Their presence is so pervasive that the local governments of the receiving state have been forced to adapt in many ways, providing additional services, linguistic and otherwise, to address the needs of the growing foreign population.

The preceding portrayal is now a familiar one in the United States, and the scenario it describes is a source of significant tension. Citizen groups throughout the United States have mobilized to protest the presence of Mexican immigrants in their cities. Cadres of minutemen militia are patrolling the southern U.S. border. Towns in the state of Georgia have passed regulations prohibiting taco stands and soccer. In 2006, Pahrump, Nevada, outlawed flying a foreign flag unless it is flown alongside and below the American flag. Numerous cities and states throughout the United States have declared English the official language, and the U.S. Congress is considering federal legislation that does the same (Jonsson 2006). And on October 26, 2006, President Bush signed into law a bill to construct seven hundred miles of fencing along the southern border with Mexico. Meanwhile, politicians and media pundits in the United States build lucrative careers railing against the economic, political, and cultural dangers associated with immigration—particularly that from Mexico. Besides being tarnished with the charge that "they" take "our" jobs and lower "our" wages, immigrants are also accused of not respecting U.S. culture and clinging too tightly to their own (Chacón and Davis 2006). Yet, the immigrants described in the opening paragraph and throughout this book are not Mexicans living in the United States; they are U.S. citizens living in Mexico.

The project presented here joins countless others in investigating why migrants move, how they adapt to life in a new land, the degree to which they stay connected to their homeland, and the implications for the sending state, the receiving state, the migrants, and the societies that host them. The familiar focus on migration northward, however, is reversed. Americans, as will become clear in the pages that follow, are moving to Mexico in growing numbers. They cross the same geographic border as their Mexican counterparts, but are headed in the opposite direction and typically with access to a more advantageous array of economic, political, and cultural resources. They remain closely attached to and promote the values of the United States through organizations that include the Democrats and Republicans Abroad, the American Legion, and the Sons and Daughters of the American Revolution. These migrants use Voice Over Internet Phones (voip), e-mail, satellite television, and satellite radio to stay connected with loved ones (and financial advisors) in the United States. They establish social organizations to build community with other Americans in Mexico and to ease the transition for new arrivals. Surprisingly few of these Americans speak Spanish, including some who have lived in Mexico for a decade or more; and most rely heavily on the willingness of their servants, waitstaff, and other Mexican professionals to adjust accordingly. Meanwhile, and despite Mexico's constitutional prohibitions against the involvement of foreigners in the country's politics, Americans living in Mexico lobby local governments on a range of issues including development, security, sanitation, and historical preservation.

Relative to the volumes of scholarship that focus on immigrants heading north across the U.S./Mexico border, the scholarly or political attention in the United States or in Mexico to the flow of U.S. citizens moving south to Mexico is scant. The size of this human movement southward is smaller than the reverse flow, but still significant (and growing) in number and in political and theoretical relevance for Mexico, the United States, and academics focusing on globalization, transnational migration, and changing forms of cultural and political belonging. This book will reverse the lens of so much contemporary scholarship to focus on the under-studied case of American migrants in Mexico.

Using the term "American" as an exclusive referent to people from the United States is admittedly problematic because inhabitants of North, Central, and South America are all technically Americans. Unfortunately, the English language does not contain an appropriate term for people from the United States that functions in the way "Colombian," "Mexican," or "Nicaraguan" does to identify individuals who hail from those countries. Due to the lack of a preferable alternative, and the fact that "American" is so widely used as a referent for individuals from the United States, I will use it that way here as well. The chapters that follow explore which factors pull Americans to Mexico and push them from the United States; how technology is reconfiguring the relevance of territory for Americans in Mexico who live their lives across international borders; the ways in which American migrants practice a form of extraterritorial citizenship in a country where they retain political membership, but do not reside, and in a country where they reside, but do not have formal citizenship; and how migrants of relative privilege negotiate belonging in a global, post-modern world.

The aims of this book are threefold: empirical documentation, conceptual application and refinement, and political enlightenment. The empirical contribution lies in focusing on a relatively invisible migration flow from an advanced industrialized country best known for importing immigrants to a less developed country better known for exporting them. Drawing on intensive fieldwork, the chapters that follow detail the intriguing story of Americans who leave the United States to settle in Mexico, and offer vivid portrayals of life in two Mexican towns heavily populated by Americans: San Miguel de Allende in the state of Guanajuato and the Lake Chapala re-

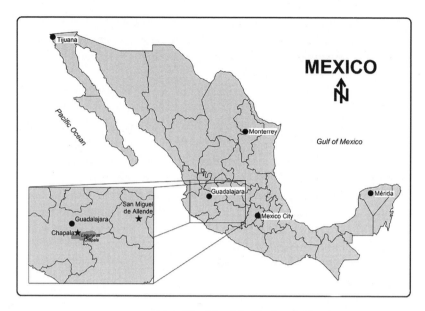

MAP INTRODUCTION.1   *Map of San Miguel de Allende and Chapala,*
Mexico. Courtesy of Dr. Claire Gomersall.

gion in the state of Jalisco—specifically the small village of Ajijic. As with
most case studies of migrant streams, this discussion will include a focus on
what motivates these migrants to move and how they live their daily lives
across borders.

In recent decades, scholars of migration have updated conventional conceptual and theoretical frameworks to account for the growing tendency
of migrants to remain closely connected to their homelands while establishing themselves in the country of settlement. The growing frequency
and intensity of immigrant transnational practices and transnational social fields have challenged the model of immigration as an abrupt rupture
with the past. The bulk of the burgeoning scholarship on immigrant transnationalism has been applied to migrants who leave a less developed country for one that is more so; and theorizing on the topic of transnationalism
has been premised almost entirely on assumptions of power imbalances between politically and economically weaker sending countries and more ad-
vantaged receiving ones, and between marginalized immigrants and their
more well-off host society. This analysis of U.S. migration to Mexico bor-
rows heavily from that scholarship, but applies it to a case study of migrants
of privilege. The project is interested in how the academic literature on
immigration, transnationalism, globalization, and the politics of identity

and belonging applies to the case of Americans in Mexico, but also how this somewhat peculiar case may call for refinements in existing theory. This effort at conceptual application and refinement begs the question of terminology. Should Americans living in Mexico be characterized as "immigrants," or something different: "expatriates," a "diaspora," "settlers," "sojourners," "legal or illegal aliens," "colonists"? As discussed below, the terms are not neutral. They are not neutral in what they convey politically and culturally, nor in the related bodies of scholarship they call forth.

Finally, this project is also not politically neutral. The patterns and practices described in this book have significant political and policy implications for both Mexico and the United States. Moreover, given the maelstrom swirling around Mexican migration to the United States, this book is motivated by the hope that "reversing the lens" on migration will open the eyes of some in the United States (politicians, policy makers, pundits, and disgruntled citizens) to the countless and sometimes invisible forms of border crossing that globalization has inspired, or at the very least, facilitated. U.S. citizens, in other words, are migrants too.

THE LENS

If all identifying characteristics were eliminated from the opening paragraph of this introduction, the portrayal would read like so many others that fill the pages of books, journal articles, and conference reports on transnationalism and migration. We are living in a world in motion. In 2005, more than 190 million people lived outside of their country of birth, up more than 100 million from three decades prior (United Nations Population Division 2005). If this group of migrants comprised their own country, it would constitute the fifth most populous in the world (International Organization for Migration 2007). Globalization has played a powerful role in propelling this intensified human movement. The faster and freer flow of goods, services, and capital, and the social disruptions that result, have compelled, sometimes forced, people to leave their country of birth in search of enhanced security and stability. Sophisticated advances in communications and transportation technology have facilitated that movement, as well as the maintenance of ties to the homeland. Worldwide migration is not, however, merely a consequence of global interconnectedness, but also a powerful force driving it as migrants carry with them ideas; languages; and cultural beliefs and practices, values, and preferences, and adopt and develop new and different ones in the act of migration. All of this movement and transformation have captured tremendous political and scholarly attention. Many hundreds of books have been written on the topics of globalization and migration and identity, and thousands of such articles have been published in scholarly journals. Countless governmental commissions have been convened nationally, regionally, and internationally to address the topic of migration, and numerous think tanks have formed to compile data and analyze the trends.[1]

Why, then, has the case of U.S. citizens migrating to Mexico not captured the attention of scholars or policy makers the way so many other cases (Colombians, Dominicans, El Salvadorans, Haitians, and Mexicans moving to the United States, for example) have? Of the possible explanations for this oversight, perhaps the most obvious, and one that is not totally without merit, is that the number of Americans leaving the United States for Mexico is smaller than the number of immigrants arriving in the United States from the opposite direction. Yet, as will become clear, the size of the migrant flow from the United States to Mexico is not insignificant; and the available data reveal some interesting parallels. For example, Mexican immigrants in the United States comprise the largest proportion, 30 percent, of the total foreign-born population (Grieco 2003); and U.S. immigrants in Mexico comprise the largest proportion of that country's foreign-born — 69 percent (*General Census of Population and Housing of Mexico XII* 2000). In other words, while the absolute numbers of Mexican immigrants in the United States may be higher, the relative size and impact of Americans in Mexico may be as great, or greater. Moreover, size is not the only, or even necessarily the best, measure of the significance of a migration flow. Other studies have shown that migration flows that might not be numerically significant at the national level can have profound effects at the local level (O'Reilly 2000; Rodriguez et al. 1998). For example, of the millions of Latino immigrants who have arrived on U.S. shores over the past fifty years, Cubans comprise but a small fraction. By 2000, the U.S. Census reported 35.3 million Hispanics living in the United States. Only 3.5 percent of that total Hispanic population was of Cuban origin. Mexicans comprised 58.5 percent. Yet the political, economic, and cultural impact of Cuban immigrants on the United States generally, and South Florida specifically, has been notable, and not constrained by their relatively smaller numbers (Population Resource Center 2002).

Some readers might aver that the lack of attention paid to U.S. immigrants living in Mexico reflects not necessarily their smaller numbers, but their positive, or at least not negative, impact on the host society. This hypothesis of American migrants' benign impact on Mexico will be discussed in the chapters that follow, but suffice it to say that although assessing the question is complicated, the impact of the migration flow southward is arguably mixed. Moreover, to accept the allegedly benign impact of U.S. migration to Mexico as an explanation for why so little attention is paid to the topic is problematic for additional reasons. Such an explanation, when considered in the reverse, tacitly accepts that the magnitude of attention focused on Mexican immigrants in the United States is a direct consequence of the empirical harm they cause to the U.S. economy and culture. It assumes that social and political realities mirror perfectly an established set of objective, empirical facts. This proposition is highly debatable (and much debated). For example, the rise of anti-immigrant sentiment in the United States tends to correlate with periods of economic or political insecurity in the country, but tying directly the real or perceived hardships of the native-born to immigration or immigrants is next to impossible.

Analysts have been more successful at establishing psychological and political explanations for nativism in the United States than providing empirical proof that immigrants harm the economy and that anti-immigrant attitudes are a consequence of that harm. Curiously, some of the most fervent anti-immigrant sentiment in the United States has bubbled up in states with the smallest number of immigrants, and among population groups least likely to be affected by immigration (Cornelius 1982; Esses et al. 2002; Fetzer 2000). Moreover, and to return to the case of Cubans, the amount and type of scholarly and political attention paid to immigrant groups in the United States have never been solely a function of their perceived negative impact. Cuban immigrants, like some Asian immigrant groups, have been spotlighted at certain historical moments as model minorities whose human and social capital stimulated the U.S. economy and contributed positively to U.S. society (Levine and Asís 2000; Stepick et al. 2003; Rieff 1993). In other words, explaining which migration flows capture public attention and what kind of attention requires that we look beyond factors like the size of the migrant population and that we interrogate more fully the politics behind widely circulating social perceptions.[2]

A more helpful explanation for the relative disinterest in Americans migrating southward (and a central premise of this book) is suggested in this introduction's opening quotation. "Immigrants," in the minds of U.S. politicians, academics, media, and public at large, are not "white." They are not U.S. citizens. They do not leave wealthy and powerful countries, completely voluntarily, to live in poorer and less powerful ones; and "immigrants" do not typically arrive in the new land possessing greater economic, political, and cultural power than the majority of their hosts. The opening quotation also reminds us of the importance of what Thorstein Veblen (1914) termed "trained incapacity." In one of the earlier examinations of transnational communities, sociologist Robert Smith invoked Veblen to illustrate how long and deeply held assumptions about citizenship, migration, and assimilation had trained analysts to focus on certain phenomena to the neglect of others (1998, 197). This same trained incapacity has likely blinded us to a recognition of Americans as transnational migrants too. Moreover, the processes by which some issues capture widespread public attention and others do not, or by which some circumstances are defined as "problems" and others not, are rarely politically neutral ones. Political scientists, sociologists, and philosophers have demonstrated that power often resides in the ability not to openly exercise power (Digeser 1992). Put differently, power and privilege are often at their most potent when they are the least visible.

From this perspective, understanding why some questions are asked and topics explored, while others are overlooked or ignored, requires a recognition of power as deeply embedded in social discourse, and as something highly decentralized that works through us, and not merely on us (Edelman 1988; Foucault 1980). Anthropologist Mark Pedelty offers as an example the fact that in the United States people are often quick to observe the work of ideology on individuals in other societies, be those chiefdoms, dictatorships, or socialist states, but are unable or unwilling to recognize how they themselves live under the influence and in the service of capitalist ideology (2004, 293). In the case of Americans living in Mexico, power and privilege have contributed to allowing a significant social reality to persist under the guise of the mundane. Why, some readers and observers will ask (and many U.S. citizens residing in Mexico did ask), is it important or interesting to study Americans in Mexico? "We" are not exotic. "We" are not like the "others" who consume the attention of scholars in the United States. These assumptions and trained incapacities are precisely why it is important to study Americans who migrate to Mexico. Interrogating the seemingly mundane is a valuable intellectual endeavor that can yield meaningful theoretical and political insights.

THE METHOD

Returning again to the quotation that opens this introduction, I am not, formally, an anthropologist, nor is skin color a prominent theme in this book, but I did set out to study a group that qualifies, at least in many respects, as what Crocombe might characterize as "my own people." I lived in Mexico for eight months—in June 2005, June 2006, and January through June 2007—in San Miguel de Allende (in the mountains of the state of Guanajuato), in the village of Ajijic (on the shores of Lake Chapala in the state of Jalisco), and in Mexico City. During this time I immersed myself in the lives of Americans living in Mexico. I conducted in-depth interviews. I read daily and did archival searches of local English-language newspapers, blogs written by American immigrants, and Internet lists catering to Americans in Mexico. I attended meetings, fund-raisers, church services, and parties. I went on bus trips and bike tours with Americans living in Mexico, and I spent many hours sitting in public spaces where the American communities in these Mexican towns congregate, engaging any and every one I could in conversation about U.S. migration to Mexico. These experiences, which were immeasurably rewarding and fascinating (but also at times challenging), inform the analysis that follows.

San Miguel and Ajijic/Lake Chapala form the primary focus of this study. Americans are living in cities and towns throughout Mexico, along the borders and on the beaches, but these two sites rank at the top not only in the absolute and proportional size of the immigrant population, but also in terms of their notoriety and established history as American settlements. In both locales, I combined reputational and snowball sampling techniques to identify research participants who were residing permanently in Mexico.[3] The interviews with these Americans ranged in length from forty minutes to two hours, and in many cases I was invited to join the respondents at another time for a meeting of their club or organization, or for a dinner party in their home. These semistructured interviews, guided by open-ended questions, aimed to assess the following: what led these Americans to leave the United States and settle in Mexico (which factors pulled them or pushed them across the international border); in what ways do they stay connected to the United States (how often do they visit, communicate with loved ones, access U.S. news sources, vote); what is the nature of their daily existence in and/or adaptation to Mexican society and culture (do they speak Spanish, socialize with Mexicans, celebrate Mexican holidays, stay abreast of or participate in the cultural and political life of the Mexican town in which they live); and how do they perceive their impact on the Mexican people and Mexican towns they inhabit, and the reception they are extended by their Mexican hosts?

I also sought out individuals whose positions or professions were particularly relevant to the themes of this study: real estate agents; current and past officers of the prominent civic organizations and clubs; contributors, owners, and editors of the English-language periodicals; and authors who have written about San Miguel and Ajijic. Because the political transnationalism of Americans is a significant focus of the book, I interviewed officers and members of the Democrats Abroad and Republicans Abroad in San Miguel, Ajijic, and Mexico City, and when the need for further information warranted it, I communicated with their national officers in D.C., and in one case with an officer of Americans Vote Abroad who resides in France. The interviews in Mexico City were designed primarily to gain insights and information from individuals in positions of political or social leadership within the American community in Mexico who could provide background on national-level (meaning throughout Mexico) activities and trends related to Americans abroad. The length of time the respondents had lived in Mexico ranged from one year to fifty-seven years; and these research participants ranged in age from thirty-eight to eighty, with the overwhelming majority over fifty-five years of age. Chapter One provides more extensive background on who these immigrants are and why they move.

The in-depth interviews were a valuable source of information, but so, too, were countless activities that fall under the heading of "participant observation." I worshipped with the Unitarians in San Miguel and at the Lake Chapala Society's Sunday morning "Open Circle." In Ajijic I attended a Rotary meeting, had brunch with the local chapter of the Daughters of the American Revolution, and joined members of the local Republicans Abroad and others on a bus trip to a nearby town for the annual Candelmas celebration (a festival that commemorates the purification of Mary forty days after giving birth, as well as the presentation of Jesus in the temple). In San Miguel I attended the monthly meeting of the local chapter of Democrats Abroad. At the public library, or *biblioteca,* I sat in on a meeting of the community security advisory committee (a group, formed during the 2006 serial rapist crisis, that sought to improve communication between Mexican officials and the foreign community on issues of security in San Miguel). I joined a group of mainly foreigners at El Charco del Ingenio, a large nature preserve just outside San Miguel, to celebrate the full moon with a bonfire, incense, chanting, and drums. In Mexico City, I pedaled through Chapultepec Park with the Young Democrats Abroad, attended a gathering of the Newcomers group, and had cocktails with the Mexpats (both of the latter social networking groups for foreigners, and predominantly Americans, in Mexico). Throughout these months in Mexico, I enjoyed the generous hospitality of many Americans who invited me to join them for impressive meals in their equally impressive homes, and to sip tequila while soaking up the spectacular views of mountains and lakes from their rooftop terraces.

In addition to interviews, social and political events, and the many hours I spent sitting in cafes, parks, libraries, and other public spaces participating in and overhearing conversations with Americans living in Mexico, a variety of published sources also provided significant current and historical information on this migration phenomenon. Since 1975, residents of San Miguel have had access to the English-language weekly *Atención*. The paper provides a schedule of upcoming cultural and civic events, announces the opening of new restaurants and art galleries, publishes news about the town, and prints social, political, and cultural commentaries by local residents. The foreign community in San Miguel comprises the bulk of the paper's readership, and that community is predominantly American. *Atención* is currently available online and maintains electronic archives. Bound copies of all of the previous year's editions are housed on the second floor of the *biblioteca*. An additional and particularly illuminating look at the lives of Americans in San Miguel comes from Internet groups, discussion forums, and bloggers—of which, as discussed in Chapter Two, there are many.

The residents of Ajijic and other villages along Lake Chapala also have access to several English-language publications. The *Guadalajara Reporter* is an American-owned, English-language weekly that has been in operation since the 1950s. Although operated out of nearby Guadalajara (another site that is home to a large population of American migrants), the paper publishes a special section devoted to the Lake Chapala community. The *Guadalajara Reporter* is online and maintains an efficient electronic archive. Two other English-language periodicals are published monthly by and for "Lakesiders" (as the immigrants refer to themselves): the *Ojo del Lago* (Eye of the Lake) and the *Lake Chapala Review*. Both are distributed free of charge, owned by foreigners, and packed primarily with real estate advertisements. They also publish social, cultural, and political commentary by Americans and Canadians living along the lake. Finally, Americans living south of the border have written an array of books about moving to or retiring in Mexico. Most of these are of the "how to" variety, but are still revealing in terms of what they choose to emphasize about life in Mexico, and the advice they proffer to prospective immigrants.

A particularly intriguing aspect of this fieldwork concerns how U.S. citizens living in Mexico reacted to me and to this study. Their reactions can be grouped into three, not necessarily mutually exclusive, categories: enthusiasm, suspicion, and curiosity. Some Americans living in Mexico whom I met were interested in the project and enthusiastic about being interviewed. On several occasions, I attended functions that allowed me to introduce myself to large groups of people and to explain my research. Inevitably, at the close of the meeting or event, many people would approach me volunteering to help, share their stories, and offer advice on individuals I should contact and places or events I should attend. Other people whom I had already interviewed would introduce me to their neighbors and friends, explaining sometimes with a sense of pride: "We've been interviewed for a study." On occasion, I would arrive at a shop or office to introduce myself, and the person I was seeking would say, "Oh, yes, I have heard about you being in town," seeming to welcome the opportunity to contribute his or her unique perspective on the topic at hand. I very much appreciated and benefited from the generosity of these research participants.

Another category of Americans in Mexico was more hesitant to talk and somewhat suspicious, at least initially, of me, and my intentions. This was particularly the case when it came to the topic of politics. Because the political mobilization of Americans abroad is an important theme of the project, it was imperative that I interview officers and active members of groups like Democrats Abroad and Republicans Abroad. This project is not a partisan one, nor do I consider my own partisan affiliations relevant to the study. A small number of the respondents, however, did. One officer of Democrats Abroad began our conversation by asking me to clarify my own political position. On another day, as I waited outside a large iron gate on a quiet street in San Miguel for a scheduled interview at the home of an officer of the local chapter of Republicans Abroad, my host came to greet me by explaining (jovially, I think): "We have this gate here to keep Democrats out!" I spent much of that particular interview trying to steer the conversation away from critiques of "leftist" professors and "liberal" universities and back to the topic I came to discuss: American political participation from abroad. In another instance, a respondent who was initially hesitant to talk with me explained later: "Well, I *googled* you, and you do seem to be who you say you are."

I attribute these more challenging interactions to several factors. Some Republicans in these two Mexican towns feel outnumbered (and seem, perhaps, to be), and the red state/blue state tensions that have frayed nerves and hurt feelings in the United States appear to have crossed the border along with American migrants. I should also acknowledge, however, that one officer of Republicans Abroad in Ajijic and his wife, who were initially hesitant to talk with me, later invited me to their home for a delightful dinner party that not only included on the guest list active members and former officers of Democrats Abroad, but also offered some hope for respectful bipartisanship among Americans—at least those living on the other side of the fence. For their part, the Democrats Abroad in Mexico are a highly mobilized crowd and were keenly interested in how my findings might assist them in their efforts to reach American voters in Mexico. Finally, the comment about "googling" me reflected a fascinating aspect of life in these towns that is discussed further in the next chapter. I was warned repeatedly to be cautious of "border promotions": a reference to the tendency, allegedly widespread, of some people who have left the United States for Mexico to embellish their previous rank, status, position, or profession once south of the border. "San Miguel," Nicholas Bloom writes, "is where the dead sergeant's wife becomes the admiral's widow" (Bloom 2006, 198). Hence, strangers like me who arrive in Mexico announcing some particular set of credentials may initially be viewed as suspect.

The most intriguing response I encountered during my fieldwork, and a common one, was curiosity as to why this issue—Americans living in Mexico—was worthy of academic analysis. Many of the Americans with whom I spoke saw nothing particularly interesting or peculiar in their decision to migrate. In fact, few, if any, thought of themselves as immigrants; and many bristled at the idea of being objects of study. These last two reactions stimulated engaging conversations and, for me, important thought processes about the political implications of terminology (a point developed below), and the ways in which power and privilege allow significant and potentially revealing social phenomena to persist in the guise of the mundane. Academics and journalists, typically North American, dissect regularly the lives of immigrants living in the United States, Canada, and Western Europe. Why these immigrants come, where they reside, and how they lead their daily lives are just a few of the legitimate and familiar topics of analysis. Rarely does anyone question the value or fascination of the subject matter. I have no sense, nor have I seen addressed, how those immigrants, typically originating from the global South, feel about being objects of analysis; or whether having the social, political, and psychic space to even reflect on that question (or at least to reflect openly) is itself a function of power and privilege—reserved for migrants like the Americans headed to Mexico, or academics like myself.

It would be disingenuous to characterize this fieldwork in Mexico as grueling in any respect. "Work" does not come much better than traveling to beautiful locales with idyllic climates and facilitating leisurely conversations with a constituency that is overwhelmingly bright, interesting, and willing to talk. Pleasure aside, however, the methodology is a serious one, and at times challenging. The qualitative case study method based on in-depth interviews, participant observation, and careful analysis of published materials has proven time and again to be a valuable source of information and insight not derived easily (if derived at all) from conventional survey research. During her ethnographic study of British migrants in southern Spain, sociologist Karen O'Reilly attempted a survey and reported a disappointing 14 percent response rate. She offered several explanations. In addition to her general conclusion that these migrants do not want to be bothered, or asked personal questions, she also noted that some want specifically to avoid being identified in any official records—whether because they are residing or working in Spain without the proper permits or because they simply want to escape bureaucracy, "Life in Spain is about freedom and escape rather than supervision, documentation and control" (2000, 155–156).

A few researchers have attempted to survey Americans living in Mexico and encountered similar challenges. Geographer David Truly, who has studied retirement migration to Lake Chapala, described difficulties associated with the lack of accurate statistical data on Americans in Mexico from either the United States or Mexico, and "the somewhat uncooperative nature of some of the expatriate residents." Describing the refusal of some immigrants to participate in his study, Truly cites one resident who said: "I won't answer your survey or your questions . . . that's why I left the United States" (2002, 269). In 1991, a sociology professor from the University of North Carolina, Richard Dixon, attempted a survey of Americans living in San Miguel. Dixon published his questionnaire in the English weekly *Atención,* seeking information that included demographic background, level of Spanish-language skills, and reasons for moving to San Miguel. Immigrants were asked to return the survey to the public library or one of the mail delivery companies in town. The response rate, according to Dixon, was too low to warrant proceeding with the study (e-mail exchange, August 22, 2006). Solutions Abroad (www.solutionsabroad .com), a Web-based resource for foreigners living in Mexico attempting a basic survey of its sixteen thousand users in 2006, reported a disappointing 6 percent return rate (field interview, May 22, 2007). And in 2006, the Overseas Vote Foundation (OVF) conducted a survey of American voters abroad regarding their participation in the U.S. midterm elections. The OVF report included a subsection, "Notably Absent—Mexico," noting the disappointing response of only 1 percent of U.S. voters residing in Mexico (Overseas Vote Foundation 2007).

Survey research has a valuable contribution to make to this topic, but what follows is inspired more by anthropologist Clifford Geertz's (1973) notion of "thick description." Thick description refers to an interpretative, ethnographic approach that does not simply recount occurrences of, but aims to capture the symbolic meanings of, social discourse and everyday events by situating and analyzing them in reference to complex webs of meaning. The emphasis is on exploring the nature of particular social phenomena, as opposed to setting out to test hypotheses. In an ethnographic study, the data are more "unstructured" than coded, for example, the number of cases is small, often one, and the analysis of the data collected takes the form of "explicit interpretation of the meanings and functions of human actions" rather than quantification or statistical manipulation (Atkinson and Hammersley 1998, 111).

This study managed to avoid some of the pitfalls that tend to plague qualitative researchers, but confronted obstacles still. Ethnographers have long struggled with the challenges of representation and exploitation. How can a cultural outsider have the authority and maintain the objectivity to represent accurately a subject population of which he or she is not a part—or is it even possible? Do the inequalities in power and position between researchers and their subjects (typically drawn from vulnerable populations), and the process of establishing close personal relationships with research participants, lead to exploitation (Denzin and Lincoln 1998; Irwin 2006)? Heeding Crocombe's call to study people with whom I generally shared racial classification, nationality, culture, and class (and working with a population that was not particularly vulnerable) lessened the potential for exploitation and misrepresentation. This "fieldwork among the familiar" conforms to what has been called "anthropology at home" (Peirano 1998), in spite of the fact that I was interviewing Americans for whom "home" is now in many respects Mexico. The commonalities I shared with Americans living in Mexico also facilitated participant observation—it was typically easy for me to blend in to whatever social or civic engagement I attended. On the other hand, and a point O'Reilly makes well in her ethnography of the British migrants to southern Spain, the lines between observer and participant can easily blur. She recounts an episode during her fieldwork on the Costa del Sol of visiting a local disco and overindulging in vodka. The people she met that night and the insights she gained were valuable to her study, but she acknowledges that she had not in that instance "been much of a detached observer" (2000, 13).

I will spare the reader any details of my own inebriations in Mexico, but acknowledge that this blurring of boundaries, and several points O'Reilly makes about the challenges of the chosen methodology, mirror my own experiences studying Americans south of the border. One evening as I enjoyed fine food and drink in the home of an American couple who had just finished remodeling their first home in San Miguel (the second house they had purchased just up the path would be used as a real estate investment), the woman host said: "My daughter is really pro-Latinos, and she told me, 'Mom, please don't participate in the gentrification of Mexico.'" Chuckling, the American immigrant continued, "And I told her, 'Well, honey, it is a hard job but somebody's got to do it'" (June 23, 2006). As the room filled with laughter, I had to choose between excusing myself to the bathroom to record the poignant moment and my reactions to it on the small notepad I carried with me everywhere, or staying put so as not to disrupt the camaraderie into which I had been warmly welcomed. On several occasions I bowed my head in prayer when I otherwise would not do so in order to avoid offending a host. On one particularly uncomfortable afternoon, I endured, for the sake of an interview, an American immigrant in Lake Chapala ranting about "Muslims," and proposing that "we" take away their children in order to stop the spread of Islamic fundamentalism to the next generation (her viewpoint was in no way representative of the Americans I met in Mexico) (field interview, January 30, 2007).

I discovered, as did O'Reilly, that "Interviews often involved being told what people wanted me to know, rather than what they thought I wanted to hear" (2000, 13). Many individuals and groups had their own agendas and saw my research as a way to advance them. A member of the Overseas Vote Foundation was deeply committed to having the U.S. government better respect the rights of its citizens overseas—whether in terms of limiting undue tax burdens or easing the hassles of voting from abroad—and as a result she wanted to discuss little else. I also observed how participant observation sometimes revealed insights different from or contradictory to the interviews. When I joined the Young Democrats Abroad for a bike ride in a Mexico City park, one American woman who is active in the Newcomers group (formed to provide assistance to, and a social outlet for, expatriates in Mexico) said, "We just know there are other Americans out there like us who are sitting at home crying but we don't know how to reach them" (February 24, 2007). When I later interviewed her individually about what it is like to live in a foreign land, she said: "Oh, everything is just great. I love it here" (field interview, March 4, 2007). O'Reilly's reflections on her research with British citizens living on Spain's Costa del Sol mirror my own fieldwork experiences among Americans in Mexico. She writes:

I learned not to attempt serious discussions in "fun" contexts;
I learned to want to stay in Spain forever; I bought a pair
of gold-coloured sandals and discarded the casual (scruffy?)
clothes which had been more befitting of a university setting.
. . . However, I experienced severe role ambiguity—a feeling
that I was not being true to my self. (2000, 15)

TERMINOLOGICAL DILEMMAS

In addition to role ambiguity, I also found myself trip-
ping over terminology in the course of this fieldwork. Before leaving for
Mexico, I had been referring to Americans living in Mexico as "expats,"
without being properly acquainted with the literature on expatriates or
having given much thought to what precisely the term was meant to convey. For their part, a surprising number of Americans in Mexico referred
to themselves as "gringos," a term I had assumed was pejorative. Mexicans
tended to refer to Americans as "*norteamericanos*," and not to use the term
gringo—at least not in open conversation with Americans. Both Americans and Mexicans used the phrase "foreign community," or *comunidad ex-
tranjero*. Nobody used the term "immigrants" to describe Americans living
in Mexico.

Early in the project, I attended a service of the Unitarians in San Miguel
de Allende. The group had invited a speaker to discuss Mexican immigration to the United States. He framed his talk in terms of the factors that
push migrants to leave Mexico and pull them to the United States. It occurred to me that this familiar academic framework might be helpful to me
as I invited U.S. citizens to discuss their own migration decisions. I tested
it out during brunch after the Unitarian service, and again the following
week with a group of American women in San Miguel who meet regularly
for Saturday morning breakfast. While most Americans were very willing
to share with me what had drawn them to Mexico, it was clear that they
were not generally accustomed to, or interested in, thinking of themselves
as immigrants. When presented with the immigrant analogy, one American woman responded in an annoyed tone: "Our situation is completely
different from theirs" (June 17, 2006).

As the chapters that follow will make clear, the situation of Americans in
Mexico is indeed different in many respects from that of most immigrants,
but in other respects it is not. As to why the label "immigrants" was not appealing or comfortable to most Americans, I can only speculate (I chose not

to push this issue with respondents for fear that any semblance of judgment on my part would jeopardize the interview). Immigrants, as they are often portrayed publicly in the United States and in other developed countries, are poor. They are desperate, they are dirty, and they are brown (Cashmore 1994, 188; O'Reilly 2000, 140). Some Americans may have wanted to distance themselves from this image of inferiority. Others may have wanted to acknowledge openly their privilege relative to "immigrants," as the term is commonly used. Some may have recognized that if they, too, were immigrants, then their presence in Mexico could be used to highlight hypocrisies in the public debates and discourse surrounding Mexican immigrants in the United States. The most accurate explanation for the resistance to the term is likely some combination of all of the above.

If these U.S. citizens living in Mexico are not immigrants, who, then, and what, are they? The question is significant not only for semantic reasons (which term do I use in this book to refer to the subject population?), but for analytical reasons as well. What does the choice of terminology, when used self-referentially, convey about an individual's sense of cultural and political belonging; and what do commonplace uses of one term as opposed to another, whether by scholars, politicians, the media, or the actors involved, reveal about the workings of power and privilege? For example, many Americans responded to the question of a label by stating, "I am just an American living in Mexico." However accurate that description might be, the possibility that Mexicans in the United States would offer a similar response—"I am just a Mexican living in the U.S."—is what many politicians, pundits, and other analysts in the United States rail against. If you are living in the United States, the familiar assimilationist argument goes, you had better adapt to and identify yourself with U.S. culture, society, and government. In fact, when Mexican president Ernesto Zedillo visited the United States in 1995 and told a group of American politicians of Mexican descent: "You're Mexicans—Mexicans who live north of the border," some conservative U.S. politicians and academics reacted strongly to a perceived threat of dual allegiance on the part of these immigrants or descendants of immigrants (Fonte 2005, 9).

"Migration," in the most general sense, refers to population movement, and "migrants" to the people who move. Because the reasons for and contexts in which people move vary tremendously, an array of terms have emerged to capture the heterogeneity of human movement: aliens (legal and illegal), diasporic communities, expatriates, exiles, immigrants, minorities, refugees, settlers, sojourners, tourists, and transmigrants. In reality, the distinction among these groups is often muddled. Is a person who is fleeing economic deprivation a refugee in the same sense as a person who is trying to escape political or religious persecution? Where international law and the control of state borders are concerned, legal definitions do exist to determine who and what are designated by which term. Yet even those lines blur and their application is open to interpretation. In academic and popular usage, the various terms listed above intersect and overlap, are used in contradictory and inconsistent ways, and can rarely be tied to firm or uncontested definitions and operationalizations. In the most basic sense, a migrant is one who moves. When that movement takes place across international borders, "immigrant" and "emigrant" are the commonly used terms. The very same border-crossing migrant is an immigrant in the country she arrives in, and an emigrant in the one she left.

The term immigrant is used extensively, but it is applied erroneously, and its meaning seldom interrogated. In the United States, Puerto Ricans, for example, are often referred to as immigrants when, according to U.S. law, they are American citizens. Nor do immigrants arriving from non-U.S. territories typically lose the label "immigrant" once they have become naturalized U.S. citizens. In fact, even many American-born citizens of an ethnic or racial background other than those currently recognized as "white" live their lives in the United States responding to the query "Where are you from?" When Keith Ellison, Minnesota Democrat, criminal defense lawyer, and Muslim, was elected to the U.S. Congress in 2006, he preferred to use the Koran rather than the Bible for his private swearing-in ceremony. Believing that the election of the first Muslim to Congress threatened the nation's values, Republican Virgil Goode of Virginia was one of several outspoken critics who quickly used Ellison's case to point a finger at immigrants:

> I fear that in the next century we will have many more Muslims in the United States if we do not adopt the strict immigration policies that I believe are necessary to preserve the values and beliefs traditional to the United States of America and to prevent our resources from being swamped.

What Goode seemed to misunderstand was that Congressman Ellison, although a Muslim, is not an immigrant (Swarns 2006).

Among the factors typically used to differentiate among terms that refer to human movement are: the intended permanence of the move, the motivation for it, and the degree of privilege that underlies it. The nature and centrality of any of these factors are, of course, open to interpretation. One person's diaspora is another's settler colony or foreign invader (think Jews and Palestinians in the West Bank, Afrikaners and black South Africans in South Africa, or Europeans and indigenous peoples throughout the Americas). Moreover, the meanings associated with these terms are rarely static. Diaspora is used today in ways that differ fundamentally from its usage a century ago, as is the term expatriate. An immigrant is defined today as "a person who migrates into a country as a settler" (*Oxford English Dictionary* 2007). The intent to settle in the country of destination is central to this and most definitions, and immigrants are typically distinguished from tourists and sojourners by the permanency or long-term nature of their move (O'Reilly 2000, 43; Warnes 1991, 53). Sojourners, as sociologist Edna Bonacich contends, are those migrants who consider their stay in the host country a temporary one; "settlers," she maintains, come with an intention to stay permanently (1973).

Recent scholarly interest in transnationalism has further confounded the question of terminology. If we are living in a world where migrants are crossing back and forth across borders and maintaining close ties with their homelands while also building new lives in a new land, then what does this convey about immigrant settlement and its permanency? Recognizing the significance of the change, scholars like Linda Basch and her colleagues (1994) contrasted the term immigrant with transmigrant. The former was said to convey a permanent rupture, "the abandonment of old patterns of life and the painful learning of a new culture and often a new language" (Basch et al. 1994, 3). The latter term, "transmigrants," was intended to capture a new category of immigrants "who develop and maintain multiple relationships—familial, economic, social, organizational, religious and political—that span borders" (Basch et al. 1994, 3). Although increasing numbers of migrants today fit this latter definition, including many Americans living in Mexico, the term transmigrant never really caught on among scholars or policy makers.

The emphasis on the maintenance of ties with the homeland, and the institutions that arise to link people across borders, evokes another term that refers to population movement, but has historically conjured very different imagery. Diaspora is a term that has become particularly prominent in academic literature in recent years, so much so that some scholars speak of a "shift from ethnicity to diaspora as master tropes of social diversity and migration" (Amit and Rapport 2002, 48). At first glance, a term that originated to characterize ethnic and religious minorities forcibly expelled from their homelands, most notably Jews and Armenians, would seem to bear no relation to U.S. citizens choosing to relocate to Mexico. Nonetheless, since the 1960s, the term diaspora has undergone a "genuine inflation," such that it is now used to designate all manner of population dispersion: expatriates, exiles, refugees, immigrants, and minorities (Schnapper 1999, 225). To some extent, the term continues to differentiate between migrants of privilege and those lacking it, referring mainly to populations moving from the developing to the developed world, but as Kachig Tölölyan emphasizes, in everyday speech "diaspora" has become so misused that it even gets applied to executives of multinational corporations who disperse around the globe for their careers (1996). Both Schnapper and Tölölyan reject the inflation of the term and offer guidelines for greater precision. Schnapper maintains that "To render the concept of diaspora operative for research, we must reserve it for populations that maintain institutionalized ties, whether objective or symbolic, beyond the borders of nation-states" (1999, 251). Unfortunately, this specification does not take us far from Basch and colleagues' definition of transmigrants.

The term "expatriate" appears in contemporary scholarship on transnational migration in ways that further frustrate terminological precision. In distinguishing what constitutes transnationalism as a new and distinct phenomenon, and what does not, Portes et al. write that "occasional contacts, trips and activities across national borders of members of an expatriate community" do not constitute transnationalism (1999, 219). What is not clear, then, is what is an "expatriate community." For Americans, this term was popularized after World War I in association with American artists and writers such as Josephine Baker, Gertrude Stein, Ernest Hemingway, and F. Scott Fitzgerald who left their U.S. homeland to live in Europe. These well-known examples of Americans living abroad captured two significant senses of the term expatriate—that migration was largely voluntary, but also that it involved an element of withdrawal from or disassociation with one's native country (*Oxford English Dictionary* 2007). Over time, however, the term "expat" has come to be applied more broadly—to business professionals; diplomats, military personnel, and other governmental representatives; academics and scientists; and retirees. It has also tended to lose its association with disconnecting from or abandoning the homeland. In one of the most comprehensive treatments of the topic in a special issue of *Current Sociology,* Erik Cohen writes: "'Expatriate' is, admittedly, a loose or 'fuzzy' term, capturing that category of international migrants who fill the gap between the tourist, on the one hand, and the semi-permanent immigrant, on the other" (1977, 7).

Although Cohen ultimately offers a very basic definition of the "national expatriate community"—"the citizens of one country living in a given locality of another country" (1977, 24)—he sharpens the term's precision by emphasizing *transiency* and *privilege* as what distinguish expatriates from immigrants, settlers, and sojourners. "The more developed a country," Cohen maintains, "the greater the chance that its citizens living abroad will be expatriates in our sense of the term. This is particularly the case with U.S. citizens abroad, who only rarely become fully-fledged immigrants to other countries" (1977, 14). In the footnote that elaborates, Cohen explains that very few U.S. citizens pursue citizenship in foreign countries where they reside. In this regard, and breaking with conventional uses of the term immigrant, Cohen seems to suggest that "full-fledged immigration" is determined by the pursuit of formal citizenship in the country of settlement. Expatriates who extend their stay in a foreign country indefinitely may become sojourners or even settlers, Cohen acknowledges, but they are still distinguished by their relative privilege (1977, 19). They are, in his words, an "'inverted minority'—which gains status by its entrance into the host society and hence tends to defend the exclusiveness of its enclave and its institutions from the hosts, whereas other, lower-status minorities often have to struggle to preserve their right to seclusiveness from the hostility of the host society" (1977, 24). He goes on to maintain: "They are surely the best-cared for, pampered and well-heeled group of migrants there ever was" (1977, 56).

Irrespective of their privilege, expatriates themselves are typically quick to clarify that they are not "tourists." Writing self-referentially as an expatriate whose husband's work in international finance took them around the world, Dorothy Backer draws a firm distinction: "The tourist may be a lifetime gadabout, but he is not an expatriate. The tourist visits; the expatriate lives" (2001, 269); and expatriates who live in popular tourist destinations, she argues, "wait in dread for the annual invasion" of tourists (2001, 270). Ultimately, she offers a description that confirms Cohen's emphasis on privilege: "Expatriatism is power, freedom from all the restraints of home. One is uncommitted, yet cannot be judged. One is an exception to every rule, a freckled blond among the swarthy, a free man among the slaves, a person in movement among the fixed" (2001, 273).

The purpose of this detour into the issue of terminology is not only to attempt to clarify the language used in the book, but also to highlight that the terms, beyond being fuzzy and imprecise, are endowed with political significance. This became clear in 2006, for example. As the U.S. Congress was battling over immigration policy, journalists were battling over the proper and politically neutral terminology to use in covering the debate: "undocumented" or "illegal," "immigrant" or "alien" (Zeller 2006). Ultimately, no term seemed free of political baggage. When it comes to Americans in Mexico, some terms available for describing population movements or dispersed peoples are clearly inadequate—exile, for example, or refugees. Other terms like diaspora that would at first seem like a poor fit have come to be used in such expansive ways that they could technically be made to fit. Doing so, however, fails to enhance our understanding of the case study, and further dilutes the utility of the concept diaspora. "Sojourner" is a term that works for those Americans who view their stay in Mexico as temporary, but a large and growing number do not. A survey of American retirees living in Mexico conducted by the University of Texas between January 24, 2007, and April 6, 2007, found 86 percent of respondents answering "no" to the question "Do you plan to return to live permanently in the United States?" Only 14 percent responded "yes" (Connolly 2007a). In my own interviews, I encountered some individuals who left open the possibility of returning to the United States, but nearly every American living in Mexico with whom I spoke was living there with the intention of staying. "Expatriate" is a useful term for Americans if, as Cohen does, we place the emphasis on privilege. His characterization of expatriates as "the best-cared for group of migrants there ever was" applies well to Americans in Mexico, as does Backer's portrayal of expatriatism as "power and freedom." Yet, to the extent that the term "expatriate" presumes transience or disassociation from the homeland, it does not accurately characterize a large population of Americans now residing in Mexico.

Ultimately, it makes the most sense to acknowledge a continuum of human movement stretching from tourism to exile, with varying degrees of agency and privilege located along the spectrum (O'Reilly 2000, 44). No one can say definitively where one position ends and another begins. The individuals to whom the terms apply have varied perceptions of where they fit, and population groups, as well as the individuals contained within them, change places on the continuum. So, if "expatriate," as commonly used today, essentially implies immigrants of privilege, it seems preferable to simply call them that. Although the term "immigrants" will not typically call to mind U.S. citizens settling in Mexico, to shun applying this label further endows groups like these with power, prestige, and privilege (O'Reilly 2000, 143)—this is particularly true given the political climate now surrounding Mexican migration to the United States. This book will, for the most part, use the term immigrants to refer to U.S. citizens living in Mexico. When another term is used by an interviewee, in a published article, or otherwise, I will transcribe it accordingly.

An additional terminological dilemma that plagues this and other treatments of transnationalism results from trying to simultaneously capture fluidity, mobility, and transcendence while acknowledging and confronting, as do migrants, the persistent significance of actual and specific places and conventional forms of belonging. Scholarship on transnational migration, social fields, and communities is filled with dichotomous terminology like home/host society, sending/receiving state, and community of origin/community of destination that implies a more static and unidirectional structure to migration flows than what scholars aim to portray. Additionally problematic, as David Fitzgerald observes, is the fact that the term "sending state" denies agency to migrants who are not sent, but send themselves (2000, 6). Similarly, "host society" implies a degree of welcome that is often missing in the sites where immigrants settle. As is the case with the term "American," no preferable alternatives yet exist, so I will rely on the problematic ones with which scholars and practitioners are most familiar.

Last, but far from least, this study is restricted by its focus on a specific category of Americans living in Mexico. Every U.S. citizen whom I interviewed for this study, and with only a handful of exceptions, every American I met in Mexico, was born and raised in the United States and racially "white." This is not to suggest that my sample is peculiar or unrepresentative of U.S. citizens living in Mexico, but it does exclude a significant population of persons of Mexican descent who are also Americans who migrate to Mexico. They are Americans either by virtue of having been born in the United States to parents of Mexican heritage (whether citizens or not, documented or not) or by virtue of having acquired U.S. citizenship through naturalization. They migrate to Mexico as U.S. citizens of Mexican heritage or as dual citizens who never relinquished their Mexican citizenship or who acquired it/reacquired it after establishing U.S. citizenship. The motivations for and experiences associated with migration likely differ for this group of Americans when compared to the population I studied, and a fuller understanding of migration and belonging in North America will require a closer focus on these migrants of Mexican or mixed heritage. In the meantime, this migrant population offers an important reminder that Americans are also, and increasingly, "brown," and provides a poignant illustration of the complexity of examining fluidity, mobility, and transcendence armed with concepts and terminology deeply rooted in cultural, political, and territorial stasis.

ROAD MAP

I began this project with some predetermined interests and ideas, and structured my initial inquiries with Americans in Mexico accordingly. Having written previously on the implications of globalization for various forms of belonging (Croucher 2003), I was interested in what this under-examined case would reveal about the meaning of citizenship and nationhood for a population of people living their lives across the border of two states. In the course of the fieldwork, other themes emerged that I had not anticipated: for example, the significance of technology in facilitating a transnational and transterritorial existence for Americans in Mexico. The chapters that follow contribute to telling the relatively unknown story of American migrants in Mexico. Each does so with a particular focus and draws upon varied but interrelated bodies of literature on migration, transnationalism, globalization, and identity formation. Chapter One introduces the two Mexican towns, Ajijic and San Miguel, which form the focus of this research and where large numbers of U.S. citizens are settling. The chapter also offers the reader some insight into the difficulty of determining exactly how many Americans live in Mexico. The bulk of Chapter One recounts the prominent pulls and pushes underlying U.S. migration southward, and provides a sustained glimpse into the nature of life within the foreign communities living in Mexico. Other studies of foreign communities provide related insights and some limited opportunity for comparison.

Chapter Two illuminates how the lives U.S. migrants are leading in Mexico confound conventional notions regarding the significance and centrality of territory and place; and how advances in communication, information, and transportation technologies facilitate, for Americans as with other immigrants, this transnational, transterritorial, and in some cases translegal existence. One of the most vivid illustrations of this transcendence of borders and of familiar forms of belonging takes place in the realm of politics and the exercise of citizenship. Chapter Three focuses on the practice of extraterritorial citizenship on the part of U.S. citizens who reside in Mexico but continue to participate actively in the politics of the United States. These American migrants also exercise political influence in the towns and cities where they reside, although few pursue formal membership in the Mexican state. Chapter Four pulls together the themes of Americans' transnationalism developed in previous chapters, but does so with a specific focus on how migrants—in this case, migrants of privilege—negotiate a sense of belonging in a global, postmodern world. Chapter Five summarizes the analytical insights gleaned from this case study and the relevant political and policy implications for Mexico and the United States. Just as the flow of migrants from Mexico to the United States shows few signs of abating, so too with the migration flow southward from the United States to Mexico. Both countries have the opportunity to address the topic of migration and its sociocultural, economic, and political implications in a constructive manner, or not. By adding information on an under-studied dimension of North American migration and belonging, this book aims to contribute to those policy debates, and to the scholarly discussion of transnationalism more generally.

PHOTOGRAPH 1   *View from Aldama Street in San Miguel de Allende at the back of the town's famous* parroquia, *or parish church. Photograph by Sheila Croucher.*

PHOTOGRAPH 2   *Foreign residents gathered in* el jardín, *the central garden plaza in San Miguel. Photograph by Sheila Croucher.*

PHOTOGRAPH 3   *Foreigners mingling in San Miguel's popular* jardín. *Photograph by Sheila Croucher.*

PHOTOGRAPH 4   *The RE/MAX realty office in San Miguel's historic center. The office occupies the southeast corner of the town's central plaza. Photograph by Sheila Croucher.*

PHOTOGRAPH 5 *A sign posted in San Miguel's popular hotel and courtyard restaurant, Posada Carmina, announcing the broadcast and celebration of the 2007 NCAA basketball championship tournament in the United States. Photograph courtesy of Marie F. Putnam.*

PHOTOGRAPH 6   *Friday morning's English-language weekly,* Atención, *stacked outside San Miguel's* biblioteca, *or public library. Photograph by Sheila Croucher.*

PHOTOGRAPH 7   *A view of Lake Chapala, Mexico's largest lake, from the north shore in Ajijic. Photograph by Sheila Croucher.*

PHOTOGRAPH 8   *Donas Donuts, along the* carretera, *or main thoroughfare, in Ajijic, is a popular gathering spot for immigrants located next to the RE/MAX office. Photograph by Sheila Croucher.*

PHOTOGRAPH 9   *One of many English-language signs in Ajijic along the north shore of Lake Chapala advertising upscale property for sale. Photograph by Sheila Croucher.*

PHOTOGRAPH 10   *An Ajijic cantina popular among foreigners announces drink specials during the 2007 Super Bowl. Photograph by Sheila Croucher.*

PHOTOGRAPH 11   *Foreign residents regularly shop at Ajijic's Wednesday morning tianguis, or open market. Photograph by Sheila Croucher.*

PHOTOGRAPH 12   *Foreigners in Ajijic gather daily at the Lake Chapala Society to peruse informational booths and bulletin boards. Photograph by Sheila Croucher.*

PHOTOGRAPH 13   *Along the bypass leading from Ajijic to Guadalajara, a housing development catering to Americans, Chula Vista North, towers above a shack inhabited by local Mexicans. Photograph courtesy of Rich Bailey.*

PHOTOGRAPH 14   *U.S. citizens living in Mexico show up in Ajijic on February 5, 2008, to vote in the first-ever global presidential primary organized by Democrats Abroad. Photograph courtesy of Jim Stork.*

One   SOUTHERN PULLS AND
      NORTHERN PUSHES

*The cost is so low that it doesn't make sense not to employ a maid
unless you love cleaning the toilet.*
—DOUG BOWER, AMERICAN RESIDENT OF MEXICO
AND AUTHOR OF *THE PLAIN TRUTH ABOUT LIVING
IN MEXICO*

*It is paradise. If you need help living or coping, this is the place
to be. I don't know that there is such a thing back (in the USA),
and certainly not for this amount of money.*
—JEAN DOUGLAS, AMERICAN RESIDENT OF A
MEXICAN NURSING HOME

Located in the mountains of southwest Mexico, just south
of Guadalajara, is Mexico's largest lake—Lago Chapala. The lake is sur-
rounded by quaint fishing villages, including Ajijic—a Nahuatl name that
means "the place where the water springs forth." Walking through Ajijic
today, a visitor will be struck by the natural beauty of this strip of land
nestled between mountains and the lake, by the colonial churches and
narrow cobblestone streets, and by the picturesque piers from which local
Mexican fishermen still head out in the early morning. Strolling north
from the lakeshore into the village, the visitor will pass Mexican señoras
selling candy from small sidewalk tables outside their thickly walled
homes, and will also encounter an abundance of real estate offices lining
the same streets. Glossy advertisements in glass display boxes announce,
in English, "homes for sale," with names like "Casa Smith" and prices like
$449,000 USD. If the same visitor had passed through Ajijic in February
2007, she might also have been surprised to see signs posted outside several small cantinas in this Mexican village announcing, in English: "Super
Bowl Happy Hour, 3–5, 2 Beers × 20 pesos." American resident Karen Blue

described being assaulted by related contrasts when she first settled in Ajijic in 1996: "A sombrero'd man, holding a cellular phone to his ear, delivered milk on a donkey. Young Mexican boys with buckets of dirty water washed a Mercedes and horse, side by side" (Blue 2000, 8).

Hundreds of miles to the east, in the mountains of the Mexican state of Guanajuato, similar peculiarities exist in the colonial city of San Miguel de Allende. In the town's central garden plaza, or *el jardín,* conversations taking place on the shaded wrought iron benches are as likely to occur in English as in Spanish. The shelves of a nearby grocery store are not stocked with fresh tortillas or chiles, but with specialty granolas and Silk brand soymilk. RE/MAX Real Estate occupies one prominent corner of the town's central colonial square, also announcing in English an array of featured proper-ties with prices in U.S. dollars far beyond the average Mexican's budget, and, in recent years, exceeding the budgets of many Americans as well. Walking through the narrow cobblestone streets, a visitor will pass several international mail delivery services advertising monthly package deals that include a post office box in San Miguel and one in Laredo, Texas, regular mail delivery from the Texas box to the one in Mexico, special discounts on international shipping, and access to high-speed Internet. Occasion-ally a donkey loaded down with his Mexican owner's wares lumbers along the same streets, reminding onlookers of a time when transportation and communication were much less convenient in San Miguel than they are today. At the *biblioteca,* or local public library, among the many activities from which patrons can choose are seminars, in English, on "Breaking the barrier of the self" or "Laughter as healing." As Nicholas Bloom correctly notes: "Those who move beyond the marketed version of San Miguel de Allende ['an unspoiled colonial gem'] find that it is not a city untouched by time but a thriving and complex point of contact between the United States and Mexico" (2006, 191).

Sociologist Peggy Levitt begins her book *The Transnational Villagers* by highlighting odd juxtapositions she encountered in the village of Miraflo-res in the Dominican Republic. In a town where most people live in small, two-room wooden homes with outdoor toilets, a handful of partially com-pleted mansions have curiously appeared, set back behind large iron gates, bearing unfamiliar architecture, and seeming to mock onlookers. Farther outside of town, at the edge of a large uncultivated field, the "overwhelm-ingly beautiful" Dominican countryside is interrupted by a billboard ad-vertising travel to Boston. The explanation for these contradictions lies in transnational migration. Levitt's book is an analysis of the close-knit, cross-border ties that Dominican migrants to the United States have established between the village of Miraflores and the neighborhood of Jamaica Plains in Boston, Massachusetts. She traces the processes and patterns through which these transnational villagers establish new lives and identities in Boston, while maintaining their sociocultural, political, and economic ties to the Dominican Republic. "Instead of loosening their connections [to the homeland]," Levitt explains, "and trading one membership for another, some individuals are keeping their feet in both worlds. They use political, religious, and civic arenas to forge social relations, earn their livelihoods, and exercise their rights across borders" (2001b, 3).

Americans in Mexico are also transnational villagers. They live in Mexico but remain closely connected to the United States. They do so physically through visits across the border, virtually through high-speed Internet connections, and psychically through their continued attachment to the homeland—an attachment that manifests in countless ways, not the least of which is the annual celebration in Mexico of U.S. national holidays: the Fourth of July, Thanksgiving, and Veterans Day. Their impact on their home villages in the United States is not as pronounced as in the case of Miraflores's emigrants. In fact, remarkably few of their compatriots in the United States are aware that a growing number of Americans are building new homes and lives south of the border. Yet these transnational villagers vote in U.S. elections, raise money for victims of Hurricane Katrina, and commemorate in Mexico the American lives lost in Vietnam and on 9/11; and like those Dominican immigrants in Boston, Americans living in Mexican cities like San Miguel and Ajijic have "re-created their pre-migration lives to the extent that their new physical and cultural environment allows" (2001b, 3). And as the pages that follow attest, the environment in these towns has allowed a near perfect re-creation of what these Americans valued in their premigration lives, and a notable improvement upon what they feel those lives lacked.

American migrants to Mexico, like Mexican immigrants in the United States, are pulled and pushed across the two-thousand-mile border by a variety of factors. They make individual decisions to move, but do so in the context of specific structural circumstances. This chapter illuminates some of the important dimensions of this southward migration flow: who is moving, and why? The introductory section offers a brief historical background on the migration relationship between the United States and Mexico and the specific history of foreigners in the towns of Ajijic and San Miguel. These are by no means the only Mexican cities that host American immigrants, but they are among the most significant in terms of the size, visibility, and established history of the foreign population. Moreover,

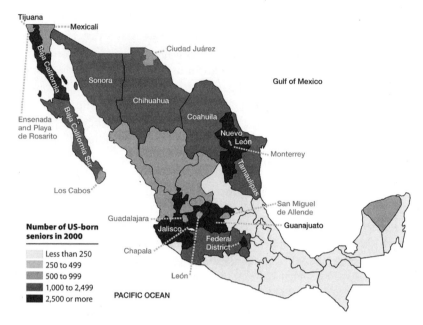

Number of US-born seniors in 2000

- Less than 250
- 250 to 499
- 500 to 999
- 1,000 to 2,499
- 2,500 or more

MAP 1.1   *United States–Born Senior Population in Mexico, 2000. Source: Migration Policy Institute, data derived from the 10.6 percent sample of the* General Census of Population and Housing of Mexico XII, *2000.*

a recent study by the Migration Policy Institute (2006) identified both locales as home to among the highest proportions of U.S. seniors moving to Mexico—suggesting that as the retirement-age population north of the U.S.-Mexican border burgeons, so too will the immigrant populations in these two towns.

This chapter also tackles the question of how many Americans live in Mexico, offering less of a definitive response than an explanation as to why the question itself is so difficult to answer. The remainder of the chapter explores the economic, cultural, and social factors that underlie contemporary U.S. migration to Mexico.

HISTORICAL BACKGROUND

As immigrants in the United States and their supporters often point out, defining who is an immigrant is a complicated task when referring to two geographic regions whose political, economic, and cultural histories are as closely intertwined as those of the United States and

Mexico. Human beings traversed the continent of North America long before the formation of either of these two modern nation-states or the delineation of the geopolitical border that now separates them. After the formal independence of the United States from Britain in 1776 and Mexico from Spain in 1821, people continued to migrate, and so did the borders. In fact, some individuals of Mexican descent in the United States are prone to remind their detractors that the contemporary southern border of the United States crossed them, not the reverse. For over two hundred years, people of Mexico and the United States have continuously crossed the two-thousand-mile border—moving back and forth from both directions. The pattern of Americans crossing into Mexico temporarily, for leisure and adventure, in border towns and at the beaches, is well known. Vacationers in San Diego take "exotic" day trips into Tijuana to bargain for colorful blankets and piñatas and to pose for photos in oversized sombreros. Teenagers from the United States regularly and notoriously traverse the border into Mexican towns such as Juárez to avail themselves of inexpensive and unregulated opportunities for inebriation, and their well-heeled adult counterparts pursue similar, albeit more costly, adventures in Cabo San Lucas. And Cancún long ago replaced Ft. Lauderdale as the preferred site for Americans' spring break debauchery. Much less well known, however, is the history of Americans living on a more permanent basis in Mexico City and throughout the country's heartland.[1]

Since its independence, Mexico has received American entrepreneurs, adventurers, missionaries, artists and writers, students, veterans of foreign wars and of domestic political tension in the United States, and retirees. In the early 1820s, American entrepreneurs could be found throughout Mexico operating precious-metal mines, planting coffee, and running steamboats (Alcocer-Berriozábal 2000; Wilkins 1970). Not long after Mexico's independence in 1821, Anglo settlers from the United States began colonizing the Mexican territory of Texas. Lured by cheap land and low taxes (a magnet that figures prominently throughout the history of U.S. migration to Mexico), Americans arrived initially with the good wishes of the Mexican government; but ultimately the immigrants declared the Mexican territory their own. In the 1860s, the first Protestant missionaries from the United States headed to Mexico. They proselytized, sold Bibles, founded schools, and opened the first branch of the New York Masonic Lodge in Mexico (Alcocer-Berriozábal 2000). In the late 1880s, an initial wave of American writers began to visit and find inspiration in Mexico, including William Cullen Bryant and Stephen Crane (Simmen 1988). Foreshadowing a trend that continues today, these sojourners were initially drawn by reading a travelogue of some sort that praised the country's land, people, culture, and climate, and they in turn penned an account of their own that lured more Americans southward. On the whole, these U.S. citizens were warmly received in Mexico, and in some cases, they arrived at the invitation of Mexican leaders. The welcome extended to foreigners from the north became even warmer under the leadership of Mexican dictator Porfirio Díaz.

Díaz ruled Mexico from 1876 until the Revolution of 1910 and had as a central pillar of his administration attracting foreign capital and foreigners to Mexico. Díaz succeeded in many respects at modernizing Mexico, although not without notable costs—namely corruption, repression, and growing social inequality. Rapid railway transit, mining, and oil drilling surged in Mexico during the Díaz years; and American investors, owners, and operators were key players in this development. American investors contributed an estimated 80 percent of the capital to build railroads in Mexico, and by 1908, 840 of the 1,000 foreign mining companies operating in Mexico were American-owned (Alcocer-Berriozábal 2000, 135; Wilkins 1970, 120). In the 1880s, Americans with connections to the transcontinental railroad began to settle in Mexico in large numbers. In 1888, the American School Foundation was founded in Mexico City by U.S. investors who wanted to provide for their children's education. In 1890, the first English-language newspaper appeared in Mexico, and in 1904, the Society of the American Colony was organized to promote the welfare of Americans living in Mexico. According to Mary Alcocer-Berriozábal, the "American colony" in Mexico increased notably in numbers and significance between 1880 and 1910. "Foreigners were truly welcomed to Mexico," she contends, and they figured centrally into Díaz's plan to make Mexico a truly modern nation (2000, 139). Writing in 1980, reporter John H. Davis noted: "What few outsiders realize is that an American colony has existed in Mexico City for well over a century, with its own social hierarchy, clubs and venerable traditions" (Davis 1980, 65).

In spite of improvements made during the Díaz dictatorship, his willingness to turn so much control of the country's resources over to foreigners contributed to his eventual downfall. Various factors inspired Mexico's Revolution of 1910, but concern about foreign control of Mexico and her resources, particularly by the United States, was central. This fear manifested itself, among other ways, in Article 33 of the 1917 Mexican Constitution, which expressly prohibits foreign involvement in the country's political affairs. Mexico and the United States endured some tensions during this post-Revolutionary period, primarily around the issue of oil, but ultimately the Mexican Revolution did little to lessen the entanglement of the two countries (Knight 1986). Nor did their southern neighbors' revolution stop U.S. citizens from moving to Mexico—although it may have contributed to luring a slightly different crowd. In the post-Revolutionary period, businesspeople were joined by a growing number of writers, artists, and eventually left-leaning Americans pushed by McCarthyism and other forms of intolerance in the United States and pulled by Mexico's more hospitable political and cultural climate. D. H. Lawrence, Katherine Anne Porter, Tennessee Williams, Langston Hughes, and John Steinbeck were some of the American writers who spent time in Mexico, drawing inspiration from the country's culture, climate, history, and landscape. Steinbeck was intrigued by the "primitiveness" of the country and cognizant of the deep class divide. Hughes's parents moved the family to Mexico in 1919 to escape racial tensions in the United States. Both *The Big Sea* (1940) and *I Wonder as I Wander* (1956) were influenced by Langston Hughes's experience in Mexico.

World War II saw a strengthening of Mexico-U.S. ties. Mexico was a committed U.S. ally—offering not only military support to the extent that it could, but also access to strategic resources: zinc, copper, lead, mercury, and graphite (Meyer and Sherman 1995). And U.S. entrepreneurs continued to be lured south by Mexico's economic potential during this period. During the presidency of Avila Camacho (1940–1946), 360 new industries arrived in Mexico, bringing 400 million pesos of new investment (Niblo 1995, 154); and in 1947, Sears and Roebuck opened its first store in Mexico City to enthusiastic shoppers numbering in the many thousands (Moreno 2003). The American community living in Mexico also signaled and solidified its presence during this period. Motivated by the threat of war, a group of Americans living in Mexico formed the American Society of Mexico in 1942. The organization's stated purposes were ("Dollars and Sense . . ." 1974, 5):

1. To keep alive a patriotic spirit toward our country, the United States of America, and to promote its interests.
2. To foster friendly relations between Mexicans and Americans.
3. To assist in developing cultural relations between the two countries.
4. To promote acquaintanceship among its members.

An "Era of Good Feeling" continued to characterize Mexican-U.S. relations in the 1950s and 1960s, and altered only slightly in the 1970s as a result of growing Cold War tensions and economic downturns in both countries. Still, U.S. citizens migrated to Mexico. Some came seeking economic fortune, others adventure, and some escape — whether from cultural repression in the United States, political intolerance, or the long arm of the U.S. law. Books like *How to Invest and Live in Mexico* (James 1960) promoted Mexico as a limitless industrial frontier. Meanwhile, Beat Generation writers like William Burroughs, Allen Ginsberg, and Jack Kerouac left the United States for Mexico in search of a different sort of frontier, "seeking freedom, less expensive drugs and sex, and a less expensive way of life" (Alcocer-Berriozábal 2000, 162). When Burroughs, fleeing a drug charge in the United States, arrived in Mexico, he wrote to Kerouac that the move across the border was like taking off a straitjacket of cultural repression (Alcocer-Berriozábal 2000, 163). The expatriation of other U.S. citizens during this period was less voluntary. The Red Scare in the United States during the 1950s, and the persistence of Revolutionary ideals in Mexico, motivated other U.S. citizens to cross the border for political freedom (Anhalt 2001). Finally, yet another group of Americans who began arriving in significant numbers after WWII were retirees, including U.S. veterans of foreign wars who could use their GI Bill benefits to live well (read: cheaply) in a healthy climate with access to affordable health care (Palma Mora 1990).

By 1980 a number of large American corporations were operating successfully in Mexico. Chrysler employed 7,500, Ford Motor Company 7,100, General Motors 6,500, and Anderson Clayton 4,000. The 1980s was also the decade during which Mexico abandoned the economic strategy of import-substitution industrialization (an inward-looking protectionist model of development) and opened its economy widely. One analyst described Mexico's economic opening as "bold" and "breathtaking," and the period from 1988 to 1993 as "a veritable rush to liberalization" (Weintraub 1993, 71–72). The most well-known symbol of this opening was the 1994 North American Free Trade Agreement (NAFTA). The free movement of people was notoriously left out of the agreement (due to U.S. fears of intensified Mexican migration north), but changes associated with and predating NAFTA still fueled U.S. migration southward. In 1994, U.S. newspapers ran a story about the flow of Americans headed to Mexico as a result of NAFTA (Oppenheimer 1994a, 1994b). Mexican officials acknowledged that the number of U.S. citizens applying for residency visas had grown by 20 percent during the previous year. One of these American immigrants, Maxim Free, 27, a recent recipient of a master's degree from California State University, explained: "To teach at a university in Los Angeles, you need a Ph.D. Here, I can teach at a local university, and gain experience" (Oppenheimer

1994a, 1994b). NAFTA also facilitated the entrance into Mexico of U.S. chain stores such as Costco, Home Depot, and Wal-Mart—which provided U.S. immigrants greater access to familiar products at cheaper prices (Migration Policy Institute 2006, 51). Jonathan Heath, HSBC's chief economist for Latin America, sees NAFTA as one of the main reasons for the burgeoning influx of U.S. immigrants into Mexico: "They come here, they live here, and they can still buy the same things. All they have to do is go to Wal-Mart" (Emmond 2008, 14).

In 2003, one observer estimated that in the previous decade alone, more than a half million U.S. citizens moved permanently to Mexico: "Not since the end of the American Civil War—when thousands of Southerners emigrated to Mexico—have so many Americans moved to Mexico" (Nevaer 2003). By 2007, Americans living in Mexico could enjoy an array of English-language periodicals and could commune easily with their conationals in Mexico through an extensive network of social organizations. The *Miami Herald's El Herald* was publishing a Mexico insert in its Sunday edition that listed the weekly events of clubs such as the American Benevolent Society, American Chamber of Commerce, American Society of Mexico, Mexpats, and Newcomers. In 2007, two Americans living in Mexico founded the popular monthly magazine *Inside Mexico: The English Speaker's Guide to Living in Mexico*—with a distribution of fifty thousand. Young adults, some of whom became familiar with Mexico during family vacations and spring breaks, are among this immigrant flow from the United States (Nevaer 2003), but particularly notable is the large and growing number of U.S. retirees. These immigrants are settling in towns and cities throughout Mexico, from Baja California to the Yucatán Peninsula, but their presence is especially notable and noticeable in Ajijic, along the shores of Lake Chapala, and in San Miguel de Allende, in the mountains of Guanajuato.

The histories of Ajijic and San Miguel mirror, albeit in somewhat magnified form, the general patterns of American migration to Mexico outlined above. Foreigners have a notable presence in the history of both of these central Mexican towns; and both towns have their favorite foreign sons and daughters who are proudly invoked by current American residents who delight in reciting the list of notable cultural and literary figures from the United States who at one time also called these Mexican towns home. Artists, writers, adventurers, entrepreneurs, and retirees have all migrated. The news of their lives south of the border spreads via travelogues and tour companies and lures still more U.S. migrants across the border. Today, both towns are widely known for idyllic climates, breathtaking landscapes, quaint colonial charm, and the large, socially active foreign communities.

American residents of both Ajijic and San Miguel are prone to compare and contrast their Mexican mountain town of choice with the other. The immigrants living in San Miguel are certain they made the better choice of the two locales, and Americans in Ajijic feel the same about their village on the lake. In reality, the history of foreign settlement in both of these towns is remarkably similar. Both have been transformed immeasurably by the influx of immigrants, and foreign residents in these towns now tend to bemoan the changes taking place in their "authentic" Mexican havens.

Ajijic

The history of the settlement of Ajijic dates back to the second half of the eleventh and the first half of the twelfth centuries, and it revolves around a legend of white tribes arriving from the north.

> There was a place far to the north called "Whiteness," and, from its seven caves, seven tribes set out towards the south. All seven tribes came from Aztlan (which is "whiteness" in the Nahuatl tongue) and all the seven tribes were called Azteca, the people of Whiteness. They came down from Aztlan and wandered southward with many stops, deviations and adventures. (Summers 1998)

The particular migration described here far predates the arrival of any European on the continent, but is prescient in its foreshadowing of another influx of immigrants that would take place along the shores of Lake Chapala centuries later.

The limited scholarly analysis of the American community living along Lake Chapala, or Lakeside as it is known to its foreign residents, has tended to characterize foreign settlement there in terms of distinct stages (Stokes 1981; Truly 2006). An initial Discovery stage reportedly lasted from the late 1800s to the turn of the twentieth century. During this period, Lake Chapala figured prominently into dictator Porfirio Díaz's grand plans for promoting international tourism in Mexico. Foreigners were encouraged to visit and build homes along the lake, and many did, including American aviator Albert Braniff, who was known for hosting elaborate fiestas from his home in Chapala. The vastly improved rail service in the region also promoted development during this early stage. Next followed the Founder stage, said to last from the early 1900s to the mid-1950s. In addition to rapidly improving rail service, road travel flourished during this period and reduced the time needed to make the trip from Guadalajara to the lake from days to hours. Notable artists and writers began to arrive at Lakeside during this Founder stage. D. H. Lawrence penned his famous novel *The Plumed Serpent* from his home on the shores of Lake Chapala, and the novel, set in Revolutionary Mexico, was filled with vibrant evocations of the country's pre-Hispanic past. It was also during this period in the 1940s that American Neill James, of Mississippi, settled in Ajijic and began a life of service that made her, to this day, the most influential foreigner to call Lakeside home. Known as the Godmother of Ajijic, James founded a public library, worked hard to cultivate the arts, developed a water purification plan for the town, and secured scholarships for local Mexican students. She also bequeathed her home and the beautiful gardens on which it was situated to the influential Lake Chapala Society—an association of foreigners founded in 1955 and dedicated to "helping non-Mexicans living at Lakeside, newcomers and old-timers, both full-time and part-time residents, to have a more enjoyable and worry-free life here" (http://www.lakechapalasociety.org). The relationship between the foreign immigrants (predominantly American) and the Mexican locals during this Founder period has been described as positive and symbiotic: "The immigrants offered economic opportunity to a subsistence-based local population, and they in turn offered assistance and security to this eclectic bunch of immigrants" (Truly 2006, 172).

Several events dating from the mid-1950s to the early 1970s led Stokes (1981) to label this period the Expansion stage. Retirees increased as a proportion of the immigrants residing in Ajijic, and prominent among them were military pensioners. The American Legion has thirteen departments in Mexico, three of which are in the Lake Chapala area and remain active today. The year 1955 saw the founding of the English-language newspaper *The Colony Reporter* and the Lake Chapala Society—an organization whose centrality to the foreign community and influence in the town have increased steadily ever since. Writers continued to be drawn to the area. American author Erik Erikson wrote *Young Man Luther* in Ajijic in the early 1960s; and in 1965, Willard Marsh published *A Week with No Friday*. It was also during this stage that the area's first subdivision, Chula Vista, was built, boasting a nine-hole golf course. Lake Chapala and Ajijic came to be featured in a growing number of travel guides and tourist promotions. Some accounts of Lake Chapala from this period continued to characterize the area as a "bohemian-artistic-intellectual colony" and contrasted its residents to the "great mass of [American] retirees" living in Guadalajara (Davis 1980); but others noted that the foreigners arriving during this period were less interested in blending into the local population than previous immigrants and more motivated by the pursuit of a bargain (Stokes 1990; Truly 2006). Beverly Hunt and her husband, Allyn, former owners of the English-language *Guadalajara Reporter*, have been living in the Lake Chapala area for over forty-five years. Both remember the mid-1970s as a time when the composition of Ajijic's foreign population began to shift away from adventurers and toward retirees. This was also the period when they chose to leave town for a more isolated area in the nearby village of Jocotepec: "There were," as Allyn explained, "just too many people in Ajijic" (field interview, February 9, 2007).

These patterns of migration and development along the lake intensified during the subsequent Established Colony stage, lasting from the mid-1970s to the late 1980s. Subdivisions sprang up everywhere, along with pizza and hamburger restaurants. Travel books continued to focus on Ajijic as a place where foreigners could live very well for very little; and the symbiotic relationship between immigrants and the native population that had reportedly characterized earlier stages was under increasing strain (Truly 2006, 176).

Along with the ratification of NAFTA, the 1990s ushered in the next phase in the evolution of foreign influence on Lake Chapala. A Wal-Mart and Home Depot were built in nearby Guadalajara; and other modern conveniences, including satellite access to North American television, continued to alter life along the lake. During this Modern stage (the early 1990s to the present), real estate boomed, prices soared, and the numbers of Americans migrating to Ajijic continued to grow. Judy King, who moved to Ajijic in 1990 and now runs a popular online resource, Living at Lake Chapala (www.Mexico-Insights.com), comments on the impact of an Internet boom beginning in 1995 and the explosion in Web sites on tourism and travel in Mexico that featured Ajijic as a unique gem. She also remembers that after the American Association of Retired Persons (AARP) published a 2004 article on Lake Chapala, "La Vida Cheapo," her Web site received over five thousand e-mails in the first four months from U.S. retirees interested in moving to Lakeside. In 2003, International Living opened a branch in Ajijic, and office directors Susan Haskins and Dan Prescher explained: "We have about 30,000 subscribers to our newsletter and another 160,000 people who get our free e-letters. They all have an interest in living the life of their dreams somewhere offshore. And we think Ajijic/Chapala and this part of Western Mexico are great options for them" (*Guadalajara Reporter* 2003). Contemporary American residents of Ajijic mark this period as the time when the once sleepy *carretera,* or main highway thoroughfare, transformed into a perpetual stream of traffic (and became nearly impossible to cross on the weekends). Some residents also characterize, pejoratively, the immigrants arriving during this period as dressing and acting "as they would in their home country, wearing expensive jewelry and driving new expensive SUVs" (Truly 2006, 178). To the east, in the mountains of Guanajuato, similar transformations were under way.

San Miguel de Allende

The history of San Miguel de Allende is intricately tied up in the history of Mexico's independence from Spain. The town sits nestled in a region known as the "Cradle of Independence," adding to the irony that it is now also widely known as a North American colony. Participants in and observers of San Miguel's history of foreign settlement are less explicit than those in Lake Chapala about the demarcation of distinct stages, but they tell a similar story about the foreign community's evolution. An American named Stirling Dickinson is to San Miguel what Neill James is to Lakeside. In 1937, this tall, shy Princeton graduate from Chicago arrived in San Miguel by train. Dickinson had become acquainted with Mexican-born, internationally acclaimed opera singer José Mojira, whose mother lived in San Miguel. When Dickinson stepped off the train in San Miguel, he fell in love with the town (an experience that would repeat itself for thousands more Americans in the decades to come). Dickinson also initiated another trend that has become widespread among the American immigrants who succeeded him: within ten days of arriving he bought a property in San Miguel, and did so for the bargain price of $90 USD (Yasui 2005). My interviews with Americans in San Miguel suggest that the truncated time frame for house shopping persists, although the price tag for properties has grown substantially. Dickinson also began a life devoted to philanthropy among the town's native inhabitants and to the promotion of art, culture, and language. He founded a baseball team and helped to establish the public library, or *biblioteca*. He is most often remembered, however, for the role he played in the Escuela de Bellas Artes (School of Fine Arts) and the renowned art and language school, the Instituto Allende. These institutions drew influential writers, painters, and sculptors to San Miguel, including the well-known Mexican muralist David Alfaro Siqueiros, and established the town's reputation as an artist colony.

The period between the 1950s and 1970s has been described as a "Golden Age" for San Miguel. Hundreds of young people arrived from the United States, using their GI bill benefits to study at the Instituto Allende. During this time, the town's first art gallery was inaugurated. In 1954, American immigrant Helen Wales joined forces with Dickinson to found the town's public library. In 1959 the library, or *biblioteca,* began its now famous tours of local homes to raise money to support the library and its charitable works. To this day, the library, located in a former slaughterhouse, forms the nucleus of the foreign community's social and civic life, and is to Americans in San Miguel much like what the Lake Chapala Society is to those in Ajijic. The local house tours continue, drawing hundreds of participants every Sunday to tour extravagant abodes, typically owned by foreigners and decorated with the best Mexican-style furniture and art that U.S. dollars can buy.

It was also during these Golden Years that Jack Kerouac and fellow Beat Generation writers spent time in San Miguel. In fact, in 1968, Neal Cassady, the inspiration for Kerouac's protagonist in *On the Road,* Dean Moriarty, died by the train tracks just outside of town. Roads and rail service improved significantly during this period, and Americans interested in heading south across the border could conveniently take a Pullman from St. Louis to San Miguel. The first edition of the English-language weekly *Atención,* then called *Esta Semana en San Miguel,* was published on May 30, 1975. The paper consisted then of eight pages: four in English and four devoted to the Spanish translation of the English text. Longtime residents remember this as a period of active engagement between the foreign community and the people of San Miguel, and San Miguel native César Árias recalls substantial intermarrying between foreigners and Mexicans in the town (Yasui 2005). In 2005, when the local and American-run Center for Global Justice sponsored a forum, "Fifty Years of Foreigners in San Miguel," it invited three old-timers who had lived and worked in San Miguel since the 1950s. Each of the three had been a partner in an intercultural marriage. Nevertheless, some longtime residents recall witnessing, as early as 1961, the arrival of "Americans driving into town with poodles with big rhinestone necklaces" (Bloom 2006, 196).

Today, there is a pervasive view among the town's residents that San Miguel has changed markedly. Summing up the forum "Fifty Years of Foreigners in San Miguel," American resident Holly Yasui writes: "By the end of the century, the foreign community began to coalesce into an increasingly isolated English-only enclave, and San Miguel's reputation as an artistic-cultural center was becoming eclipsed by its fame as an 'American colony' with inflated prices, 'chic' bars and boutiques and runaway development" (2005). Another American immigrant who had been living in San Miguel since 1986, and who owns a home in El Centro, the town's historic center, recalled:

This street was all Mexicans. There used to be kids playing
on the roofs, and roosters. These houses are all owned by
foreigners now. Mexicans can't afford to live in El Centro. . . .
And they are making the police wear silly uniforms and ride
horses. They just do that for the tourists. (field interview,
June 22, 2006)

Changes in San Miguel over time can be traced through the pages of the
English-language newspaper *Atención*. From its founding in 1975 to today,
the paper grew from eight pages to eighty. With the exception of one or
two feature articles translated into Spanish, the paper is published entirely
in English. In 1975, the paper covered mainly social news in town, reported
the week's duplicate bridge scores, and included only an occasional real
estate advertisement. Today the paper is filled with brightly colored full-
page real estates listings, announcements of newly planned gated communities, and advertisements for upscale furniture stores, plastic surgeons,
spas, and cross-border mail services. By 2001, announcements appeared
regularly advertising a van service that would ferry San Miguel residents
to the new Wal-Mart in the nearby city of Queretaro. By 2007, the van
service was no longer necessary, since similar superstores had opened in San
Miguel. Nevertheless, *Atención* continues, to date, to faithfully publish the
weekly bridge scores.

Looking back over these more than thirty years of life in San Miguel
through the lens of the local English paper, I am most struck by two ob-
servations. First, "affordable luxury" has long been a selling point in the
town: one advertisement in 1975 listed a "colonial home" with five bedrooms, a large kitchen, and patio for $40,000 USD; another raved about a
six-bedroom colonial abode with a heated pool for $65,000 USD (*Atención*
1975). Second, concerns about growth, new arrivals, and rising prices are
a consistent theme. Writing in 1975, an American resident of San Miguel,
John M. Johnson, described longingly the old days back in 1948 when there
were few foreigners in San Miguel and he and wife rented a house in El
Centro for $30 USD a month, which included electricity, phone, and fur-
niture (Johnson 1975). Six years later, in 1981, an editorial titled "Surreal
Estate" referred to a recent survey of five prominent real estate agencies in
town that revealed that "prices of houses, lots, and undeveloped land have
soared in the last two to three years." One house that sold for $55,000 USD
in 1979 now sold for $125,000. The editorial speculated on the future of San
Miguel: "Will the unmoneyed artists and writers be forced to move out?
. . . Will native artisans be pressured to sell their long-held family proper-

ties . . . ? Will San Miguel become another St. Tropez?" ("Surreal Estate" 1981). Ten years later, in 1991, another longtime American resident, Harold Black, who arrived in San Miguel in 1958, also harked back to the good old days when the population was 15,000, automobiles were not even noticeable, there were only a few phones in town, a haircut cost the equivalent of sixteen U.S. cents, and maids were paid $8 USD a month (Black 1991).

One sentiment that clearly does not change over time in San Miguel is the concern about change. Still, in spite of more people, more cars, and higher prices, American writers and artists continue to be drawn to San Miguel. In 2001, author Tony Cohan fueled San Miguel's popularity with his book *On Mexican Time,* a narrative of his and his wife's move south from California and their evolving love affair with Mexico. Beverly Donofrio, author of the cult classic *Riding in Cars with Boys* (1990), is a full-time resident of San Miguel, and her more recent work, *Looking for Mary, or the Blessed Mother and Me* (2000), reveals notable influences of her life lived south of the border. Today the town boasts abundant art galleries, holds regular writers' *salas,* and hosts prominent artists and authors.

Although San Miguel is proud of its writers, many people fear more publicity. When I approached Americans in Mexico for interviews, some, most notably in San Miguel, responded in an exasperated tone: "Please don't write another travel book. We don't need more people flocking here." Since the early days of foreign settlement, San Miguel has been featured in magazines, brochures, travelogues, and now Web sites — all of which lure more migrants southward. Stirling Dickinson once recounted an event, which has been much repeated since, involving a reporter who arrived in town in 1947 to write an article on San Miguel. Not long after the piece, entitled "Luxury Living on 45 Dollars a Week," appeared in *Coronet Magazine* in 1948, Stirling Dickinson described receiving an initial bag of 3,600 letters from interested Americans and potential immigrants (Dickinson 1975). From that point on, U.S. periodicals of all sorts have regularly reported on San Miguel's charms and bargains. The demographic profile of the immigrant flow from the north has, however, evolved a great deal over the past sixty years. World War II veterans studying art were joined by refugees from McCarthyism, beatniks, Vietnam War draft dodgers, hippies, and New Age practitioners, who, by the end of the millennium, found their proportion of the immigrant population giving way to retirees and real-estate investors (Yasui 2005).

As interest in Ajijic and San Miguel continues to grow, along with the communities of immigrants settling there, a central question emerges: how many Americans do live in Mexico, or, specifically, how many are residing in well-known American colonies like Ajijic and San Miguel? Before turning to a more in-depth discussion of the factors that have pushed and pulled Americans to Mexico, the section below focuses on the question of numbers—which, as it turns out, is a remarkably difficult one to answer.

HOW MANY ARE THERE?

After countless hours of researching, reading, surfing the Internet, interviewing or seeking to interview government officials, and poring over documents and reports from U.S. and Mexican agencies, I regret that I must join the chorus of voices who proclaim, as did recently the Migration Policy Institute in Washington, D.C., that "data about the numbers of US citizens abroad . . . are meager and incomplete" (Migration Policy Institute 2006, 23). Observers with varying degrees of qualification are willing to offer estimates, but just as many are quick to point out that "to get exact numbers is very difficult" (Rehm 2007, 6). A study of the feasibility of extending Medicare to Americans in Mexico noted: "One of the most difficult questions addressed by our project has been determining a good estimate of the number of Medicare-eligible persons residing in Mexico" (Warner 1999, 52). Guidebooks for towns like San Miguel have poked fun at the paucity of firm data on the number of Americans living there and the wildly divergent estimates (Harmes 2004). The question has also been fodder for blogs by Americans in Mexico who spar in cyberspace over which estimates are more accurate. Bill Masterson, a longtime American resident of Mexico, became interested in this issue a few years back, and recounts in a widely referenced Internet essay a quest that took him from the U.S. Census Bureau to the U.S. State Department to the U.S. Embassy in Mexico and back again. Likening the search for verifiable numbers on Americans in Mexico to "a case for Sherlock Holmes," Masterson eventually received from Mexico's Instituto Nacional de Inmigración (INI) an estimate that 124,082 U.S. citizens were residing in Mexico—a number far lower than the estimates of 500,000 to over 1 million that had circulated widely since the 1990s (Masterson 2000). In a second essay on the subject, Masterson criticizes the U.S. government, which, in his words, "hasn't a clue," and accuses a Mexican university professor who has written one of the few academic works on this subject of "sloppy research" (Masterson 2002). Meanwhile, another popular site, Mexfiles, critiques Masterson himself as having greatly exaggerated other researchers' failings and characterizes his numbers as unreliable (Mexfiles 2006).

This quandary about the numbers of Americans living abroad is not new. Writing in 1966, statistician Ernest Rubin attempted to provide a comprehensive overview of Americans abroad. He noted various limitations in existing sources of data on this population and concluded with a plea:

> The importance of the American presence abroad is related to our foreign-policy aims, to United States business operations, and to our cultural objectives. Because of this it may, perhaps, be appropriate to voice a statistical plea here for better data and information about American [*sic*] abroad. (1966, 10)

In the forty years since Rubin issued his plea, remarkably little progress has been made on the issue. Estimates of how many U.S. citizens actually live in Mexico continue to "vary widely and wildly," from as few as 150,000 to as many as more than 1.5 million (Kernecker 2005, 146). Some commentators choose to blame Mexico for the lack of reliable data. One U.S. reporter in Lake Chapala wrote: "This being Mexico, no one is quite sure how many foreigners there are, nor does anyone seem to know the total population of these lakeside towns" (Toll 2006, 75). The United States, however, provides no better data on its emigrants than Mexico has on its foreign-born, and seems surprisingly disinterested in the question. Below I will provide what data are available, but begin with a brief discussion of some of the challenges involved in answering the elusive question.

Censuses everywhere are estimates, and they vary widely in their accuracy and reliability. Countries regularly confront obstacles when it comes to determining with precision the number of citizens, residents, and inhabitants within their borders and distinguishing among them (Blastland and Dilnot 2007). When it comes to counting Americans in Mexico, the challenges are multiple and relate to questions of terminology, proper documentation, and a seemingly ambivalent commitment to data collection and compilation (the United States being no better than Mexico). With regard to terminology, what does it mean, for example, to "reside" in Mexico? Does six months of the year qualify? Are retirees who live in Mexico on U.S. income distinct from American employees of U.S. corporations or governmental institutions with offices in Mexico? Should we distinguish Americans who are married to Mexicans, or Mexican Americans who migrate south with U.S. citizenship whether acquired at birth or through naturalization?

The presence of this latter group begs the question touched upon in the

Introduction of what, or who, exactly is an "American." Beyond the misuse of the label "America" as referring exclusively to the United States is the question of the large number of people residing in Mexico who are "ethnically" and "culturally" Mexican (or as some observers said to me, "of Mexican stock"), but who have U.S. citizenship—acquired either through naturalization while in the United States or through birth in the United States to Mexican parents. Citing comments by Mexican demographer Agustín Escobar Latapí, Robert Smith notes: "U.S.-born children of Mexican migrants are the largest foreign-born group in Mexico outside Mexico City" (2006, 9). In November 2006, the English-language monthly *Inside Mexico* reported that Mexican Americans are one of the fastest-growing subsets of Americans moving to Mexico (Shetterly 2006, 19). The significance of this category of Americans had not occurred to me when I began this project. My own image of "Americans" in Mexico was skewed by narrow and racialized assumptions of what the term signifies. As international migration and transnational participation intensify, conventional terminology and the assumptions on which terms are based will increasingly fail to capture what they aim to represent. Take, for example, Juan Hernandez, who in 2001 was named to head former Mexican President Vicente Fox's Office of Mexicans Abroad. In an article titled "American in Fox Cabinet Aims to Protect Mexicans Here," *The Houston Chronicle* described Hernandez as "the first American to serve in a Mexican president's Cabinet" (Hegstrom 2001). The life of Hernandez, born to a mother from the United States and a father from Mexico and raised in Texas and Mexico, reflects a reality more complicated than this static terminology conveys.

Adding to the complexities of terminology is the fact that the agencies in the United States that would seem to have an interest in the question of Americans abroad choose neither to expend the energy or resources nor to report what they know. Among the U.S. agencies that might be expected to maintain such data are the U.S. Embassy in Mexico, the U.S. State Department, the U.S. Department of Commerce, the U.S. Justice Department, the U.S. Department of the Treasury, and the U.S. Census Bureau. Representatives of the U.S. Embassy in Mexico City and the American consulates in places like San Miguel point out that registering with the U.S. Embassy is a voluntary act. Some Americans living abroad do so, but the majority do not. Compiling data from this source is also complicated by the fact that some short-term visitors register with their embassy while on holiday, for example, and rarely does anyone deregister (Migration Policy Institute 2006, 23). When I arrived in San Miguel in June 2006 I immediately registered with the local U.S. consulate (motivated largely by the fact that I would be living alone in a town where foreign women were being terrorized by a serial rapist), but most of the Americans I interviewed laughed at the idea that they would ever bother to register. One woman told me: "We are trying to get away from the government, not help them keep track of us" (field interview, June 6, 2006). Confirming the prevalence of this sentiment, Richard Gonzalez of the American Consulate in Mexico City acknowledged that "for each American that registers in the American consulate in Mexico City, there are up to five who do not" (Alcocer-Berriozábal 2000, 234).

Americans are also not required to notify the U.S. State Department of their move abroad, nor is there a system of passport controls in place that tracks the numbers of passports issued in relation to the place of destination. As Kernecker writes: "[H]olding a valid U.S. passport allows a citizen to go anywhere, with neither side of the border keeping specific and co-ordinated track of the paper slips left behind in the immigration booth on entering Mexico" (2005, 146). Passage of the recent Western Hemisphere Travel Initiative (WHTI), which requires citizens of the United States, Canada, Mexico, and Bermuda to present a passport upon entering or re-entering the United States, could facilitate record keeping in this regard (Ferguson 2006). Nevertheless, in the past, the U.S. State Department has issued estimates of the numbers of Americans abroad and their locations, but now cites post-9/11 security concerns as a reason for no longer doing so (Migration Policy Institute 2006, 23). The Departments of Commerce and Justice have both published data on Americans abroad in the form of the *Statistical Abstract of the United States* and the *Statistical Yearbook* of the Immigration and Naturalization Service, but stopped doing so in 1995 and 1957, respectively (Alcocer-Berriozábal 2000, 232–233). The U.S. Treasury Department can shed some light on the issue in terms of Treasury checks. In 2003, the Department estimated that 750,000 checks (Social Security, Veterans Administration, and tax refunds) were mailed to Americans in Mexico (Nevaer 2003). This measure misses, however, the many Americans who live in Mexico but retain a post office box or some other address in the United States.

The U.S. Census Bureau excludes private citizens residing abroad from its decennial count. It recognizes, said Kathleen Styles, project manager for the Census Bureau Overseas Test, that, "In an increasingly global economy, we have a lot of Americans who are living overseas." But, she proceeded to explain, "There is no central registry, and we don't have any good way to reach out to them" ("Census Bureau Finds . . ." 2006). In 2004, however, motivated by lawsuits (including one by Utah alleging that the failure of the 2000 Census to count 11,000 Mormon missionaries overseas cost the state a congressional seat) and by lobbying efforts on the part of groups like American Citizens Abroad, the Association of Americans Resident Overseas, and Democrats and Republicans Abroad, the Bureau agreed to test the practicality of enumerating Americans abroad. The Government Accountability Office (GAO) was charged with monitoring the implementation of the pilot project. Tried in three countries believed to be home to large populations of Americans—Mexico, France, and Kuwait—the test ultimately proved prohibitively expensive and the results disappointing. The Census Bureau printed 520,000 forms and received back only 1,783. Domestically, the Census Bureau spends an average of $56 per person to count the resident population. The overseas count cost the U.S. government a staggering $1,450 per response. Ultimately, the Census Bureau and the GAO determined that including Americans abroad in the Census would not be cost-effective, and they advised the U.S. Congress to drop the idea (Government Accountability Office 2004; "Census Bureau Finds . . ." 2006).

Given the difficulties the U.S. Census Bureau and other U.S. agencies face when it comes to counting U.S. citizens in Mexico, it is not surprising that the Mexican Census and other comparable Mexican sources are also considered somewhat unreliable in this regard. One American I interviewed in Ajijic seemed to remember hearing about the Mexican Census, but was not surveyed. Another said she came home to find the official Mexican Census sticker on her door indicating she had already been interviewed, when, in fact, she had spoken to no one. Yet a third said, "Oh, yeah, they came by but our maid just answered for us." Then she chuckled, "She told them my husband was thirty-eight!" (field interview, January 29, 2007). Her husband was in his late fifties. Nevertheless, the Mexican Census is one of the most reliable sources for data on foreigners living in Mexico, although it most certainly undercounts the number of Americans residing there. In addition to the Mexican Census, two other Mexican agencies maintain helpful data on the country's foreign population. The Instituto Nacional de Inmigración (INI) issues visas to foreigners and maintains some statistics on migration flows; and the National Institute of Statistics, Geography and Information (INEGI) coordinates the collection and dissemination of statistical data on the land, people, and economy of Mexico. Yet, complicating the efforts of these agencies are the numbers of Americans who secure a visa that does not properly reflect their status in Mexico, or who secure no formal documentation at all.

According to a staff member of the U.S. Embassy in Mexico, "There are certainly MANY Americans who cross into Mexico via land border who never register with immigration. We at the consular services see a great number of Americans who have been here as long as a year without so much as a passport" (Masterson 2000; emphasis in original). This situation with undocumented immigrants captured increased attention after the signing of NAFTA in 1994. At that time, Mexican officials estimated that at least 200,000 Americans were living illegally in Mexico. Some observers in Mexico referred to these illegal immigrants as "drybacks," or *espaldas secas.* A twist on the derogatory term "wetbacks" used to refer to Mexicans who crossed the Rio Grande, "drybacks" are Americans who arrive in Mexico without documents, but do so via the comfort of a car or airplane. One Mexican official remarked: "The number of drybacks is growing steadily. Maybe it's partly because we have never really gone after them" (Oppenheimer 1994a). Eleven years later in an interview with the *Dallas Morning News,* Mauricio Juárez, spokesperson for the Mexican Migration Institute, confirmed that the problem persists: "The United States isn't the only country that has problems with illegal immigrants. We have our own" (Corchado and Iliff 2005). Beyond the problem with illegality, some Americans travel to Mexico with a tourist visa, or FMT (readily available at airports and other border crossing points), and either overstay the six-month limit or renew the visa indefinitely. As one American immigrant and lawyer living in Mexico explains, for Americans interested in formalizing their residency in Mexico, the FM-3 visa has become a popular option in recent years. Designed to serve the interests of immigrants who are not seeking employment in Mexico and can demonstrate access to sustainable income or resources from outside of Mexico, the FM-3 is valid for a year and allows the immigrant to import from the United States a reasonable amount of household goods and one automobile. Nevertheless, "many long-term foreign residents do nothing to formalize their residency, merely obtaining a new tourist card every six months. Certainly, that's the cheapest and most hassle-free method" (Rose 1996).

In spite of these many challenges, the data that are available from U.S. and Mexican government sources and from researchers on both sides of the border provide a relatively sound basis for statements regarding what we do know about the number of Americans living in Mexico. First, of the estimated 4 to 6 million Americans living outside the borders of the United States, the largest proportion, estimated at over 1 million, reside in Mexico. In 1999, the Bureau of Consular Affairs in the Department of State estimated that of the over 4 million Americans living abroad, 1,036,300 were living in Mexico (AARO 2007; *Overseas Digest* 1999; Migration Policy Institute 2006, 23). Organizations like the Association of Americans Resident Overseas, Overseas Vote Foundation, American Citizens Abroad, Democrats Abroad, and Republicans Abroad also recognize Mexico as home to the largest number of U.S. citizens living abroad[2] (see Table 1.1). Second, within Mexico, U.S.-born residents comprise by far the largest proportion of the country's foreign-born—an estimated 69 percent (see Table 1.2). Moreover, the Mexican Census also reports a large number of residents (roughly the same as the entire foreign-born population) whose country of birth is unknown. It is safe to assume that Americans comprise at least part of that population (Migration Policy Institute 2006, 26 n. 44). Third, the numbers of Americans living in Mexico have increased steadily over time. Despite the likely undercount of the total number of U.S.-born residents (in 2005, Mexican industrial giant Cemex put the number of Americans in Mexico at more than 1 million—triple the Census estimates), the Mexican Census shows a clear and significant trend upward in this population (see Table 1.2). It is also important to note that the 2000 census, from which many current estimates are drawn, misses what is now an additional nine or ten years of U.S. migration southward. From all indications, this period has been a very significant one in terms of U.S. migrants, particularly retirees, crossing the border.

Finally, we also know that U.S. migrants tend to cluster in particular regions and locales of Mexico, including the two that form the focus of this book—Lake Chapala and San Miguel. The challenges of collecting data countrywide in Mexico are compounded when the unit of analysis is a municipality or village. Nonetheless, some of the sources cited above provide useful information on Chapala and San Miguel as well. In 2006, and based on preliminary figures from Mexican immigration authorities, city officials in San Miguel adjusted upward their estimates of the number of foreigners living in town. An immigrant population that had been calculated at somewhere between 8,000 and 10,000 was estimated to have increased, since the year 2000, to somewhere between 11,000 and 12,000. Thus, the foreign population, more than 70 percent of whom hail from the United States, now makes up as much as 15 percent of San Miguel's 80,000 residents (Schmidt 2006a). Estimates of the number of Americans living in Ajijic vary. Judy King, editor of Mexico Insights, puts the number of full-time foreign residents at 5,000, with about an additional 10,000 part-time seasonal residents each year. This is based on the entire north shore of Lake Chapala, whose total population is an estimated 150,000. Ten years ago, Mexican government sources offered a similar estimate of

TABLE 1.1. UNITED STATES CITIZENS LIVING ABROAD

Region

Americas	2,113,295	51%
Europe	1,169,438	28%
Asia	517,800	12%
Middle East	295,645	7%
Africa	67,632	2%
Total	4,163,810	100%

Country (Top Ten)

Mexico	1,036,300	24.89%
Canada	687,700	16.52%
United Kingdom	224,000	5.38%
Germany	210,880	5.06%
Israel	184,195	4.42%
Italy	168,967	4.06%
Philippines	105,000	2.52%
Australia	102,800	2.47%
France	101,750	2.44%
Spain	94,513	2.27%

Source: Schachter 2006, Table 1.

5,000–6,000 full-time foreign residents living along the lakeshore (Truly 2002). In 2001, the *Washington Post* ran an article that put the total foreign population at 7,500 (Jordan 2001); and *Discover Mexico Magazine* estimates that 10,000 foreigners live along Lake Chapala (2007).

Particularly helpful with regard to municipal-level estimates is a recent study by the Migration Policy Institute (2006) focused specifically on U.S. retirement migration. Using data from the 2000 census in Mexico, the Migration Policy Institute report concludes that the population of U.S. seniors (age fifty-five and above) living in Mexico increased by 17 percent between 1990 and 2000. Specific states, however, experienced more dramatic increases. The state of Jalisco saw its U.S.-born senior population increase by 138.6 percent; and the municipality of Chapala (which includes Ajijic) saw a phenomenal increase of 581.4 percent. The population of U.S. seniors in the state of Guanajuato increased by 26 percent, and by 47.7 percent in the municipality of San Miguel (Migration Policy Institute 2006, 28). Jalisco

The Other Side of the Fence

TABLE 1.2. FOREIGN POPULATION IN MEXICO: 1900–2000

	Mexican Population	Foreigners	Americans	Percent Americans
1900	13,607,259	58,179	15,266	26.24
1910	15,160,369	116,527	20,639	17.71
1920	14,334,780	108,482	21,740	20.04
1930	16,552,722	140,564	36,306	25.83
1940	19,653,552	177,375	9,585	5.40
1950	25,791,017	182,707	83,391	45.64
1960	34,923,129	223,468	97,902	43.81
1970	48,225,238	191,184	97,246	50.87
1980	66,846,833	268,900	157,117	58.43
1990	80,908,821	340,824	214,719	63.00
2000	97,483,412	492,617	339,717	68.96

Sources: Salazar Anaya 1996, 99–106; *General Census of Population and Housing of Mexico XII* 2000.

and Guanajuato were also the states where significant proportions of the U.S. immigrants residing there were new arrivals (having migrated within five years of the Census) (Migration Policy Institute 2006, 29).

This problem of counting emigrants and immigrants is a serious one, but notably is not restricted to the case of Americans in Mexico. In her ethnography of British immigrants living along the Spanish Costa del Sol, Karen O'Reilly describes how Spain, having long been a country of emigration, was unprepared for its role as a country of immigration. In particular, local officials and the Spanish state were slow to gather reliable figures on the numbers of immigrants. For reasons very similar to those described here, official figures of British citizens living in Spain do not accurately reflect the foreign presence. Ultimately, O'Reilly explains:

> Many British migrants are undocumented . . . pensioners are claiming British pensions which are still paid into British bank accounts. Moreover, younger, working migrants sometimes work informally within the British migrant community. It is not surprising therefore that existing data in Spain and Britain . . . do not accurately reflect the fluidity or extent of British migration to Spain. (2000, 50)

Southern Pulls and Northern Pushes

Scholars, policy makers, and pundits will continue to struggle with the collection and verifiability of these data, but beyond dispute is the fact that a large and growing number of U.S. citizens are migrating to Mexico. What, then, are the factors driving this migration trend?

PULLS AND PUSHES

Six out of every ten Americans I interviewed in Ajijic and San Miguel responded to my query "Why did you move to Mexico?" with some version of this response: "I arrived here on a Saturday and bought a house the following Wednesday." Some immigrants described giving the move south more careful thought, but it is commonplace when talking with Americans in these towns to be regaled with tales of instant love affairs with either Ajijic or San Miguel, and seemingly rash decisions to settle there. American immigrant Carol Schmidt's book *Falling in Love with San Miguel* (Schmidt and Hair 2006) and Web site by the same title (www .fallinginlovewithsanmiguel.com) convey this sentiment explicitly, as did American Judy King, who lives in Ajijic and edits the online magazine *Living at Lake Chapala.* King described arriving in Ajijic and being swept up by the feeling that "I just knew I was meant to live here" (field interview, February 6, 2007). When pushed to elaborate on the nature of these love affairs with Mexico, American immigrants recite a variety of factors that lured them across the border, and some that compelled them to leave the United States — or at least contributed to their decision to do so.

The notion of push and pull factors has a long academic history and continues to figure prominently into scholarship on migration. Nevertheless, applying the framework today warrants certain caveats. The distinction between push factors and pull factors can be a fine and blurry one. When a Mexican national migrates to the United States in search of better wages, is he being pushed by economic hardship in Mexico or pulled by the promise of a better quality of life in the United States? The answer is both, as it is with respect to an American retiree facing an insecure economic future in the United States who learns of incredible real estate deals and affordable health care in Mexico. The use of the push/pull framework also runs the risk of oversimplifying a complex set of factors, and specifically the interrelationship between what social theorists refer to as *structure* and *agency.* Any application of a push/pull framework must be careful not to portray individual migrants as making rationally calculated decisions in an economic, political, or cultural vacuum. Nor should an emphasis on the role of structural variables, such as unemployment, in the country of emigration or immigration diminish the agency of individual migrants who choose to move. The push/pull dichotomy can be useful for analytical purposes, and will be employed here, but with the explicit awareness that migration, whether it is Mexicans moving north or Americans moving south, is a complex phenomenon influenced by a range of economic, political, and sociocultural factors, individual calculations, and historical and structural forces. Based on her ethnography of British citizens living in Spain, O'Reilly discovered that push factors (reasons for leaving Britain) could be either personal (divorce) or general (the social or political mood of the country or an inhospitable climate). Pull factors could be natural ones (Spain's welcoming climate), traits of the foreign community residing there (ample social opportunities), or a function of the host community and culture (the warmth of the Spanish people or the less hectic pace of life). Similar motivations underlie the migration of U.S. citizens to Mexico.

Related to the push/pull calculus, but defying simple categorization as either one or the other, are what O'Reilly and other scholars have labeled "trigger mechanisms." Trigger mechanisms that influence migration decisions include: deaths of a spouse or other loved one, divorce, financial crisis, job loss, or trouble with the law, all of which can influence a decision to migrate (Wiseman and Roseman 1979). It is important to keep in mind, when probing respondents for migration motivations, that the explanations they offer for their migration decisions are often "no more than post-hoc justifications, constructed from the perspective of the new context within which they have found themselves" (O'Reilly 2000, 28; see also R. Cohen 1996). For example, feeling a sense of cultural liberation may follow from the migration experience, without necessarily having been a motivating factor. Writing about American writers who left the United States for the Left Bank between World War I and World War II, historian Foster Dulles notes that these emigrants, such as Gertrude Stein and Ernest Hemingway, are known for having fled American materialism for the more free and cultured atmosphere of Paris; but, he writes: "That many of them found the cheap living costs of the quarter quite as appealing as its freedom, there is no question" (Dulles 1966, 18).

The Economic Calculus

Although six of every ten Americans I interviewed in Mexico recounted stories (accurate or not) of arriving in Mexico one week and purchasing a house the next, ten out of ten identified economic considerations as an important factor in their decision to migrate. Other research confirms this finding (Sunil, Rojas, and Bradley 2007), including a survey of Americans in Mexico by the University of Texas which found that 75 percent of respondents in San Miguel specifically cited cost of living as a main reason they migrated (Warner 1999, 40). Time and again Americans living in Mexico shared with me examples of the remarkable real estate deals to be had south of the border, pointing out, for example: "You can get an amazing place here—three or four bedrooms, a garden, a terrace for as low as $200,000 US. In the U.S. you can't buy anything anymore in the $200,000 to $300,000 range" (field interview, June 3, 2006). Also appealing are Mexico's remarkably low property taxes. On average, property taxes in Mexico range from 0.01 to 0.4 percent of the assessed value of a property (Migration Policy Institute 2006, 17). Those already low taxes are made even more affordable by a common practice of listing the sale price at something much lower than it actually was, and by home appraisers who assign significantly lower-than-market values. As a result, one reporter explained, "tax bills of $200 a year for a $100,000 plus condo are common" (Burns 2001). Several people mentioned this in interviews, and Tony Cohan describes such an occurrence in his colorful saga of home ownership in San Miguel (2000).

Real estate bargains and cheap property taxes lure Americans southward, but many migrants are also impressed with their ability to afford an array of Mexican servants at minimal cost. The quotation about toilet cleaning at the beginning of this chapter is but one example, albeit a crass one. A financial reporter profiled American retirees in San Miguel in 2001 and noted that the most common payment cited puts the price of a Mexican maid at less than $200 a month. Monthly rent in San Miguel, for those who do not purchase homes, averages $300 a month, and that includes all utilities and a full-time maid (Burns 2001). In the article "La Vida Cheapo," *AARP Magazine* quoted an American in Ajijic who exclaimed: "A maid in New Jersey, if you can afford one, can be $100 a day. Here, it's $5 to $10 a day" (Golson 2004).

Beyond the low prices, American immigrants in Mexico are also generally pleased with the quality of service they can procure at bargain rates. One respondent marveled at her cook's willingness to hand-squeeze two separate pitchers of fresh orange juice each morning—one for her husband, who does not like pulp, and another for her because she does. Another American described how the Mexican maid, who was initially puzzled by her foreign employers' odd ritual of sanitizing fruits and vegetables in an iodine solution, quickly took it upon herself to learn the proper measurements per liter of water so she could assume the daily task herself. A third respondent was impressed with the maid's commitment to ironing even blue jeans: "I have barely tossed them on the bed, and she has them washed and ironed and put back in the closet" (field interviews, June 2006).

Americans living in Ajijic and San Miguel boast regularly about how inexpensively they live and exchange tips for how to reduce those costs even further. One sixty-one-year-old woman living alone in Lakeside estimates her monthly cost of living at $800, which includes her rent: "My Uncle Joe brags that he lives here on $500 a month. That's fine, but I get my nails done, my hair done, I buy clothes, and I eat out maybe once a day." She goes on to exclaim that for a tummy tuck at the hospital in Guadalajara, "I paid only $1,000 and that included ten ultrasounds" (Blue 2000, 166, 170). Ken Luboff, author of *Live Well in Mexico: How to Relocate, Retire, and Increase Your Standard of Living* (1999), writes in his book, "Friends of ours rent a house for about $500 a month and live well for about $1,200 a month, total, including the cost of a part-time maid and gardener. Barbara and I own a house and live a more luxurious lifestyle for less than $20,000 a year" (quoted in Burns 2001).

The Web site Falling in Love with San Miguel (the subtitle of which is "How to Retire in Mexico on Social Security") regularly informs readers when prices in town rise or fall, and where to find the best deals. Describing a night out at the new eight-screen movie theater in town, Carol Schmidt writes:

> Back at the MM Cinema: the signs over the snack bar make it look as if there is a promotional deal of 14 pesos for a large popcorn and two soft drinks instead of the usual 66 pesos. Instead, the 14 pesos is how much you save in buying the combo instead of each item separately. But the tub of popcorn seemed equal in amount to the jumbo at the Gemelos that was 30 pesos, and the soft drinks looked bigger for the same price, so it's about the same. We used to sneak in our soft drinks in our purses at the Gemelos. Now that we know the good deal isn't so fantastic, we'll do that again. (Schmidt 2007a)

The centrality of economics as a factor in the decision of U.S. citizens to migrate south is also evidenced in the numerous retirement and travel articles and books written about Mexico by Americans and intended for an American audience. Since San Miguel resident Stirling Dickinson's experience of receiving bundles of letters from the United States in 1948 after publication of the article on "luxury living on $45 a week," this theme "how much you can get in Mexico for how little" has been a persistent one for Americans. In July of 1995, *Fortune* magazine did a cover story on retiring abroad. "Mexico," Justin Martin and Henry Goldblatt wrote, "is bargain numero uno." The article focuses on an American couple who retired in Lake Chapala in 1989. For the bargain price of $170,000, they built a four-bedroom house with a swimming pool, fishpond, and fountain. They live on less than $18,000 a year, which includes flights to the United States, a maid and a gardener, and membership in a country club. Immigrant and retiree Bob Bowles remarked: "In the States, retiring with even a semblance of our previous lifestyle would have been impossible. Here we've actually improved on it" (Martin and Goldblatt 1995, 94–95).

The flip side of the affordability of life in Mexico, or a push factor, pertains to what many migrants describe as the unaffordability of life in the United States. I heard this complaint many times in interviews with Americans in Mexico, and read it in various published commentaries. The reality of the problem hit home for me in a poignant way, however, after I published a short article on this research project in the political journal *Dissent.* The journal editors informed me that my article had captured the attention of readers beyond their usual audience. Some of those readers wrote letters to the editor, a few of which were forwarded to me. Below is one message I received on March 30, 2007:

> Hello Ms. Croucher, we are disillusioned over the thoughts of retiring in America on a $50k/yr combined pension. What kind of lifestyle could we expect in San Miguel for that amount? I am 60 and retired; my wife is 54 and working, but wants to quite [*sic*]. Any help you could offer would be appreciated; there is already a line of retirees waiting for a job at the local Wal-Mart.

My article was not written as, or intended to be, a "how to" guide for retiring to Mexico. It was intended to utilize the case of Americans in San Miguel to highlight the hypocrisy and shortsightedness of the current immigration debate in the United States. But what was of primary concern to this particular couple, and I assume many others like them, was the quality of life, or lack thereof, that they could expect in the United States as retirees. The U.S. immigrants living in Mexico whom I interviewed were more likely to describe being pulled to Mexico than being pushed from the United States, but when I asked specifically about push factors, rising economic costs in the United States, particularly in the realms of health care, prescription drugs, and the difficulty of living on Social Security or a meager retirement pension, were the most popular responses. Describing the decision he and his wife made to leave the United States in 2003, Doug Bower explains: "I had become too sick to live in America. Even with private insurance, even with Medicare, we couldn't keep up with our medical bills. So we found a country where we could, and we left" (2005). A growing number of cash-strapped retirees are also leaving the United States to move into Mexican nursing homes. At least five such facilities already exist in the Lake Chapala area. One American who made such a move, Harvey Kislevitz, 78, of New York, explains: "You can barely afford to live in the U.S. anymore" (Hawley 2007). Kislevitz, the Bowers, and other U.S. citizens who have moved to Mexico are not alone in their fears. A Gallup Poll revealed that 40 percent of U.S. residents are somewhat or very worried about not having enough money during retirement (Gallup Poll, June 13–19, 2005, cited in Migration Policy Institute 2006, 6).

Their fears are not unfounded. A study conducted by Harvard Medical School found that 50 percent of bankruptcies filed in the United States in 2001 were medically related and filed by middle-class home owners with health insurance (Himmelstein 2005). Dr. David Himmelstein, director of the study, exclaimed: "Unless you're Bill Gates, you're just one serious illness away from bankruptcy." His coauthor, Elizabeth Warren, concurred: "It does not take a medical catastrophe to create a financial catastrophe. A larger share of American workers are going to have insurance that's like a paper umbrella. It looks good, and might even protect you in a sprinkle, but it melts away in a downpour" (cited in Bower 2005). The U.S. Congress recognizes the problem, as do various civil society groups such as the AFL-CIO and Americans for Secure Retirement. In 2004, the U.S. Senate's Special Committee on Aging held hearings to address the issue: "Retirement Planning: Do We Have a Crisis in America?" The testimony suggested overwhelmingly that the answer is yes. Dr. John Goodman, president of the National Center for Policy Analysis, reported, for example, that 61 percent of all workers in the United States between the ages of twenty-four and sixty-four have no retirement savings account. Of the 42.5 million workers who do have an account, the median balance is a mere $14,000 (Senate Special Committee on Aging 2004).

Without question, financial factors play a central role in American migration to Mexico, but economic concerns are not the only motivation for the move. American immigrants in Ajijic and San Miguel also report being pulled and pushed by cultural longings and frustrations.

Cultural Ambivalence

"I can't remember the last time someone asked me for a business card. I love that about Mexico." This particular migrant to San Miguel, an American man in his late fifties, did not use the same straitjacket metaphor that Burroughs did when writing to Kerouac about the allure of Mexico in contrast to the United States, but he and many other Americans living in Ajijic and San Miguel expressed related sentiments. They spoke of various aspects of culture and climate in Mexico that they found appealing and often contrasted these with aspects of life in the United States that they found distasteful or stifling.

American immigrants repeatedly describe their lives south of the border as more tranquil than they were in the United States. Many explain their decision to migrate in terms of wanting to escape the "rat race." This was the case both for the minority of respondents who were still employed, either in transnational enterprises of some sort or in Mexico, and for the overwhelming majority who were retired. On several occasions I heard the following anecdote, or some version of it: "Friends call us from the States and ask us, 'What will you all be doing today in Mexico?' We laugh and tell them, 'We don't know yet, but whatever it is it will take us all day to do it.'" This punch line is not meant to critique the state of efficiency in Mexico (although that critique is frequently issued as well). Rather, these Americans mean to project an ethos of leisure. In that same vein, many people also reported walking more in Mexico, eating healthier, and taking time to enjoy things they otherwise would not have in the United States. Some respondents mentioned significant weight loss since moving to Mexico. Adding another dimension of tranquility to life in Mexico, Americans are impressed with what they perceive as a different attitude toward anger in Mexican culture. I was told in several interviews that in Mexican culture to lose one's temper is a bad thing, a sign of weakness, unlike in the United States, where open displays of anger can be an effective, even admired, means of exerting and displaying power. Each American who mentioned this aspect of Mexican culture did so with a tone of admiration. Absent from these American immigrants' interpretations and portrayals of Mexicans as calm and tolerant is any recognition that an entitlement to anger, or its open display, may itself be a function of power and privilege. This is not to suggest that Mexican culture is not indeed more tolerant than U.S. culture (I am not qualified to issue such a verdict), but rather a reminder that the isolated and imbalanced relationships the American immigrants maintain with their employees are a poor basis for general proclamations about Mexican culture.

In addition to the warm and sunny climates of Ajijic and San Miguel (which were identified consistently as key factors pulling the migrants to Mexico), Americans are drawn to a people and culture they experience as warm. One American living in Lakeside explained: "The thing that keeps us here is—more than anything—we love the climate, but the people enter into it. That's a strong factor, and I find the people to be very gentle; they're very friendly" (Banks 2004, 368). Another American woman identified several reasons for coming to Mexico, including cost of living, but went on to say: "I stay because I am learning new lessons from the Mexicans. . . . They're much less materialistic than we are and infinitely more spiritual" (Blue 2000, 35). An American woman in San Miguel marveled to me: "The kids here are happy with any kind of toy; they don't have to have the latest Game Boy" (field interview, June 18, 2006). Another in Ajijic said: "They are beautiful people, the Mexicans. I hope we don't ruin them" (field interview, February 10, 2007). Caren Cross, a painter, retired psychotherapist, and American immigrant in San Miguel, notes: "I found that I could be more present, less harried, more attentive to whatever I'm doing rather than living in the past or the future. And I think Mexicans are really good at that" (Shetterly 2006, 18).

Americans living in Ajijic and San Miguel also frequently expressed admiration for the attitudes they encounter among Mexicans regarding children, families, and seniors. "Mexicans love their children, and enjoy them— you can really see that" (field interview, June 5, 2006). Even more frequently, and not surprising given the large percentage of these immigrants who are retirees, I heard references to the different cultural attitudes about aging in Mexico. This mirrored Karen O'Reilly's findings among British immigrants in Spain—one of whom exclaimed: "You aren't discarded here when you retire, not like we were in Wales" (2000, 71). Similarly, American migrants described various ways they felt cared for in Mexico. The comments about attentive maids willing to take extra care with the immigrants' clothing or food were not simply stories of a good bargain, but also conveyed from the perspective of these Americans a valued relationship with their Mexican employees that was not merely instrumental. One American immigrant recounted: "It is hard to say who helps who more. We have done a lot for [our maid's] family, but they are loving people. They give us back so much" (field interview, June 7, 2006). They repeated similar stories with regard to their experiences with health care in Mexico. Contrary to some common perceptions in the United States, every American with whom I spoke who had received medical care in Mexico was impressed. Mexican doctors, nurses, and clinics were described not only as highly competent and affordable, but Americans repeatedly emphasized a feeling of being well "cared" for. "It's amazing," one American man noted. "The doctors still make house calls here" (field interview, January 31, 2007). Another American woman recounted a recent and very positive experience at the doctor's office in Ajijic: "He took time to just talk to me first, about nothing. I did not feel rushed and it seemed like they really care about people" (field interview, February 1, 2007).

For many American immigrants in Ajijic and San Miguel, Mexico's cultural appeal has a gendered dimension. American women in their sixties or older frequently commented on experiencing more favorable attitudes toward senior women while living in Mexico. In a conversation with a group of sixty-something American women in San Miguel, one commented: "Older women are respected here, even by teenagers. It is horrible being an older woman in the U.S." The others concurred (field interview, June 18, 2006). Karen Blue, an author and American resident of Lake Chapala, devoted her book *Midlife Mavericks: Women Reinventing Their Lives in Mexico* (2000) to exploring the trend of American women in their forties and fifties moving to Ajijic. Running throughout the life stories of these different immigrant women are various trigger mechanisms that motivated their move to Mexico—divorce, death of a loved one, loss of a job. Mexico offered these women the hope of starting over, adventure, and escape, as well as a sense of safety and comfort: A woman in her late fifties living at Lakeside explained to Blue: "I feel protected and safe here" (Blue 2000, 115).

In her documentary *Lost and Found in Mexico*, American emigrant Caren Cross interviews fellow "expats" in San Miguel to better understand why so many foreigners have moved there. Most of her subjects are women who emphasize gendered pulls to Mexico and pushes from the United States. One American woman living in San Miguel shared this contrasting view of the two cultures: "I find it [the U.S.] a fairly masculine, kind of point to point culture, and I feel a little bit, sort of, out of step. I don't really fit in and when I came here, it's like sitting down on, you know, your favorite old chair. It's like I'm home" (Cross 2007). Another American woman, a native of Philadelphia who had been living in Mexico for eleven years, discussed what it had been like for her "growing up in a very male, intensely male culture . . . I was looking to escape being a nobody because I'm a female and I didn't have a place in that culture and I think I felt like that whole culture let me down" (Cross 2007). A recent exposé by *More* magazine on American women living in San Miguel echoed these same themes, referring to the town as "a reinvention destination for scores of midlife women" (Fraser 2007).

For many American women living in San Miguel, this sense of security was shattered in 2006 as the town's residents endured the torment of a serial rapist. The rapist, age 58, Mexican, and a veteran of a U.S. prison, was targeting foreign women in their fifties and sixties who lived alone in San Miguel. By the time he was apprehended in July 2006, he had raped five women, all foreigners, and was charged with the attempted rape of a sixth. The ordeal caused a great deal of tension in this otherwise tranquil town and revealed cultural chasms that typically remain muted. Many American women felt the Mexican police were not taking the crimes seriously, and some of the victims complained that they were treated disrespectfully by Mexican officials when they reported the rape. Pablo Gonzalez Sierra, district attorney for the State of Guanajuato, offered this all too familiar defense of how local Mexican authorities were handling the case:

> A girl comes and tells us she was raped, but in a second declaration, perhaps two hours later, she says the person that raped her was her boyfriend, that she went voluntarily into his car. The boyfriend comes and says that, indeed, they did have sexual relations but it was consensual and they had a fight. We ask the girl again, and she says that is the way it happened. (Garcia-Navarro 2006)

During an hour-and-a-half shuttle ride from the Guanajuato airport in Leon to San Miguel in June 2006, I made the mistake of asking the male driver about the rapes. In addition to practicing my Spanish, I hoped for some good news about the rapist's capture. Instead, the driver unleashed a mini-tirade against the victims—characterizing them as "American women known to hang out in bars with younger men"—and against the police for arresting innocent Mexican men in a desperate effort to appease the powerful foreign community. He also lamented the impact on tourism—his and the town's lifeblood. Contrary to his and the district attorney's portrayals of women and Americans, all of the victims were attacked in their homes while asleep alone in their beds. None was acquainted with the rapist. One of the women was legally blind. Nevertheless, once convicted, the rapist, too, claimed in his defense that he did not rape the women but that they consented, because "Americans are very liberal" (Schmidt 2006b).

Neither the reactions of the foreign community in San Miguel nor those of local Mexicans were uniform. One of the victims spoke openly about the respectful and professional treatment she received from the local authorities upon reporting the rape, and she called on the foreign community in San Miguel to cease criticizing local Mexican officials. Some Mexican women were impressed that American women were so willing to speak publicly about the crime without shame and so adamant in their demand for justice. Other Mexicans, however, resented what they saw as an inordinate amount of attention being focused on these crimes against foreign women when Mexican women are raped every day and rarely do authorities react with such force or speed. In the midst of all of this, the fact that American women had felt safe and cared for in Mexico was clear. One American woman explained: "The United States to me is like an adolescent. Mexico is like a grandmother—and it's safe, and nurturing, and warm—that's why we moved here" (Garcia-Navarro 2006).

Gender also figures into the migration experience of American men in interesting ways. While many women were likely to mention feeling more respected and safe in a culture they perceive as valuing women and older people, male migrants also shared experiences that convey a kind of openness not typical of their lives in the United States. Several men, particularly in Ajijic, white, middle-class, heterosexual men in their late sixties or early seventies, baby boomer men from Michigan, Ohio, and Tennessee, men who once sold insurance or balanced financial accounts, talked openly of surrendering, and then becoming addicted, to the pleasure of a pedicure: "At first I was like, 'no way,' but then I tried it, and, man, is it incredible. Now she comes to our house every other week, and I can't wait" (field interview, February 9, 2007). A few of these same heterosexual male immigrants also commented on the unexpected ease with which they had formed friendships with fellow members of the American immigrant community who were gay. One man joked, "I have learned now that I am supposed to say, 'partner.'" Another noted: "You know, if we had a party here [his home in Ajijic], say with thirty people, as many as ten of them would be gay. That wasn't the case back home" (field interview, February 8, 2007). Scholars have written insightful accounts of how gender influences, and is influenced by, the migration of Mexicans and other Latin Americans to the United States (Hondagneu-Sotelo 1994, 2003). Although distinct in terms of the context, related dynamics are at work among American immigrants in Mexico.

Whether it is safety, warmth, openness, or tranquility, when Americans identify the pull factors that drew them southward, they also implicitly, and sometimes explicitly, refer to what pushed them from the United States. American migrants to Mexico describe leaving a culture of stress and consumption in the United States for one that is more laid-back and loving, and less materialistic: "I left Mississippi, and that's an angry state. I came down here and found a friendly people. . . . They're polite to each other, and they're polite to strangers. That's a new experience and one that I really like" (Banks 2004, 368). One eighty-one-year-old woman who had been living in Ajijic for six years commented: "I like visiting my friends and family, but I am always anxious to come back home [Mexico]. In the States, everybody's so uptight and in a rush" (Blue 2000, 148). In these ways American migrants point to a cultural void they experienced in the United States that was being (or was more likely to be) filled in Mexico.

If culture (or what gets identified as culture) is one factor pulling Americans to Mexico and pushing them from the United States, to what extent are these migrants assimilating into the culture that reportedly helps lure them across the border? As is already apparent from the discussion above, the answer to this question is: very little. With every American I interviewed, I asked questions designed to assess this issue of assimilation: "To what extent do you interact socially with Mexicans? Do you have any friends who are Mexican? How often are Americans and Mexicans in attendance at the same social events? Do you speak Spanish?" Several Americans mention receiving invitations from Mexicans to baby showers. Others identify one or two Mexicans in town who are likely to be present at predominantly gringo functions. Yet, in keeping with what Cohen (1977) and others have written about expatriate communities, these Mexicans are typically members of the upper class whose professions—real estate, law, and tourism—put them in close contact with members of the foreign community. Overwhelmingly, American respondents agree that Mexicans and Americans in Ajijic and San Miguel interact very little beyond serving and being served—a pattern that is confirmed by earlier and more recent studies of these towns (Banks 2004; Bloom 2006; Stokes 1990).

Almost a third of the Americans I interviewed appeared to regret their limited social contact with Mexicans, attributing it, in part, to the belief that socializing in Mexico takes place primarily in the family and that unless you marry into the Mexican family you are not likely to be truly embraced within the inner circle. One American explained to me: "Mexicans are very shy. It is hard for them to trust anyone outside of family" (field interview, June 16, 2006). In his interviews with retirees in Lake Chapala,

Banks also found Americans invoking Mexicans' exclusivity as the explanation for limited friendships between the two groups:

> Everyday Mexicans are nice warm friendly. They're not like American friendly. You know we could be friends and you'd be coming to our house to dinner and blah-blah-blah and it'd take about a week. In Mexico it's not gonna happen, if you're not family you're not gonna get past a certain point. (2004, 371)

A likely explanation for the lack of intercultural socializing, although one rarely mentioned by Americans, has to do with language. Shockingly few of the Americans living in Ajijic and in San Miguel speak Spanish. And this is not unique to only the more recent arrivals, but includes some Americans who have been living in Mexico for a decade or more. A study of Lakeside in 1996 found that only 12 percent of immigrant retirees rated their Spanish as "more or less fluent," and only 6 percent described their Spanish as "good," or "fluent" (Otero 1997). A 2006 Migration Policy Institute study of American retirees in San Miguel found that few retirees were fluent in Spanish and that the ability to get by speaking only English was one of the things that drew them to San Miguel (2006, 57, 53). My interviews confirmed this point as well. Moreover, when I had the occasion to encounter an immigrant who did profess to speak fluent Spanish and then witness him or her doing so with a Mexican employee, I realized that some immigrants' self-assessments of their language ability can be quite generous.

It is important to note that many of the factors that typically contribute to the assimilation of immigrants in their countries of settlement are absent in the case of Americans in Mexico. For example, assimilation is generally a process that takes place over generations. Children, schools, and workplaces are central sites and resources in the process of incorporation into a new culture and society. For a majority of the immigrants living in Lake Chapala and San Miguel, none of these is present or prominent, which contributes to the perpetuation of what Cohen (1977) and others describe as an "environmental bubble." This bubble impedes assimilation, at the same time that it continues to draw southward immigrants who are attracted to the close-knit nature of the foreign community and the easy access to familiar cultural comforts.

"YOU GO TO FLORIDA TO DIE, BUT YOU COME TO MEXICO TO LIVE."

Stories of immigrants who do not or cannot assimilate into their host society are often stories of hardship and isolation; but very little about the lives of Americans in Mexico can be characterized in terms of hardship or isolation. After only a couple of weeks in Ajijic and in San Miguel, anywhere I went I bumped into someone I had already met. In Ajijic, I arrived on a Sunday and began my interviews on Monday. Tuesday, I was invited to dinner at a popular local restaurant. Wednesday, I joined several American women living in town at an exercise class. Thursday, I was invited, and given a complimentary ticket, to attend a major fund-raising event for handicapped children in town. On Friday, a group of Americans welcomed me on their bus tour of a nearby town; and on Saturday night, I attended a dinner party in a magnificent home, hosted by a couple who had moved to Ajijic two years before, after selling their vineyard in Northern California. The following week proceeded in much the same way, as did the time I spent in San Miguel. In San Miguel, one American couple living there learned I had arrived from Cincinnati and invited me to their home that very week for Skyline Chili. (This is a "cuisine" Cincinnati is well known for, and the couple had acquired the package of special seasoning from an Ohioan living in San Miguel.)

Tempting though it might be for me to feel personally flattered by this abundance of social activity, the truth is that the majority of Americans living in these Mexican towns are a very friendly and socially active crowd. The close-knit nature of the foreign communities and the ample opportunities for social engagement rank high among the factors Americans identify as drawing them to Ajijic and to San Miguel. I was told on more than one occasion: "You go to Florida to die, but you come to Mexico to live." When Americans praise the social virtues of these towns, they also draw a contrast to the lives they left behind—a contrast that confirms some of the scholarship on a decline in civic engagement in the United States. Yet, unlike many of their counterparts in the United States, these Americans in Mexico are not, to use political scientist Robert Putnam's phrase, "Bowling Alone" (2000). Social networks, in addition to economic and cultural factors, play a crucial role in migration across the Mexico/U.S. border—no matter which direction.

A typical day in Ajijic offers a glimpse into the vibrant lives American immigrants are living in Mexico. One February morning in 2007, I meandered through the narrow streets of Ajijic on my way to the Lake Chapala Society (LCS) — an organization that forms the backbone of the foreign community living along Lake Chapala. I had quickly learned that by simply sitting down at one of the many tables on the property's beautifully manicured gardens, I would soon be drawn into engaging conversation. Sometimes I met individuals or couples who were relative newcomers to town and stopping by the LCS to seek assistance with the logistics of settling into their new home, such as learning how to get the electricity hooked up. On other days, I would chat with old-timers who regaled me with tales of how things used to be in Lake Chapala "back in the day." On two different occasions, when I happened to be wearing a brown blazer, American visitors shopping for a retirement spot approached me, assuming I was a real estate agent. That particular day was warm and sunny, the bougainvillea was in full bloom, and hummingbirds buzzed about. I was keenly aware of the good fortune of all of us in Ajijic, because most of the states we hailed from north of the border were in the midst of a frigid cold spell of snow, ice, and record low temperatures. The people in the garden of the Lake Chapala Society, however, seemed pleasantly oblivious. Off to my far left, a steady stream of patrons lined up at the ticket booth to purchase tickets for an upcoming fund-raiser. Directly in front of me, a table was being used to administer free blood pressure tests. At another table, a young Mexican attorney was providing North Americans with complimentary consultation on immigration issues. One older American gentleman sat at this English-speaking Mexican attorney's table for over an hour—seemingly more interested in having company than securing any legal advice. The snack bar area was full, as usual, with a jovial crowd enjoying morning coffee and muffins from the popular gringo hangout, The Secret Garden. A sizable group milled about the bulletin boards that serve as classified advertisements for used furniture, apartment rentals, and pets needing homes. The video library also did a brisk business that day. A sign reading "New Acquisitions February 1" announced the arrival of *The Devil Wears Prada, Little Miss Sunshine,* and *Talladega Nights.* Meanwhile, the people from the Costco in Guadalajara were busy at their appointed table signing up new members and distributing the company's most recent merchandise catalogue.

The centrality of common institutions—an association, a club, a school, and to a lesser extent, a church or religious institution—is a recurrent theme in studies of expatriate communities. "The expatriate associations, clubs and schools," as sociologist Erik Cohen writes, "are not only the most ubiquitous but also the most important expatriate communal institutions; internally, they focus and structure the life of the expatriate community;

externally, they symbolize its separateness" (1977, 41). Foreigners' establishment of and reliance upon clubs and associations in areas of their settlement have a long history dating to the early days of European colonization. Analyzing the expatriate clubs in Tanganyika before its independence (when the country became Tanzania), Tanner explains: "The social life centered around the club, whose membership was confined to Europeans, all of whom were expected to join" (1966, 296). Centuries later, among communities of U.S. citizens living in Mexico, these sorts of organizations still play a crucial role in absorbing new members, providing support for individuals, and structuring the social life of the community. Moreover, and as a testament to the fine line between "expatriates" and those referred to as "immigrants," these social clubs and civic organizations formed by Americans in Mexico share many commonalities with immigrant hometown associations in the United States (Orozco and Rouse 2007).

Any discussion of social life in either Ajijic or San Miguel would be incomplete without a focus on the prevalence of philanthropic organizations and activities. Affiliation with and dedication to charitable work are a defining dimension of life for Americans living in Ajijic and San Miguel. In all but a very few interviews, Americans shared with me unsolicited accounts of their involvement in different philanthropic organizations focused on improving the lives of people (and animals) in Mexico. Both towns boast a wide array of charitable organizations and associations. The commitment to philanthropy and the immigrants' pride in it led one scholar to label San Miguel "the most earnest and self-righteous of the American colonies" in Mexico (Bloom 2006, 192). The Lions Club buys eyeglasses for Mexican children. Patronato Pro Niños raises money for their medical care. Mujeres en Cambio (Women in Change) helps disadvantaged women in rural areas outside of San Miguel, many of whom have husbands and sons working in the United States. Nicholas Bloom offers a poignant personal account of a typical fund-raiser in San Miguel:

> This event brought well-heeled Texans and summer crowds, social noise, and an aggressive auctioneer. . . . He encouraged his audience to "take another drink and bid one thousand dollars" because it was "money for the niños." The countless cocktail parties for large groups sold at the event would evidently lubricate group bonding among the American, particularly the Texan, elite of the town (one of the items up for sale was lunch with the governor of Texas). (Bloom 2006, 198)

As earnest and self-righteous as San Miguel may be, in Lake Chapala, the array of social service organizations and the commitment to charitable work are equally impressive. In February 2007, I attended a fund-raising gala in Ajijic quite similar to the one Bloom describes. The organization, Niños Incapacitados, raises money for handicapped children in the local region. That night's theme was "Baubles, Bangles, and Beads," and a large crowd of well-dressed foreigners showed up for "*botanas*" (appetizers), a cash bar, and a live dinner auction. Attendees bid on the likes of a "N'awlins Dinner for Eight," a "Backyard BBQ for Twelve," and "Cocktails for 25." The event raised over $20,000 USD, and when I left at 11 P.M., a sizable crowd of Americans and Canadians, many years my elders, were just beginning to warm up the dance floor (February 1, 2007).

In addition to charity for fellow human beings, Americans migrating to Mexico bring with them a culture of pampering animals that has placed many of the dogs and cats in these immigrant towns among the most well cared for in Latin America. In San Miguel, the well-funded Society for the Protection of Animals provides a reception and adoption center for lost and unwanted animals and low-cost veterinary services; Amigos Animales focuses on neutering and owner education; and Save a Mexican Mutt (SAMM) coordinates an adoption service. In both San Miguel and Ajijic, the foreign community has devoted itself to building and maintaining several animal shelters and clinics as well.

Some scholars have speculated about the function philanthropy serves for its organizers. According to Stokes, "Philanthropy, idealized by Lakesiders and recipients alike, is an instance of institutionalized prestige management" (1990, 178). She draws from early social exchange theory (Mauss 1967) to make the point that prestige is a payoff for gift-givers in asymmetrical transactions: "Gift-giving by Lakesiders is reciprocated by sentiments and expressions of admiration, loyalty and respect. . . . The retirees have no jural authority but the role of patrón is a metaphor of power and authority in Mexico" (1990, 178). Analyzing the function or impact of philanthropy is a complicated issue. I have no reason, or capacity, to judge the motivations of these Americans. Nor are complex and contradictory motivations for charitable work peculiar to Americans in Mexico. Certainly many, if not most, practitioners seem quite sincere and bring with them impressive human (as well as financial) capital. Perhaps Bloom puts it best in his discussion of San Miguel when he writes:

> Although many of these activities are needlessly showy, reflect aspects of guilt compensation, and seem to be more closely

focused on status competition within the American community (rather than just good works), many of them have made a great difference in the lives of local Mexicans. (2006, 192)

The array of activities outlined above—social, civic, philanthropic—and the countless organizations and clubs are a major factor in pulling American immigrants to these Mexican towns and keeping them there. Longtime resident and author on Lake Chapala, Karen Blue, notes: "Normally it takes me about six months to feel comfortable in a new place, to find my way around and develop a new circle of friends. But here, I felt like I belonged by the end of my first week." She goes on to explain: "No one asks, 'What did you do?' or 'Where did you go to college?' They ask, 'Where do you come from?' 'How did you find out about this place?' and 'Can you join us tonight for dinner?'" (2000, 18). American immigrants in San Miguel express similar sentiments. Writing for *Atención,* San Miguel's English-language weekly, longtime resident and columnist Connie Moore contrasted life in San Miguel with that of her hometown, Los Angeles:

> One of the biggest differences between the two places has to do with street life: there is virtually none in LA. The jardin here strikes me as the town living room with all the streets corridors leading to it. . . . To walk two blocks to the post office and encounter 16 humans who are involved in your life is in some way a heady experience. (Moore 1982)

What is clear in these quotations is that American migrants are not only drawn to Mexico, but pushed, or at least nudged, in some respects by voids they experienced at home.

For some of these migrants, life in the United States may be unfulfilling, but, and somewhat ironically, the social lives they construct in Mexico typically take the form of re-creating the comforts and familiarity of home. This is particularly the case in terms of celebrating traditional American holidays. The Fourth of July is a major event in both Ajijic and San Miguel. In Ajijic, the Lake Chapala Society sponsors the event, and in late June, the *Guadalajara Reporter* typically runs a column detailing the plans for the "U.S. Independence Day Bash." In 2005, the *Reporter* wrote: "It'll be set up with an old-time country fair flavor. . . . A silent auction will offer two Delta round-trip tickets to anywhere in the United States" (Chaussee 2005). In San Miguel, various groups organize July 4th events. In 1991 the recently founded Pack & Mail hosted the celebration for hundreds of guests with fireworks, hot dogs, potato salad, and watermelon. A spokesperson for the company explained: "We imported the hotdogs from Harlingen, Texas, so we'd have the real thing" (*Atención* 1991). Particularly popular is the gala hosted by the Democrats Abroad. In 2006, one of the town's popular Internet lists saw postings by American immigrants eagerly seeking tickets to the sold-out event.

Thanksgiving is also celebrated widely by American immigrants in Mexico. Several respondents told me how pleased they were that each year, more and more of the Thanksgiving "necessities" are available in their local Mexican grocery stores. In November of 2006, the English-language paper in Guadalajara assured American residents of Lake Chapala that they "should have no problem finding all the ingredients for traditional Thanksgiving fare at local supermarkets where shelves are crammed with all manner of stuffing mixes, canned green beans, potatoes, cranberry sauce, French fried onion rings, pumpkin pie mix . . ." (Chaussee 2006e). Stokes noted in her ethnography of Lakeside: "It is in the persistence of such familiar forms and symbols that North American culture is re-created at Lakeside, the transition to a foreign land is simplified, and formal markers of a social border are established" (1990, 173).

Notably, the interactions among U.S. citizens and the bonds they are forming in Mexico are more than mere fun and games. In Ajijic, in May 2002, a group of immigrants joined together to form the Expat Support Network. The network was initially composed of pods of eight to ten people, indicated by residential proximity or social relationships, who committed themselves to be available to each other in the case of an emergency. As one spokesperson explained: "A group leader is armed with house keys, personal medical data, financial data about who has access to accounts, family contacts, passport numbers, information concerning the individuals [*sic*] property, rental agreements, post-life planning, possessions, automobile, health insurance, wills and even information about pets" (Chaussee 2003). Meanwhile, in San Miguel, American immigrants use their Internet groups to coordinate blood donor lists to serve the foreign community in times of emergency—citing the lack of an ample and safe blood supply in Mexico (June 10, 2006, http://groups.yahoo.com/group/Civil_SMA). Sociologist Charles Tilly has recently written on the importance of trust networks to transnational migration (2007). Tilly's analysis, like most, focuses on immigration to the United States, but the phenomenon he identifies is present among American immigrants in Mexico as well.

When it comes to social relations among immigrants in Ajijic and San Miguel, all is not rosy in paradise. As scholars have found in studies of expatriate communities elsewhere, various forms of intracommunity tensions typically emerge, and infighting among different cliques is common. In his review of the existing scholarship on expatriate communities, Erik Cohen concludes: "The tightness of expatriate communities is thus conducive to a marked closure of the social horizon of the members and a preoccupation with the minutiae of daily life, to constant invidious comparison with fellow expatriates and to an intensified internal status struggle" (1977, 48). A very early study of Americans in India and Vietnam reported similar findings: "The tightness of the American community . . . may be too constrictive. The ecological concentration magnifies even trivial acts . . . transforms marginal items into ones of great symbolic value" (Useem et al. 1963, 179). In his study of Americans in Spain, Nash noted internal conflicts among the Consulate, businesspeople, the American School, and missionaries. He also described the common tendency of the "residents" to resent the tourists (Nash 1970, 91, 179). In more recent analyses of transnational migration, scholars like Thomas Faist have referred to the extremely complicated interactions between "old" and "new" immigrants, sometimes from the same country of origin (2000, 217).

All of these tensions are evident in Ajijic and San Miguel and are discussed further in Chapter Four. Old-timers regularly complain about the newcomers. Full-time residents resent the seasonal arrivals. In San Miguel, some New Yorkers were prone to complain about Texans, and vice versa. Active members of various social service groups often described to me different types of turf wars that periodically erupt within or between the organizations. For example, in Ajijic, the issue of euthanizing stray animals reportedly caused irreparable ruptures among the town's animal lovers. In San Miguel, some of the most colorful spats play out in cyberspace on the various Internet sites devoted to the town's foreign residents. One Yahoo group broke with another one, renaming itself "Civil SMA" to emphasize the expected code of conduct. And in mid-June 2006, a minor controversy erupted within San Miguel's foreign community around the issue of immigrants and their pets. One immigrant wrote an editorial in the town's popular English-language paper criticizing the increasing "number of gringas dogtrotting around town on their high heels with little toy dogs under their arms. . . . These American matriarchs are pushing their tiny, toy pets into the lives of everyone in town—not only in Centro, but in stores, churches and, most appallingly, in restaurants." As in the United States, Mexico's health department prohibits animals in restaurants, but San Miguel's proprietors are loath to alienate their wealthy customers. By 2006, some had, however, begun to do so. On June 15, 2006, several

American residents of San Miguel paraded around *el jardín,* pets in tow, to protest hostility they perceived was being directed toward them and their furry loved ones. The owners and their dogs were well dressed—in one case in matching outfits—and one American immigrant and dog owner offered this protest: "The dogs do not do anything bad, they are clean and educated, better than many people who do have access to these premises" (Noriz 2006, 11).

CONCLUSION

U.S. citizens have been living in Mexico since the beginning of that country's history as an independent state. Their numbers have increased over time, but their reasons for migrating have remained remarkably constant: cheap real estate, low taxes, ample sunshine, and welcoming hosts. From Steve Austin to Jack Kerouac to the retirees heading south today, U.S. migrants have been drawn by the search for adventure as well as by a desire to escape—whether from emotional or financial crises, or from a culture and a set of social rules and norms in the United States that they find unsatisfying. These U.S. migrants are generally quite satisfied with their migration decision. They boast about how well they live for how little (although some complain of rising prices in recent years). They feel welcomed by a people they perceive as warm, friendly, and tolerant; or, perhaps, they feel appropriately cared for and properly attended to by their Mexican hosts.

Americans living now in Mexico, like the expatriate communities Cohen and others have studied in the past, have a tendency to exaggerate the exoticness of their experience. One American immigrant living along the shores of Lake Chapala (and from all indications, quite comfortably) told me: "This [Mexico] is the most foreign country I've been in. If you can't adjust, you won't make it" (field interview, February 6, 2007). They have relocated to a foreign country and culture, but, in reality, what they encounter in the way of "strangeness" is limited by their privilege. Cohen writes: "It has often been observed that immigrant groups, middlemen minorities, as well as expatriates all over the world create their own 'enclaves'—ecological ghettos and institutional frameworks—which shelter them off from the environment of the host society" (1977, 16). Not all bubbles are alike, however, and the immigrants discussed here are a privileged group with the capacity to "make their definitions prevail in a foreign setting" and to "develop a lifestyle to their liking and create the institutions to maintain it" (Cohen 1977, 33).

The privilege of Americans in Mexico manifests itself not only materially in the houses they purchase, the cars they drive, the clothes they wear, and the restaurants they dine in, but also in their psychological outlooks. The narratives U.S. migrants tend to offer regarding Mexicans and themselves reveal a sense of cultural superiority. This superiority serves both to justify and to perpetuate the social boundaries between the migrants and their hosts, and to bolster a sense of self among a population of U.S. retirees whose identities are no longer firmly grounded in work or youth (Banks 2004; Cohen 1977; Stokes 1990). The material and psychological privilege of Americans in Mexico also seems to prevent them from seeing themselves, and others from seeing them, as immigrants in the conventional sense of the word.

Of the many conclusions that can be drawn from this overview of why U.S. citizens migrate to Mexico and the nature of their lives in a new and foreign land, two stand out, and both warrant important caveats. The first relates to the motivations for crossing the border. Without question, economic considerations are one, and arguably *the,* primary factor pulling the migrants to Mexico and pushing them from the United States. The affordable luxury homes, the cheap yet dedicated servants, and a comfortable lifestyle of dining out, movies, and manicures are among the first things U.S. citizens living in Mexico mention as pulls, alongside the push of rising costs in the United States. To end the story here, however, is to miss a significant dimension of this under-studied migration flow. A majority of Americans living in Ajijic and San Miguel also speak passionately about cultural and social longings that are satisfied in Mexico. Some of this emphasis on cultural factors may reflect what O'Reilly (2000, 28) and others label "post-hoc justifications." In other words, financial factors may have been the primary motivation underlying the migration, but, once comfortably ensconced south of the border, the immigrants also acquire an appreciation for Mexican people and come to value the social bonds they form with other immigrants. Nevertheless, the sentiments I heard expressed, some of which are recounted here, seemed quite sincere. Take, for example, a 2006 blog entry about social interactions in Mexico by a recent American immigrant to San Miguel (Schiavo 2006a):

> Leaving a store, restaurant, taxi, just about any space . . . we
> say Hasta luego—see you later—or Adiós. Mostly Hasta luego.

It seemed odd, at first, to send a cheery See you later to a
store clerk with no merchandise of interest. Felt disingenuous
to tour a village telling everyone we'd never see again Hasta
luego. Then, last evening, we experience something unset-
tling. We pay our tab and get up to leave the Limerick pub,
the bartender and manager busy with other customers. We
just walk out the door. No words, no smiles, no handshakes,
no promises to stay connected. I feel I've run off, left a friend's
home without saying good-bye, walked out in the middle of a
conversation. The full way home I can feel the lack. Reaffirm-
ing relationships in every interaction is important to me now.

The significance of cultural and social longings as an aspect of American
migration reveals something about Mexico, but also about what some U.S.
citizens, particularly retirees, experience as voids in their homeland.

A second finding revealed in this overview is that although many Americans are leaving their country of birth to settle in a foreign land, the lives
they establish in the new land appear to be, in large part, replicas of home.
U.S. immigrants living in Mexico are watching American television, celebrating American holidays, participating in U.S. politics, socializing with
other Americans, and speaking English, with only a rudimentary knowledge of Spanish. Nevertheless, to portray their lives in the new land as exact
replicas of home would be to miss important dimensions of the migration
experience for these Americans. For starters, American immigrants are, on
the whole, living more affluently in Mexico than they did, or otherwise
would do, in the United States. Rather than the decline in material lifestyle
and social and cultural status they would likely have endured at home as
retirees, they experience an enhancement of both. And as Cohen discussed
in his analysis of expatriates, they have an opportunity to become bigger
fish in a smaller pond (Cohen 1977, 39, 22).

As a corollary to the point regarding the strength of sociocultural pulls
and pushes, Americans in Mexico described to me repeatedly the pleasure they receive from meeting and forming friendships with new people
from different walks of life (albeit other foreigners like themselves) and
taking advantage of new and different experiences that they did not or
would not have in the United States (joining local theater groups, for example). I interviewed one American couple who had been living in Ajijic
for ten years. They might have been any other sixty-something, middle-
class, Anglo-Saxon retirees from the American Midwest, except for the
fact that they lived in an elaborate Spanish-style home located just blocks

from the picturesque shore of Mexico's largest lake. The male, a retired businessman, recounted, almost dreamily and after several cocktails: "You know, we have met so many interesting people here. We are always going to some dinner party at some different couple's house and trying out new things" (field interview, February 1, 2007). Moving to another country had been his wife's dream, and it was evident that she was living it to the fullest. Two different local English-language newspapers were spread open on their kitchen table, revealing where she had carefully circled and highlighted an array of upcoming events of interest—art openings, plays, and garden club meetings.

Most of the experiences Americans value in Mexico are not uniquely "Mexican" experiences, but they nevertheless credit the move to Mexico with changing and improving their lives in ways that extend beyond the financial. One travel magazine described life in Ajijic this way: "Foreigners give themselves permission to go a little eccentric . . . painting their walls in bright Mexican pinks and yellows, for example, or wearing arty, bohemian clothes that might have been frowned on when they were dressing for their neighbors back home" (Toll 2006, 76). In addition to the sense of personal and cultural liberation, a persistent theme in the lives of these migrants, and one that is developed in the next chapter, is the role of technology in influencing how they live their lives south of the border and how they simultaneously stay connected to the United States.

Two

HIGH-TECH MIGRANTS

Technology and Transterritoriality

That phone thinks it's in Houston.
— AMERICAN RESIDENT OF AJIJIC, MEXICO

It is not so much that [identities] are simply extra-territorial now,
but rather that peoples' relationship to territory is more complex,
more layered, less bounded, even if no less tangible.
— SHAMPA BISWAS, "GLOBALIZATION AND
THE NATION BEYOND"

In February 2007, I visited the home of an American couple who had been living in Ajijic for seven years. At one point, the American woman gestured to the telephone on her colorfully tiled Mexican counter-top and said, "That phone thinks it's in Houston." My initial, although un-spoken, reaction was "Who can blame it?" The Chevrolet Silverado truck parked on the dusty street out front sported U.S. license plates and a "Don't Mess With Texas" bumper sticker; a glass-encased, Texas-size American flag covered the wall behind the disoriented phone; and the flat-screen tele-vision was broadcasting audibly Fox News. Her comment referred to the fact that her telephone, like that of most U.S. migrants living in Mexico, operated with a U.S. telephone number made possible by a U.S. service provider. An international call to or from Mexico cost the same as if the communication took place between two neighbors in a Houston suburb. I had been introduced to this calling feature almost a year earlier when I first began making contacts with Americans in Mexico. I did so via e-mail from my home office in the United States, and many of these initial con-tacts graciously shared with me all the personal information I might need in order to reach them in Mexico. In several cases, they gave me telephone numbers with U.S. area codes. After assuming that either I had miscom-municated my plans, or these Americans were not actually in Mexico at the time, I learned of the wonders and prevalence of Voice Over Internet Phone (VOIP) service. Every American I met in Mexico subscribed to either Vonage or some other VOIP system. For approximately $30 a month these immigrants could select from an array of U.S. area codes, such as for Philadelphia, Houston, or Detroit, and receive a telephone number with which they could make and receive unlimited calls to and from family, friends, and business associates in the United States while residing in the mountains of central Mexico. This technology, like mobile phones, obliterates the old-fashioned notion that calling someone at a certain number reveals anything about his or her actual whereabouts. This also turned out to be just one of many ways that evolving information and communication technologies facilitate the migration of Americans to Mexico and a cross-border existence that defies conventional assumptions about the relationship between territoriality and belonging. This migration flow southward, like other, more familiar ones, challenges the significance of borders, territory, and the sovereign nation-state but, ultimately, attests to the fact that although all of these have been reconfigured in some way, none has been completely transcended.

TRANSMIGRANTS, TECHNOLOGY, AND THE TRANSCENDENCE OF TERRITORY

More people are now crossing back and forth across more borders more frequently. Immigrants today are less likely to leave behind one home and culture to commit fully or solely to a new one, and are instead more likely to sustain close ties with their homeland while building new lives and communities in a new land. Borders have become more porous, and the modern nation-state has slipped from prominence as the only, or the primary, source of cultural and political belonging. This "turbulence" (Rosenau 1990) is typically referred to as *globalization*. The term "globalization" is a contested one, but speaks to the increasing interconnectedness of the world (Croucher 2003, 10–13). Intensifying international migration—arguably both a consequence and a mechanism of globalization—has also given rise to new patterns of being and acting in the world, and new concepts designed to decipher those patterns: *transnationalism, transnational social spaces,* and *transmigrants.* The burgeoning literature giving rise to this terminology has yet to examine Americans migrating to Mexico, but promises rich insights into a rather unusual case.

Beginning in the 1990s, scholars of international migration began to identify new patterns and trends not well accounted for by existing analytical frameworks. Intrigued by these phenomena, Linda Basch, Nina Glick Schiller, and Cristina S. Blanc were among the first immigration scholars to issue the subsequently well-heeded call: "The time has come for all of us—social scientists and immigrants—to rethink our conceptions of the migration process, immigrant incorporation, and identity" (1994, 3). Basch et al. coined the term "transmigrants" to refer to those who "take actions, make decisions, and develop subjectivities and identities embedded in networks of relationships that connect them simultaneously to two or more nation-states," and they defined transnationalism as "the processes by which immigrants forge and sustain multi-stranded social relations that link together their societies of origin and settlement" (1994, 7). A robust body of literature on transnationalism emerged in the years following these early analyses. Scholars acknowledged and responded to the need for greater conceptual precision in the study of transnational phenomena (Kivisto 2001; Mahler 1998; Portes et al. 1999) and produced a range of case studies that illustrated the empirical and conceptual complexity of transnationalism (Guarnizo 1998; Levitt 2001b; Mountz and Wright 1996; R. Smith 2003, 2006).

A debate that has figured prominently into much of this discussion concerned the extent to which the phenomena being grouped as "globalization," or the patterns described as "transnational," are indeed new. On one side of this debate are those who insist that globalization is as old as humanity itself, and point to evidence of global interconnectedness dating back as far as the prehistoric period. Professor of politics Manfred Steger traces the evolution of globalization through five distinct stages, the first of which he locates between 10,000 B.C.E. and 3500 B.C.E. (2003). Sociologist Roland Robertson (1990) also identifies five phases of globalization. The first, what he labels "the germinal phase," occurs between the early fifteenth and the mid-eighteenth century. Similar claims circulate with regard to transnational immigration; and, indeed, literature dating back many decades indicates that neither the term "transnationalism," nor much of what it refers to, is entirely new (Angell 1967; Bourne 1916; Field 1971). Peter Kivisto, for example, writes: "It is quite clear that immigrants during the industrial era acculturated, but they did so on their own terms. . . . many groups continued to maintain an active interest and involvement in their homeland" (2001, 554).

Other scholars, however, have argued convincingly that many patterns and events witnessed today are indeed distinct enough to warrant new terminology and fresh analytical perspectives. Globalization as we experience it today is characterized by a qualitative and quantitative jump in the speed and intensity of interconnectedness, or as David Harvey explains, an unprecedented compression of time and space (Harvey 1990). These analysts do not dispute historical evidence of global ties, but insist that since the 1970s worldwide interdependencies have experienced a quantum leap (Marchand and Runyan 2000). Similar assessments are applied to transnational phenomena. As Portes et al. write: "While back and forth movements by immigrants have always existed, they have not acquired until recently the critical mass and complexity necessary to speak of an emergent social field" (1999, 217). According to these authors, what constitutes truly original phenomena and hence justifies a new topic of investigation are "the high intensity of exchanges, the new modes of transacting, and the multiplication of activities that require cross-border travel and contacts on a sustained basis" (1999, 219).

Ultimately, a large middle ground exists in the debate. Moreover, irrespective of where individual scholars stand on questions regarding the novelty of transnationalism, they are in broad agreement as to the centrality of technology—whether the railway, telegraph, typewriter, or Internet—to the transnational patterns being discussed. For example, political scientist Stephen Krasner rejects the novelty of globalization and the claims of the impending death of the sovereign nation-state, but he does so by arguing that the invention of the printing press in the fifteenth century wreaked far greater havoc on political authority than any of the challenges posed by today's global media (2001, 24). In an analysis of the growth of transnationalism during the 1960s, Robert Angell placed its origins further back in history than many do, and tied it to the availability of affordable air travel (1967). Thomas Faist also traced the emergence of transnational social spaces back to earlier historical breakthroughs in long-distance communication and travel, such as the invention of telegraph communication in the nineteenth century (2000, 198). From the perspective of these analysts, the roots of transnationalism may reach back in history, but those roots are always closely intertwined with the technologies of the time. Linda Basch and her colleagues are more persuaded by the newness argument, but in articulating their version of it, they, too, point to the role of technology. Although careful to caution against technological reductionism in explaining transnationalism, Basch et al. maintain that "Today's electronic technology lends a sense of immediacy to the social relations of people who are geographically distant" (1994, 23). Portes et al. concur and quite explicitly attribute the contemporary emergence of transnational practices to recent advances in technology:

Transnational enterprises did not proliferate among earlier immigrants because the technological conditions of the time did not make communications across national borders rapid or easy. It was not possible for would-be transnational entrepreneurs to travel to Poland or Italy over the weekend and be back at their jobs in New York by Monday. Nor would it have been possible for leaders of an immigrant civic committee to keep in daily contact with the mayor of a Russian or Austrian town in order to learn how a public works project, financed with immigrant money, was progressing. Communications were slow and, thus, many of the transnational enterprises described in today's literature could not have developed. (1999, 223)

Over the past decade several scholars have linked transnationalism directly to rapidly evolving information and communication technologies (ICTs) (Faist 2000; R. Smith 1998). A number of interesting case studies illustrate how the Internet, mobile phone, videoconferencing, and the like have affected the capacity of migrants to cross borders—physically and virtually—to maintain close ties with family and friends in the homeland, and to form communities and welcoming social spaces in a new land. Migrants, in fact, are often on the cutting edge of new communications and transportation technology because of the unique challenges they confront in maintaining relationships and forging cross-border networks (Karim 2003). Jamaicans living in rural regions of that country rely on mobile phones to keep in contact with relatives and loved ones across borders (Horst and Miller 2006); Salvadorans in the United States and El Salvador make skillful use of teleconferencing (Benítez 2006); and Eritreans in the homeland and in the diaspora use the Internet to debate democracy and the future of Eritrea (Bernal 2006). In the late 1980s and early 1990s, Chinese students in the United States and Canada formed cyber-communities to share news about events in China, including Tiananmen Square, to exchange information about jobs and migration issues in their countries of settlement, and to ease the adaptation to a new culture (Wu 1999). Children of Moroccan immigrants living in Holland use discussion boards on Web sites to exchange information about their country of origin, provide local news concerning migrants, and forge a sense of ethnic belonging as Moroccans while residing in the Netherlands (Brouwer 2006). Meanwhile, growing numbers of Mexican immigrants in the United States are developing Web sites about their hometowns that allow migrants to stay connected with their villages in Mexico and with fellow Mexican migrants in the United States. When Raul Briseño, an immigrant from the Mexican village of Atolinga in Zacatecas, was murdered in Chicago in 2001, the Web site www .atolinga.com served to spread the news quickly so that former townspeople from that Mexican village now living in different parts of the United States could attend the funeral in Chicago (Quiñones 2002).

In spite of a communications revolution, not all migrants have ready access to high-speed Internet connections, so must rely instead on less flashy, but no less influential, forms of transnational communications technology. In a recent Pew Hispanic Center study of Latino immigrants in the United States and their attachments to their homelands, Roger Waldinger (2007) reported that only one-third of the Hispanic immigrants in the United States use a computer even on an occasional basis, and only 15 percent use e-mail to contact friends and family in their native lands. Telephone calls are by far the most prevalent method of cross-border communication. From Steven Vertovec's perspective, prepaid telephone cards comprise the "social glue of migrant transnationalism" (2004). Inexpensive international telephone calls are particularly important to "non-elite social groups such as migrants" and offer a reminder, as Vertovec explains, of the still "grossly uneven distribution of telecommunications" access (2004, 219, 222; see also Benítez 2006). Other less novel technologies that help sustain transnational ties include "letter-writing" on cassette tapes that are carried across the border by friends and neighbors (Richman 2005); and videotapes transported across the border that allow friends and family in Mexico, for example, to stay apprised of the success of those who left, and allow those who reside in the United States to enjoy from afar the cultural and religious festivals they are unable to attend in their home villages in Mexico (R. Smith 1998).

In addition to recounting interesting anecdotes of immigrants' transnational lives, these case studies offer valuable analytical insights. Cyberspace, for example, can become a realm where some migrants establish or regain prestige outside of their homeland—even though "cybercapital" may not always translate into real life (Graham and Khrosravi 2002). In his analysis of the role of Web sites in South African expatriate discourse in the United States, Scott M. Schonfeldt-Aultman contends that white migration from South Africa has been motivated in part by a loss of privilege in a post-apartheid era. Resettlement in countries like the United States, Canada, Britain, and Australia, and the building and maintenance of community via the Internet, allow some South African migrants to recoup white racial privilege (2004). Other studies emphasize how computer-mediated communication can assist immigrant groups in resisting restrictive racial categorization and discrimination in their countries of settlement (Brouwer 2006; Nakamura 2002; Turkle 1996). Brouwer contends, for example, that the negative public image Moroccan youth suffer in the Netherlands contributes to their high degree of Internet activity: "Websites give them a chance to be heard" (2006, 1153). All of these analyses recognize that immigrant groups are heterogeneous and sometimes highly fragmented, but they nevertheless tend to unite in mutual support around their experience as immigrants, and in contrast to an "Other," which typically refers to "majority White America" (Mitra 1997).

One important disagreement that emerges from these studies concerns whether new technologies facilitate immigrant integration into the host society and culture or encourage maintenance of distinct ethnic and cultural differences. Wu maintains that among Chinese students living in North America, communications technology served to facilitate acculturation. Similarly, Robert Saunders found that regular Internet usage among ethnic Russians living outside of Russia did not fortify a sense of distinct ethnic identity or solidarity, but precipitated instead a denationalization of identity and the emergence of a postnational, globalist orientation (2006). Presenting the opposite perspective, a study of the South Asian diaspora in the West found that the use of electronic media led to an accentuation of religio-ethnic differences (Thompson 2002). Similarly, the availability of Greek satellite channels in Canada has served to revive a sense of ethnic identity and cultural distinctiveness among the Greek immigrant population living there (Panagakos and Horst 2006). Ultimately, whether the transnational practices fueled by emerging technologies result in the fortification of ethnic and cultural separateness or its transcendence depends on the specific context. How welcomed do immigrants feel in the host society? To what extent are the home government and civil society groups using technology to reach out to their conationals? To what sociocultural and material resources do the immigrants in question have access? Despite these variations, in all of the cases described above immigrants lead lives that confound conventional notions of territory and belonging.

Similar to the question of transnationalism's novelty, the continued significance of territory and the role of the modern nation-state have spurred vibrant academic debate. For some scholars, deterritorialization constitutes the very essence of globalization, while others insist that claims of fundamental shifts in the nature of space and place have been greatly exaggerated. The sovereign state is, from the first perspective, on its last leg; from the second, states are viewed as impressively adaptable entities, and hence their power may be perpetual. Again, a nuanced middle ground has emerged.

In his *Critical Introduction to Globalization,* Jan Arte Scholte maintains that definitions of globalization that focus on internationalization (increased interdependence between countries and their inhabitants), liberalization (reduction in barriers to the cross-border movement of goods, services, and financial instruments), or Westernization (processes of homogenization) are missing the point. These processes may very well be intensifying, but what is qualitatively new and different, and deserving of the term globalization, is the "far reaching transformations in the nature of social space" (2000, 46). Globalization, from his perspective, entails the "spread of supraterritoriality," or "a reconfiguration of geography, so that social space is no longer wholly mapped in terms of territorial places, territorial distances, territorial borders" (Scholte 2000, 16). International relations theorist John Ruggie agrees: "The distinctive feature of the modern system of rule is that it has differentiated its subject collectivity into territorially defined, fixed, and mutually exclusive enclaves" (1993, 151). Today, however, we have entered a new and different postmodern era, characterized in large part by the "unbundling" of territory, sovereignty, and identity (Ruggie 1993). The compression of time and space has altered how people participate and negotiate a sense of belonging in the world (Croucher 2003). In David Elkins's view, this shift away from purely territorial formations toward a greater role for nonterritorial organizations and identities constitutes "a new logic," opening up "possibilities unknown or unimagined or unattainable until now" (1997, 142).

Central to the alleged transcendence of territoriality are portrayals of a modern nation-state that has lost power in the international system, and that no longer serves as a primary site of political and cultural belonging. During the 1990s, some analysts stepped forward to proclaim the retreat, or the end, of the nation-state (Strange 1996; Omhae 1995) and the related arrival of a "post-national global order" (Appadurai 1996; Soysal 2000). Susan Strange argued, for example, that "Today it is much more doubtful that the state—or at least the great majority of states—can still claim a degree of loyalty from the citizen greater than the loyalty given to family, to the firm, to the political party or even in some cases to the local football team" (1996, 72). Arjun Appadurai concurred: "We are looking at the birth of a variety of complex, postnational social formations. . . . The new organizational forms are more diverse, more fluid, more ad hoc, more provisional, less coherent, less organized, and simply less implicated in the comparative advantages of the nation-state" (1996, 168).

These scholars were not only portending the decline of the state as a primary and autonomous actor in the international system, but also the weakening of the nation as a central source of identity and belonging. The distinction between the two, state and nation, is important and widely noted. States are the bureaucratic administrative units with sovereignty and a monopoly over the legitimate use of force. They can be marked concretely through, for example, longitudes and latitudes on a map. Nations, on the other hand, are less tangible and defined in subjective terms, but always as "the people": "a body of people who feel that they are a nation" (Connor 1978, 396); "a collective of people" (Barrington 1997, 712); "a named human population" (A. Smith 1991, 14). Any number of factors might be said to constitute the "sentiment of solidarity" that binds these communities—language, religion, blood, territory (Weber 1948)—but most scholars agree with Benedict Anderson's famous definition of nations as "imagined communities" (1991). They are "imagined" because the members of any given nation will never know most of their fellow members, but they nevertheless share a belief in belonging to a finite and distinct community of kind. Anderson tied the possibility and proclivity for such national imaginings to the convergence of specific historical forces in the late eighteenth and early nineteenth centuries. Working from this assumption of nationhood as a modern invention, some scholars naturally conclude that as the modern era fades, so too will nations and nationalism (McNeill 1986). "Nation-states and nations," as Eric Hobsbawm wrote, "will be seen as retreating before, resisting, adapting to, being absorbed, or dislocated by the new supranational restructuring of the globe" (1990, 182).

While proponents of this postsovereign, postnational perspective proclaimed fundamental shifts in the world system, others cautioned that it was much too soon to write the obituary of the nation-state (Tölölyan 1991, 5). "In spite of forecasts of the 'end of the state,' there is," wrote Ronnie Lipschutz, "little question that the 'state' will remain a central actor in world politics for some time to come. It will retain its capabilities, its material and discursive powers, and its domination of the political imaginary" (1999, 217). The same, it can be argued, is the case with nations. Globalization in its varied dimensions is altering the mechanisms with which and contexts in which national communities are being imagined. Anderson identified the emergence of "print capitalism" as a key historical factor in the birth of imagined national communities. The historic conditions today are different from those Anderson emphasized, as are the available technological tools (the Internet, satellites), but nations themselves, although altered in form, continue to be potent sources and sites of belonging and hence seem destined for "perpetual imagination" (Croucher 2003).

Finally, territory, too, has been shown to still matter in an era of heightened globalization, although it matters differently. Peter Mandaville explains:

> I think we need to examine the possibility that people are actually holding on to notions of territory and place—increasingly complex yet highly tangible senses of "here" and "there"—but are also understanding the nature and, in particular, the boundaries of territory (as well as their socio-political relationships within and across these boundaries) somewhat differently. (1999, 653)

Thomas Faist also offers a useful illustration of the continued relevance of territory by drawing a distinction between globalization and transnationalism: "There is a marked difference between the concepts of globalization and transnational social spaces. . . . Whereas global processes are largely decentered from specific nation-state territories and take place in a world context above and below states, transnational processes are anchored in and span two or more nation-states, involving actors from the spheres of both state and civil society" (2000, 192). Transnationalism, Faist goes on to explain, is "not located on a magic carpet of a deterritorialized space of flows. It only makes sense when firmly tied to specific spaces in different nation-states" (2000, 218). These discussions of the ambiguous role of technology, territory, and the nation-state in the lives of transmigrants apply in interesting ways to the case of U.S. citizens residing in Mexico, and this little-known case can help deepen the empirical foundation of the existing scholarship on transnational phenomena.

TECH-SAVVY MIGRANTS IN MEXICO

American migrants residing in Mexico, compared to immigrants living in the United States, receive relatively little political or scholarly attention; but they, too, live transnational lives powered by evolving information and communications technologies (ICTs). They have easy and affordable access to high-speed Internet connections, satellite radio and television, mobile phones with special North American calling plans, and private mail services that make daily deliveries across the border. They watch American television, read U.S. newspapers online, and communicate regularly with family, friends, and business associates in the United States. They maintain and regularly access an array of Web sites, blogs, and Internet chat groups (all in English and geared toward foreigners residing in Mexico as well as those contemplating a move across the border). Like Mexican immigrants in the United States, Americans in Mexico also use less technologically sophisticated methods of cross-border communication. In San Miguel, for example, the Unitarians and other church groups begin Sunday services asking who is headed north across the border in the upcoming week and willing to carry mail. Volunteers raise their hands, and members of the congregation pass their letters (sporting U.S. addresses and postage) across the aisles. In Ajijic, the Lake Chapala Society coordinates similar cross-border communication, and sells its members U.S. postage stamps. The Society's directory explains: "LCS offers its members a postal courier service to the U.S. Postal Service. The mailbox is situated in the LCS office. . . . Members traveling to the United States are encouraged to stop by the LCS office and ask to take as much mail as they are able. The success of this service depends on every LCS member's cooperation" (Lake Chapala Society 2006, 32). As is the case with migration from Mexico and other countries to the United States, technology influences the migration of Americans to Mexico. It does so by reducing the uncertainty associated with the decision to migrate; facilitating the maintenance of sociocultural, political, and economic ties with the homeland; and easing the transition to new and unfamiliar terrain (in part, by providing mechanisms for community building among fellow immigrants in the new land).

Writing about South African migration to the United States, Schonfeldt-Aultman explains that "When considering immigration to a country, it is not unreasonable to think that potential emigrants will surf the Internet to find information about a likely host country." He emphasizes the significant role message boards and chat rooms play in emigration/immigration decisions, and notes that "once arriving in a host country, the web may provide access to resources that help emigrants cope with the relocation, as well as reproduce and maintain their national identities" (2004, 311). All of this holds true with regard to U.S. migrants to Mexico. Although many Americans in Mexico repeat the tale of arriving in Ajijic or San Miguel one week and purchasing a home the next, others describe carefully researching the move in advance and doing so via the Internet (Migration Policy Institute 2006). A variety of Web sites, Internet groups, and blogs provide information to potential immigrants on living and retiring in Mexico. Some serve the country as a whole, and others are region- or city-specific. Some are branches of larger global companies, like International Living; others are created by private individuals capitalizing on the growing trend of U.S. migration southward. Some sites rely heavily on advertisements from hotels, real estate corporations, tourist agencies, and moving companies. On other sites, American migrants simply share (with family, friends, and anyone else who is interested) tales of their adventures in an "exotic" land (www.rollybrook.com/index.html).

Mexico Connect is a Web site that bills itself as "The Most Comprehensive Resource About Mexico, On the Internet or Anywhere, in English" (www.mexconnect.com). The site has published an e-zine since 1996 and has recorded 20,086 subscribers between 2003 and mid-2007. In recent years, Mexico Connect has grown to become one of the 5 percent of sites worldwide with the most traffic. Each month, the site averages 3,650,000 successful page requests. More valuable than a "hit," the moderator explained, a page request means someone actually clicked on a banner or link and loaded the page. These requests come from an average of 580,000 unique hosts. North Americans comprise the overwhelming majority of Mexico Connect users, with a handful in Europe and Thailand, and two in South Africa (e-mail correspondence with site owner, July 6, 2007). The site offers an array of information on living, working, and retiring in different parts of Mexico. Subscribers (and to a lesser extent visitors to the site who do not subscribe) have access to specific guidelines for obtaining the appropriate visa or insurance in Mexico, as well as information on the culture and food of Mexico. Featured columnists share regular musings about life in Mexico—such as a recent essay, "Here and There," by American Marvin West on how his life in the small village of Jocotepec, along the shores of Lake Chapala, differs from life in Washington, D.C. (West 2007). The Web site also displays a number of testimonials from American immigrants regarding how Mexico Connect influenced their decision to cross the border. One subscriber writes: "In making our decision to move down here we extensively used the resources that Mexico Connect provides, and I will tell you it was a major factor in our ultimate decision." Another exclaims: "Mexico Connect helped me realize that Mexico was indeed for me. I haven't looked back" (www.mexconnect.com [accessed July 14, 2007]).

Solutions Abroad is a company based in Mexico that bills itself as "the most complete web-based resource for expatriate foreign nationals working in Mexico, living in Mexico, visiting, retiring or moving to Mexico" (www.solutionsabroad.com). The site provides information on real estate in Mexico (both for investment and relocation), how to get a visa, Spanish language schools, and social and cultural events. Solutions Abroad was started in May 2000, and the company's president reported in June 2007 that it had 16,000 users, up from 6,000 three years earlier. He also noted that in 2000, 70 percent of its clientele were seeking information on Mexico City, but by 2007, that was the case with only 16 percent. Interest in the country's capital city had not declined absolutely, just relatively, as interest in other places such as Lake Chapala and San Miguel de Allende surged. Retirees have also come to comprise a growing proportion of the site's users (field interview, May 22, 2007). New Beginnings is a Web site developed by two retired teachers from New Jersey who moved to Mexico in 2002. It is also the name they gave to their new home in Ajijic. As they explain: "The pages on this web site document the six months that we went through the final stages: the paperwork, the packing and all the angst that [go] with retiring and moving to another country. Now it gives you personal and helpful details about life in paradise" (http://www.newbeginningsmexico .com/ [accessed July 7, 2007]). International Living, "a resource for living, traveling and investing overseas" (www.internationalliving.com), is in its thirtieth year of operation, and a recent study of U.S. retirees found this to be the most cited resource for migration decisions (Migration Policy Institute 2006, 56). The organization publishes a popular magazine and blog, sponsors online discussion forums, and averages 378,856 visitors a month to its Web site. Mexico is one of only eight countries where International Living maintains "in-country support." It also publishes an e-zine, *Mexico Insider,* and offers "The Mexico Alert," which provides free online informational updates. As of 2007, "The Mexico Alert" had 19,189 subscribers—the overwhelming majority in North America (e-mail correspondence with Mexico Office director, July 9, 2007).

More specialized Web sites, Internet groups, and blogs serve foreigners, mainly North Americans, interested in or already residing in the specific communities of Ajijic and San Miguel. In Ajijic, Mexico Insights has been a particularly popular site since 2002, and for $40 a year offers subscribers access to its online magazine *Living at Lake Chapala,* with feature articles on the region, a kitchen section with locally inspired recipes, as well as real estate and cost-of-living advice. Editor Judy King, known as the "Ajijic Storyteller," also maintains a popular blog on the site. King, a native of rural Iowa, arrived in Lake Chapala in 1990 and helped found the site in 2002. She reported 700 subscribers in February 2007—a number lower than it had been in the past. Subscribers consist primarily of people still in the United States who are planning to move to Mexico. King regularly speaks to tour groups visiting the area and conducts weekly "Living at Lake Chapala" seminars. She identifies the mid-1990s as the period when the Internet boom began to most noticeably affect foreign migration to Lake Chapala. The region was increasingly featured on different travel Web sites and publicized in popular media outlets in the United States. In March 2004, *AARP Magazine* published an article, "La Vida Cheapo," featuring Lake Chapala as a paradise for U.S. retirees. In the subsequent year, King answered 5,000–6,000 e-mail queries about life and prices in her adopted home (field interview, February 6, 2007).

In San Miguel, Americans Carol Schmidt and Norma Hair maintain a Web site, "Falling in Love with San Miguel: Retiring on Social Security," that is popular among both those who have made the move to Mexico and those who are pondering it. Like King, they post news about the town, host a discussion forum, share cooking tips, and offer advice on living in San Miguel on U.S. Social Security. They started the Web site in February 2006 and averaged, in 2007, 183 unique hits per day on the home page ("unique hits" means that the counter only registers one hit per web address a day, not repeat visits in a day). As of June 2008, they reported 580 registered forum users, 120 active posters, and as many as 100 unregistered "lurkers" reading the forum at any one time (e-mail correspondence with Schmidt, June 12, 2008). As Schmidt explains, "Most people lurk and don't even register, and most of those who register still are only lurkers and never post. And you can get to the forums directly without going through the home page and never get counted. So all our numbers are undercounts." She goes on to explain: "Most of our active forum members live in the US and are collecting information about moving to Mexico, particularly to San Miguel. But some local residents use our forums for fun and to also give back to others the way they were helped by Internet posters themselves" (e-mail correspondence with Schmidt, June 19, 2007). Portal San Miguel (www.portalsanmiguel.com) is a more commercial site that acts as a sort of Yellow Pages for real estate associations and hotels, but also provides a list of social and charitable organizations and publicizes upcoming cultural events.

Several Internet lists catering to foreigners are also active in San Miguel. Potential migrants residing in the United States use the lists to gather information on moving to Mexico — "Can I bring my car, my cat; what kind of insurance do I need?" — but Americans who have already crossed the border make frequent use of them as well. Schmidt explains:

> There are at least six internet lists in San Miguel that are made up primarily of SMA residents, exchanging information, for example, on what others are paying for a gold crown by various San Miguel dentists, what internet speed do they have that day, is there a dry cleaning service that will come out to

your house and pick up your rug, do any of the vets do pet
boarding, etc. . . . We also get into a lot of silly disputes and
some fun posts, and some of the unmoderated lists have heavy
arguments on US politics. (e-mail correspondence, June 19,
2007)

One of the more popular lists is a Yahoo group, named "Civil_SMA." The
group formed in April 2006 after many grew disillusioned with the "un-
civil" discourse on another list. The name "civil" reflects the list's commitment to respectful exchanges among members and to their stated commitment not to talk politics. By June 2008, Civil_SMA had 1,685 members and
averaged 2,000 posts per month. A smaller group of immigrants in San
Miguel who resent what they perceive as an emphasis restricting open dialogue are committed to "smacoollist." This group, first formed in November 2005, had 480 members as of June 2008, and describes its mission as
follows (http://groups.yahoo.com/group/smacoollist/):

> This is for all related to san miguel allende [sic] and general
> chat between folks related to this town one way or the other,
> not necesarily [sic] living there. The list is not moderated so
> feel free to post your ideas and remember that this list is built
> by many threads of conversation, not every thread is for you,
> so be wise and skip what offends you, if at all. The rationale
> behind this openess [sic] is that diversity is a bonus and unifor-
> mity and censorship is [sic] what make groups, countries and
> churches dull.

Most Americans who crossed the border during the past decade acknowledge, albeit some more emphatically than others, that they would
not live in Mexico without the array of communication and information
technologies currently available to them. High-speed Internet connections, e-mail, and VOIP are standard features in the homes of American
immigrants, as are satellite television and, to a lesser extent, satellite radio.
Some Americans joke good-naturedly about the irony of their "high-
tech, laid-back" Mexican lifestyles: "Yesterday at home I mixed up the ring
tones and picked up the wrong phone. Mexican land line . . . VOIP phone
. . . cell phones . . . the row of equipment on chargers blinks to us in the
dark" (Schiavo 2006b). Other immigrants boast about being able to receive
programming via satellite television from both the east and west coasts

of the United States, and those who don't have satellite radio can listen to U.S. radio programming via streaming audio on their computers. An American grandmother in Ajijic described to me how she watches daily the live video of her grandson at his day-care facility in Houston. Another American woman is able to use Vonage to participate across thousands of miles, and regulated interstate borders, in an annual slumber party reunion she and her friends from high school hold each summer. In all of these ways, U.S. citizens who move to Mexico maintain transnational ties to their homeland: following news reports and cultural events in the United States, managing financial affairs, and communicating regularly with loved ones.

For Americans in Mexico, technology not only facilitates transnational migration but is, for many, an important factor in the decision to make the move. A discussion thread on Mexico Connect in late March 2007 addressed this issue directly (http://mexconnected.com/perl/foros/gforum.cgi?post=106760;search_string=without%20internet). An American woman living in Mexico posted the following query to Mexico Connect subscribers: "Would you live in Mexico . . . without Internet? Seriously. Have been wondering about this for about eight years." Her post generated more attention than most. A few American migrants harked back to the "old days" when they had no choice but to survive in Mexico without the Internet—pointing out, for example, that dial-up did not come to the Lake Chapala area until 1997 and Prodigy was not widely available until 2001. Others responded with an unequivocal "no," they would not live in Mexico without the Internet. The most common response to the query was some version of this particular immigrant's reply: "I suppose we COULD, but would I WANT TO?—NO!!!!" Most Americans in Mexico identified as the main factors that tied them to the Internet the convenience and reliability of online, cross-border banking and the ability to sustain relationships with loved ones in the United States:

> Having done it [lived without the Internet] once a million years ago, of course, I could do it again. My husband doesn't touch the computer and he seems quite content. But . . . I love saying goodnight to my newest granddaughter over Skype at night and seeing her everyday in real time on the computer. It allows me to keep one credit account (and therefore, a credit history, etc) in the US if I should ever have to return there.

My own interviews with immigrants in Mexico revealed similar sentiments. On a February 2, 2007, bus trip from Ajijic to the nearby town
of Tuxpan, an American woman and retired investment banker who had
been living in Mexico for eight years said, without hesitation: "I could not
have lived here before technology. I am able to start my day here just like
I would in the U.S.—with the *Wall Street Journal*" (field interview, February 2, 2007). Frequently, American immigrants I met in Mexico would extend the offer "E-mail me anytime, I am always online." Judging from the
traffic on the online discussion forums, Yahoo groups, and the like, many
indeed seem to be.

Communications and information technology are allowing Americans
south of the border to stay connected to the United States, but are also
facilitating community building among these immigrants once they have
settled in Mexico. Beyond being valuable sources of information for new
and potential migrants, the Internet lists described above foster a sense
of community and connectedness among their members—some of whom
have never actually met but still refer to one another as "friends." Virtual
socializing meets actual socializing, as these lists also serve as venues for
posting announcements about upcoming events: happy hours, charity auc-
tions, and Fourth of July celebrations. When participants on one online
forum discussed whether or not they would live in Mexico without the
Internet, several posters pointed to the role of communications technology
in forging community and a sense of belonging (http://mexconnected
.com/perl/foros/gforum, March 26, 2007):

> I don't mean to sound crass but really, why would some-
> one keep coming here if their only function was to answer
> newbies questions? There has to be a community for it to be
> worth returning here once you get your questions answered.
> Creating a community is not all that easy but it exists here
> and is considered valuable by many of us.

Another immigrant agreed:

> I'm one of MexConnect's most prolific posters and view the
> site several times a day, as much for keeping in touch with the
> community here as for posting some tidbit of information or
> asking a question. I've never met most of you in "face-time,"
> but nevertheless I generally consider you to be friends, or at
> the very least, interesting folks along my life's path. Most of

you whom I have met face-to-face are good friends, people I depend on for frequent nourishment of my heart, soul, and intellect. I'd never have met most of you if it had not been for the Internet. (http://mexconnected.com/perl/foros/gforum)

Some posters become well known and respected in these cyber-communities for their experience, knowledge, and level-headed views on provocative issues. In this way, and like what Schonfeldt-Aultman (2004) illustrated in his study of the South African diaspora, technology allows Americans living in Mexico to maintain or gain a certain amount of prestige outside of their homeland or communities of origin. In the cases I observed personally in San Miguel and Ajijic, cyber-capital does translate into social capital and vice versa. Ed Clancy, U.S. consular agent for San Miguel, has significant social capital in cyberspace as well as out of it, and makes effective use of Internet lists to communicate with and assist his constituency. Carol Schmidt, creator of the site Falling in Love with San Miguel (www.fallinginlovewithsanmiguel.com), is a well-known and respected member of the foreign community in San Miguel. I personally witnessed people stop her in restaurants to introduce themselves and to express their appreciation for her online insights and assistance. The same is true of Judy King in Ajijic, who edits the online magazine *Living at Lake Chapala* (http://www.mexico-insights.com/).

A second theme in the literature on technology and transnationalism questions whether technology facilitates migrants' cultural assimilation or encourages the preservation of ethnic and cultural distinctiveness. This particular case tends to provide more support for the latter position. Americans are able to use technology to learn the ropes as they arrive in Mexico—to exchange the information they need to live comfortably and safely in Ajijic and San Miguel. They do learn some things about the people and the culture of Mexico, about recipes and festivals, but do so more as long-term tourists might. These technologies do not facilitate Spanish language acquisition, nor do they encourage closer social ties between American immigrants and their Mexican hosts. In an analysis of transnationalism, Alejandro Portes recounts an interview with an immigrant from Central America living now in Los Angeles, California. The man describes the various ways he stays connected to his home village in El Salvador, La Esperanza, and ultimately concludes: "I really live in El Salvador, not in LA" (Portes 1999, 466). No American with whom I spoke in Mexico characterized her or his life in this way—"I am really living in the United States." On the contrary, most are quite pleased, even proud, to be living in Mexico.

Nevertheless, for very many U.S. citizens living in Mexico, the daily content of their lives, the language they speak and with whom they converse, the news they consume, the entertainment they enjoy, the cars they drive, the checking accounts they withdraw from, the addresses they are identified by, the jobs they perform, are not defined—and, thanks to technology, are often remarkably unconstrained—by geographic borders and territorially grounded notions of place and space.

RECONFIGURING TERRITORY

Before departing for Mexico in June 2006, I ordered over the Internet the highly recommended *Insider's Guide to San Miguel* (Dean 2005). American author Archie Dean is well known for his firsthand knowledge of and familiarity with San Miguel—offering advice that ranges from how to get legal documents notarized in San Miguel to where to get your watch repaired. Curiously, Archie's address, where I was to mail my payment for the book, is in Texas. Given his obvious devotion to the Mexican paradise of San Miguel, I could not imagine why Mr. Dean would choose to live in Laredo, Texas. As it turned out, he is a full-time resident of San Miguel and has been since 1993. Archie Dean, like most Americans in San Miguel and Ajijic, "lives" in Laredo only on paper. Just as Vonage gives Americans abroad a U.S. telephone number, a variety of mail delivery services located in Ajijic and San Miguel provide Americans residing in Mexico with a U.S. address (typically Laredo). At a cost of roughly $25 USD per month, mail received at this Texas address is picked up by employees of companies like Mail Boxes, Etc., Pack & Mail, or Border Crossings, driven across the border, and delivered to the immigrant's post office box in Mexico. Among other things, this allows American immigrants in Ajijic and San Miguel to avoid the vicissitudes of the Mexican postal service, buy and sell on eBay, rent from Netflix, and receive their regular subscriptions to U.S. magazines. This is also one of several ways that conventional signifiers of place and identity—whether a mailing address, telephone number, license plate, or job—may, today, reveal little about a person's physical whereabouts or how that individual defines his or her sense of belonging in and to the world.

In addition to a virtual population boom in Laredo, Texas, when I arrived in the mountains of Mexico, I initially thought I had stumbled upon a little-known migration stream from the state of South Dakota. It is not uncommon for someone walking through the streets of Ajijic and San

Miguel to see cars with U.S. license plates from the border states of Texas or California; but the disproportionate number of cars with plates from South Dakota struck me as odd. Scholars of migration often uncover established migration flows between a particular village, or state, in Latin America and a specific region in the United States. These ties emerge and are sustained in large part through social networks. Robert Smith has analyzed transnational flows between a village in Puebla, Mexico, and New York City. Peggy Levitt's work does the same with the village of Miraflores in the Dominican Republic and the neighborhood of Jamaica Plains in Boston, Massachusetts. Allison Mountz and Richard Wright examine the transnational social field encompassing El Salvador and Poughkeepsie, New York. It appeared to me, at least initially, that something similar was taking place with migrants from the U.S. state of South Dakota to the Mexican towns of Ajijic and San Miguel. As it turned out, however, not one American I met in Mexico was actually from South Dakota, and very few had ever set foot in the state.

The explanation for the abundance of cars in Mexico with license plates from the Northern Plains of the United States lay in the fact that South Dakota, or at least one county in South Dakota (Clay County), is reportedly quite generous about registering motor vehicles. American immigrants living in Mexico and driving with South Dakota plates report that they are able to register their car and receive the title or registration and the plates through the mail at bargain prices without having an address in South Dakota or a South Dakota driver's license, a vehicle inspection, or proof of U.S. insurance, or ever leaving their homes in Central Mexico. As one immigrant explained: "The South Dakota folks are real laid back about this. They don't care whether you live in Pierre or Mozambique. They don't really care if you are even alive if your money is negotiable" (http://mexconnected.com/perl/foros/gforum, October 6, 2004). Some of the Web sites and online discussion forums mentioned above dispense advice and precise instructions for how immigrants can take advantage of the license plate loophole (http://www.newbeginningsmexico.com), and offer space for exchanging up-to-date information about the best strategies, car-related and otherwise, for "living" simultaneously in Mexico and the United States (http://mexconnected.com/perl/foros/gforum, March 6–12, 2007; http://groups.yahoo.com/group/Civil_SMA/, February 28, August 12, November 22, 2007).

Some Americans living in Mexico, for example, opt to register their vehicles in Texas instead of South Dakota and report doing so with similar ease—although this option does require at least one physical appearance in the state of Texas. Securing a Laredo address via one of the mail service companies in Ajijic and San Miguel is the first step. Step number two entails driving to Texas, purchasing the minimal amount of liability insurance required by the state, and getting a safety inspection at Wal-Mart or any other of a number of inspection stations. The third and final step requires going to the licensing authority and applying for Texas registration without title transfer. Americans in Mexico explain that when asked for a telephone number at this stage, they simply give the state official the number of their hotel and explain that they have just moved to Texas and do not yet have a phone:

> I registered my car in Texas with a personal mail box at a
> Mail Boxes, Etc. street address in Laredo. No questions asked.
> Had they inquired, I was prepared to say that I was moving
> to Laredo and using that address until I found an apartment.
> When they asked me for a phone number, I told them that I
> had no phone as of yet. However, you could simply give them
> the phone number of your hotel. (http://mexconnected.com/
> perl/foros/gforum, December 3, 2004)

Whether by mailing forms to South Dakota or paying a quick visit across the border to Texas, American immigrants are able to keep their American-bought cars and U.S. registration while residing on a permanent basis in Mexico. This option is preferable, they explain, because to buy a car in Mexico and pay the related taxes are relatively expensive, as is the process of registering or "naturalizing" in Mexico a car purchased in the United States. Immigrants are also able, via similar "loopholes," to watch U.S. television programming in their Mexican homes. The technology that powers satellite television is such that service providers cannot fully restrict the reach of a signal being beamed to earth from outer space. As Benjamin Barber wrote in "Jihad vs. McWorld," "Satellite footprints do not respect national borders" (1992, 58). Nevertheless, it is technically illegal, and a violation of contract with companies like Dish Network, to subscribe in one country and utilize the service in another. But enterprising immigrants and Mexican technicians have found ways around these old-fashioned notions of borders, places, and spaces. Some simply pirate the television programming, while others use their Laredo address, or a fictitious address somewhere else in the United States, to subscribe to a service provided by a U.S. company in the United States that they are actually enjoying in Mexico. One American living in Mexico explained to me in an e-mail correspondence: "Dish network is a pirated service here. You are stealing the signal. And you don't need to bring anything. There are two 'suppliers' here who will sell you all the equipment and install it. . . . What we will do to have our shows!!!" (July 12, 2007). Others explained that they were subscribing to and paying for the service, but that they had to pretend to be living in the United States to do so. Dish accounts typically include two addresses, a billing address and a service address. The first poses no problem for immigrants in Mexico who simply list their Laredo, Texas, post office box address or sign up for electronic billing and auto-payment via credit card. The service address, on the other hand, must be invented. One American woman living in Ajijic told me: "Oh, I just gave them the address of a McDonalds in Arizona" (field interview, February 3, 2007). Her strategy seemed generally to work well, but a series of posts on Mexico Connect in April 2007 revealed a potential glitch in the system. One American living along Lake Chapala posted the following:

> We recently had two of our three receivers turned off by Dish Network. We, like many other people at Lakeside, use MBE [Mail Boxes, Etc.] with a Laredo address for mail and credit card billing addresses. When we called to correct the situation, we were grilled with questions about our "apartment" in NYC, which is our service address. We were informed that all receivers would be turned off unless we sent Dish a utility bill in our name, or a certified copy of the lease for our "apartment." Of course we will not be able to produce either of these items. (http://mexconnected.com/perl/foros/gforum, April 3, 2007)

For many Americans living in Ajijic and San Miguel (a large proportion of whom are retirees), the ability to transcend (or defy) territoriality is a matter of comfort and convenience. For others, however, the ease of transnational living allows them to continue in, or pursue, careers not de-limited by offices, cubicles, staff meetings, or attendance at company picnics. Recent reports indicate that a growing number of younger Americans are migrating to Mexico without any change in their career status and in some cases without even informing employers that they have moved (Hoffman 2006b; Nevaer 2003). Some of these migrants, like Nicole and John Gordon, who are now living in San Miguel, consider themselves to be "at the forefront of a demographic trend: high-tech professionals who can work anywhere in the world." They are joined by Mike Taylor, a recent

American migrant to San Miguel who hails from San Francisco and is employed by a software company in Florida. Using a portable Internet-based phone number to telecommute, Taylor remarks: "They have no idea when they call me if I am in San Francisco, San Miguel or Miami" (Hoffman 2006b). This virtual existence was a common theme among immigrants in Mexico. Another American explained (http://mexconnected.com/perl/foros/gforum, July 9, 2007):

> I work from my home office in Mexico, telecommuting
> into the computer systems of US clients every day. Certainly
> couldn't have done that 50 years ago. As far as my clients are
> concerned, I could be sitting in an office in Silicon Valley or
> India—wouldn't really make a difference.

An American woman in her forties, and a resident of San Miguel, makes her living teaching computer science online. She, too, commented that "Nobody knows where I am. My job thinks I live in Texas because that is where I have an address. Sometimes people ask, 'How's the weather out there?' I just say, 'Fine'" (field interview, June 23, 2006).

This same online teacher said to me at one point during our interview in San Miguel, "I hope you aren't going to go putting all of this in your book!" She was joking, for the most part, and certainly nothing about her life as she described it to me violated any national or international laws. Nevertheless, when I pushed too hard for details from some immigrants regarding the specifics of their transterritorial lives, they grew hesitant. In addition to challenging conventional models of belonging to and residing in only one nation-state, a number of Americans in Mexico are bending rules and in some cases breaking laws. Chapter One noted that among the obstacles to an accurate count of the number of U.S. citizens living in Mexico is the fact that some cross the border and reside in Mexico without securing the proper authorization. Some travel to Mexico, for example, on a tourist visa (issued automatically at airports, border crossings, travel agencies, and consulates) and never leave. Others cross by land somewhere along the massive two-thousand-mile border without securing official permission of any sort. These migrants, like their counterparts who cross in the opposite direction without documents, are "illegal aliens." As I wrote this book, their counterparts throughout the United States increasingly faced raids and forced deportations.

None of the Americans I met or interviewed in Mexico fell into this "illegal immigrant" category. To the contrary, most had diligently navigated the required bureaucratic channels to secure an FM3 visa that can be renewed annually and allows the importation of domestic goods and an automobile. Nevertheless, technology and deterritoriality facilitate, for some American migrants, not just transnational lives, but translegal ones. On different occasions American migrants I interviewed in Mexico made reference, sometimes veiled, sometimes not, to the shady activities or pasts of some of their fellow migrants who hail from the United States. One American man and longtime resident of San Miguel remarked: "If you went into that *jardín* with a bullhorn and announced that you were a bounty hunter from the States, you could clear the place out in fifteen seconds flat" (field interview, June 12, 2006). He was referring primarily to tax evaders and people who have crossed the border to escape paying alimony and child support, or to avoid meeting some other financial obligation in the United States. Similar allegations are whispered about certain Americans living along Lake Chapala, although that region's most notorious criminal fleeing the United States was guilty of a much more violent crime. In 1999, Nashville attorney Perry March moved to Ajijic with his children to join his father, retired army colonel Arthur March—a longtime Lakeside resident. Perry was escaping custody claims by his murdered wife's parents, and suspicion that he himself was the murderer. In August 2005, he was extradited to the United States, and a year later was convicted of murdering his wife, Janet. His father was arrested as well for plotting to kill Perry's dead wife's parents, but received a reduced sentence in exchange for testifying against his son.

Characters like March, and those who might flee a bounty hunter, comprise a very small minority of the migrants living in Mexico and are not representative of the larger foreign community in Ajijic or San Miguel. Nevertheless, a notable number of Americans in Mexico break other kinds of laws, and are facilitated in doing so by technology and an apparent sense, at least for some, that extralegality is one of the acceptable benefits of living transterritorially. In recent years, Mexican officials in both San Miguel and Chapala have grown concerned about the prevalence of undocumented economic activities by American immigrants. Much of this activity occurs in the area of real estate, but Americans also work in restaurants without proper documentation and practice their craft, whether accountancy or psychotherapy, without the appropriate licensing (Hoffman 2006b; Oppenheimer 1994a; Quiñones 1996; Welch 2007). One high-level Mexican municipal official in San Miguel's Office of International Relations estimates that the city loses thousands of dollars in tax revenue from illegal real estate activity and explained that city officials would begin cracking down:

> Just look on Vrbo.com [Vacation Rentals by Owner]. At least 150 houses are listed in San Miguel, and 95 percent are owned by foreigners. They are not registered as rental properties. They are not paying income tax or lodging tax. They are typically not paying Mexican social security to their domestic help. (field interview, June 20, 2006)

Similarly, an administrator at San Miguel's Instituto Allende estimated that only 30 percent of the real estate business in town was being done legally: "Foreigners are working and earning money here illegally. Yes, they are creating businesses, but we need to put some order to this. Many are not paying income taxes" (field interview, June 14, 2007).

A similar situation exists in the Lake Chapala area. During January and February 2006, Mexican immigration authorities there launched an investigation of foreigners engaged in undocumented business in the real estate sector. Immigration chief José Luis Gutiérrez Miranda explained: "Real estate promotion has always been an activity that we review carefully. . . . It is probable that some people have dared to get into this activity without permission" (Palfrey 2006c). Nor is the problem new. In January of 1991, La Asociación de Comisionistas en Bienes Raices de San Miguel de Allende, A.C. (Realtors Association of San Miguel de Allende) took out a full-page announcement in the English-language weekly addressed to "The Foreign Community of San Miguel de Allende":

> It has come to the attention of the realtors association of San Miguel de Allende that many foreigners without working papers have been acting as real estate agents using Mexican corporations or names of Mexican citizens as a legal umbrella. This is prohibited by law and can result in immediate deportation. . . . Therefore, we suggest that foreign guests, visitors, and residents without working papers desist from illegal activity and that home owners and prospective clients deal only with professional, experienced and legal agents for any business involving buying, selling and renting property. ("The Foreign Community . . ." 1991)

The harm caused by pirating satellite dish signals or giving a false address to procure some service is perhaps less tangible than real estate fraud, but all constitute a violation of and attempt to transcend the authority and sovereignty of states. The participants are aware of this. On a technology-related discussion forum in 2005, one subscriber posted the following in response to repeated queries about receiving satellite broadcasts in Mexico:

> Whats [sic] with all these people wanting to get E* programming in mexico [sic] ???? It is illegal to receive US satellite programming outside the US. While it might be possible with a very large dish, we can not condone such activity on this board. If you want to know, ask a satellite dealer down there, I'm sure they can provide you the necessary equipment if it is possible. (http://www.satelliteguys.us, October 16, 2005)

Another replied:

> It's also illegal to drive 56MPH in a 55MPH Speed Zone, not to wear a seatbelt, use a radar detector in NY, talk on a cell-phone using the handset while driving in Texas or have your wife perform oral sex in 26 states. Your point? (http://www.satelliteguys.us, October 16, 2005)

Americans in Mexico are also aware that the South Dakota license plate loophole is a questionable practice and have chided each other about blowing the cover on the convenient scam. The following exchange took place among a group of immigrants in Mexico on March 6, 2006 (http://mexconnected.com/perl/foros/gforum.cgi?post=91226; search_string=south%20dakota%20plates).

Immigrant A:

> Several people have commented about the ease with which one can register a car in South Dakota by mail without having an address in the state. Today (Sunday) I got this e-mail from a man planning a move to Mexico:
>
> > "I (mistakenly) talked to someone at the South Dakota DMV today (I'm buying a new car, and thought I'd have to pay sales tax on it there if I registered there), and was told

the practice of registering cars in SD without a residence there is legally restricted to RV owners who live in the RV 365 days/year. If they crack down on this, are we going to have to start registering in TX?"

This is all I know on the subject. Anyone have any more information?

Immigrant B:

ARGHHHH If these fools don't stop screwing around they will kill the whole thing for everyone. You do NOT call the DMV. All the required info is on my website under cars page. We renewed both of ours this year no problemo and I was told that they are still accepting new applicants. And yes we did buy a new car in Texas and paid only the SD sales tax, and the dealership got all the paperwork done in SD.

Immigrant C:

Yes, there will always be those who, insist on speaking to "The Authorities", go by "The Book", and cower with lower lip trembling, accepting all from Big Brother. Fotunately, [*sic*] I have Texas plates and am not affected by it.

My intent here is not to single out Americans in Mexico as rule-breakers—that tendency is a nearly universal one. Rather, these and other examples point to a world where, on the one hand, borders have become more fluid, but, on the other, states and the principle and practice of territorial sovereignty continue to intervene in the lives of individuals regardless of how mobile and virtual their lives have become. The very reason for maintaining an address in Laredo is that formal residence within the political and economic jurisdiction of a state (national or federal and in some cases subnational or provincial) continues to affect how individuals lead their daily lives. The license plate conundrum, for example, is a reminder that states retain authority over the licensing of cars and drivers—even if technology allows for the blurring of jurisdictions. A U.S. address is also required for, or at least greatly eases the cost and inconvenience of, banking, credit card transactions, and online shopping. Responses of those asked about the advantages of maintaining a U.S. address (even when the immigrant in question has no plans to return there) generally mirrored that of this retired seventy-six-year-old American, who explained: "I have no intention of ever moving back to the USA. I've even bought my burial plot here." Nevertheless, he explained that maintaining a U.S. address was useful for these reasons:

— It makes it easier to deal with banks and credit card companies.
— I have two bank accounts in the USA—one for my social security checks and another for my IRA checks. I draw my money using ATM cards. I use only online bank statements.
— I am a very big guy, so I can't find clothes in my size in Mexico, so I buy online and have them sent to my Texas address. If I have them sent to me in Mexico, the shipping and import duty will be almost as much as the purchase. (e-mail interview, July 8, 2007)

Similar concerns about cost and convenience also explain why many American seniors living in San Miguel grew accustomed, prior to 2006, to violating international law by having family members ship their prescription drugs to the U.S. Consulate there—taking advantage of the inspection and monetary exemptions that diplomatic pouches are afforded. The consular staff contacted the immigrant to pick up his or her shipment. When U.S. Consular Agent Ed Clancy took over the post, he explained that the practice would cease. It was illegal, and post-9/11 security concerns had increased surveillance of all cross-border transactions.

Perhaps the most significant reminder of the persistent and inescapable reach of the state pertains to the collection of taxes. Many Americans abroad complain that the United States is one of only a few developed countries in the world that levy taxes based on citizenship as opposed to residency, and some resent the requirement so much that they have renounced their U.S. citizenship. By June of 2006, the number of Americans giving up their U.S. citizenship had reached 509 for the year (Carvajal 2006; "Costing more . . ." 2006). The Republicans Abroad have made the taxation of Americans abroad one of their major initiatives. In addition to efforts to simplify absentee voting, include emigrants in the U.S. Census, and extend Medicare abroad, the Republicans Abroad are working to: "Fashion a fair tax system in line with the rest of the 28 OECD countries, which tax on the basis of residence rather than citizenship" (American Citizens Abroad 2007). For American emigrants in higher income brackets, the tax bite from Uncle

Sam intensified in 2006 after President Bush signed into law tax-cutting legislation that had buried in it a provision to sharply increase the taxes on the income of Americans abroad ("Costing more . . ." 2006).

Finally, for Americans living in Mexico, particularly the growing populations of retirees in Ajijic and San Miguel, the inability to access Medicare from abroad is a stark reminder that the state giveth and the state can taketh away. Currently, in order for Medicare to cover health care costs, U.S. citizens must return to the United States for their health care. Some disagreement exists among migrants as to the pros and cons of extending Medicare outside of the United States (e.g., would the cost of health care in Mexico increase as a result?), but many share the view of organizations like American Citizens Abroad, the Association of Americans Resident Overseas, and Professor David Warner (1999), author of *Getting What You Paid For: Extending Medicare Benefits to Eligible Beneficiaries in Mexico,* that it is unjust that most retirees abroad still pay U.S. taxes and have paid all their lives into a health care system they now cannot access: "'It is a vast injustice,' one immigrant says, 'not to receive Medicare when it is taken out of our checks'" (Warner 1999, 69).

In many respects, American transmigrants in Mexico, like those elsewhere, inhabit sociocultural, economic, and political spaces that are outside of or beyond nation-states; in other respects, however, both the sending state and the receiving state continue to govern the activities of their members and residents. Scholars of the reverse flow of Mexican migration to the United States have emphasized precisely this point. After detailing the countless ways that Mexican immigrants, migrants, and Mexican Americans inhabit a "third space" beyond the cultural and political jurisdiction of either Mexico or the United States, historian David Gutiérrez issues this caveat: "This is not to argue that the sovereign state somehow has suddenly lost the power to inscribe difference on either sojourner migrants or permanent immigrants or that the state no longer influences their daily lives in powerful ways" (1999, 512).

CONCLUSION

Technology has reconfigured the significance of place and space. An individual's job, telephone number, and mailing address, for example, are not firm indicators of the person's physical whereabouts. And people's physical whereabouts—the place, town, country, nation, state where they reside—do not fully determine or delimit the spaces—cultural, social, political, or economic—that they inhabit on a daily basis. U.S. citizens in Mexico, like immigrants throughout the world, are living lives that unsettle familiar notions of territoriality and belonging. Nevertheless, and as the literature on transnationalism suggests, neither territoriality nor the nation-state has been transcended in full. Both continue to shape the lives of transnational migrants, albeit in complex and shifting ways.

That we are witnessing an ongoing struggle between modern notions of territory and belonging and postmodern ones has been evident in the events of 9/11 and since. In spite of the fact that radical Islam has been described as "backward," and the attacks of 9/11 characterized as a parochial reaction against modernization, development, and progress, what happened that day could not have occurred without the availability and use of sophisticated communications and information technologies. Al Qaeda's existence and the success of their mission relied heavily upon airplanes, cell phones, the Internet, ATMs, video recorders, satellites, and a sophisticated system of international exchange. Moreover, this enemy was not a state or an alliance of states, but a vast network of terrorists who came from more than twenty different countries and had spread their organization across and through the geopolitical borders of as many as sixty different states. In other words, much about 9/11 epitomized the role of technology in globalization, the porosity of borders, and the transcendence of states. Nevertheless, much that has happened since speaks volumes about the persistent power of states, and their armies, as actors in the international system. The military response of the United States and its allies has been distinctly state-centered (even when it is unclear which state should be held responsible); and Americans, as well as members of other imagined national communities, have frequently not been encouraged by their leaders to think globally, but rather to close ranks around the national community, turning inward to protect "our" borders, culture, language, "way of life." A sizable majority has responded accordingly (Croucher 2006).

A prime example of and vehicle for the assertion of U.S. state authority has come in the form of the Uniting and Strengthening America by Providing Appropriate Tools Required to Intercept and Obstruct Terrorism Act of 2001—signed into law by President Bush on October 26, 2001, and also known as the "Patriot Act." Much has been written and spoken about the role of the Patriot Act in extending the government's control over the lives of U.S. inhabitants; but policies being put forth by the Department of Homeland Security are also affecting U.S. citizens residing outside of the homeland. For example, Title III of the Patriot Act places heavy responsibilities upon financial institutions of all types to develop affirmative measures to track and prevent activities, broadly grouped under the heading "money laundering," by persons within and outside the United States. Specifically, banks and financial institutions are charged with establishing internal security procedures that are changing the way banks relate to and monitor their customers, accounts, and transactions (Russell 2002). Some Americans abroad are hearing from their financial institutions that legal liabilities now make it too risky and too expensive to retain them as customers. Moreover, the U.S. address that some immigrants report maintaining as a convenience has now become a necessity for opening a bank account. Although Internet technology allows Americans who already have U.S. accounts to bank online without regard to residency, a U.S. address is necessary if these migrants wish to open an account or receive credit cards, ATM cards, and hard copies of bank statements.

As a result of this legislation, some U.S. citizens living abroad are having increasing difficulty opening and maintaining bank accounts with U.S. financial institutions, and some have initiated a letter-writing campaign to inform U.S. policy makers and financial institutions of what they perceive as unfair practices:

> Banks and investment companies in the U.S. have effectively ceased to accept new accounts from U.S. citizens resident abroad, unless they create a domestic trust or falsify their residence address. Major U.S. corporations will no longer accept payment by credit card, even issued by a U.S. bank, when the billing address is outside the U.S. We are law-abiding Americans attempting to maintain our permanent roots in the U.S. while working overseas. These restrictions are an enormous burden and a violation of fundamental economic freedoms. If U.S. law denies financial services to American citizens outside the borders, it is certainly unconstitutional, a violation of Americans' right to equal protection. (Kiesling 2007)

Journalist Ceci Connolly, an American resident of Mexico, shared her recent post-9/11 experience as an American abroad in an essay in *Inside Mexico*. After fake charges forced her to cancel her U.S. credit card account with Capital One, she was unable to receive a replacement card. "We aren't allowed to mail cards to Mexico," the Capital One representative explained, "per order of Homeland Security." Days later Ms. Connolly contacted her U.S. bank, Bank of America, to request a change of address for her monthly statements. The bank manager warned her: "If we put a non-U.S. address in our system, your account will be closed. . . . Homeland security, ma'am" (Connolly 2007b, 7).

Americans living in Mexico may be transcending territory in some respects, but they do not escape engagement with borders, government regulations, or the jurisdiction of states. Even the translegal practice of having prescription drugs shipped to a consulate relies upon existing diplomatic agreements between states. And in the aftermath of 9/11, the reach of states, particularly the United States, has intensified (or at least proven not to have dissipated). The new national security context is what led, for example, to the cessation of the illegal shipment of legal drugs. In a similarly ambiguous way, technology facilitates the emergence of new forms of community and existence while allowing the preservation of old ones. Like other migrants, Americans can leave their homeland physically, without doing so virtually. Meanwhile, the same border-transcending technologies that have assisted American immigrants in leading transnational lives (electronic banking, for example) also assist states in their efforts to safeguard national security by monitoring the behavior of citizens and noncitizens alike. This is similar to a paradox evinced by mobile phone technology, which subverts territoriality, and GPS (Global Positioning Systems) technologies that can be attached to the mobile phones to, in effect, subvert the subversion by tracking a user's whereabouts.

Echoing Thomas Faist's distinction between globalization and transnationalism (the former largely decentered from nation-state territories and the latter anchored in it), Doreen Massey writes: "Living in an age of globalization refashions, but it does not deny, a politics of place" (2004, 4). A particularly poignant illustration of the persistent politics of place and centrality of states can be found in the many ways migrants continue to engage directly in the politics of their home state, although residing contentedly, and for the foreseeable future, permanently, in a new land. The next chapter takes up this topic of the transnational political activity of U.S. citizens residing in Mexico.

Three

WAVING THE RED, WHITE, AND *AZUL*

The Transnational Politics of Americans in Mexico

In the current period, we are witnessing the emergence of new forms of political action and citizenship that transcend the territorial and political boundaries of states.
—JOSÉ ITZIGSOHN, "IMMIGRATION AND THE BOUNDARIES OF CITIZENSHIP"

I go to bed at night thinking, "What if Kerry loses by 20 votes?" That's what is driving a lot of us.
—ANA MARIA SALAZAR, CHAIRPERSON, AMERICANS OVERSEAS FOR KERRY, SEPTEMBER 2004

On a warm June 4, 2006, close to a hundred registered Democrats gathered in Finnegan's restaurant for their organization's monthly meeting. Chairperson Gretchen Sullivan presided over the meeting, which included an invited speaker and agenda items pertaining to how the group would focus its fund-raising energies for the 2006 U.S. midterm elections. They had raised over $10,000 for presidential candidate John Kerry in 2004 and now debated whether to support the party as a whole or channel money to particular candidates in tight swing state races. Many members were sporting anti-Bush paraphernalia, and more was for sale at the door. The scene itself was not entirely unusual. Groups of Democrats, Republicans, Independents, and others gather regularly in cities and states throughout the United States to strategize and fraternize. But these politically active Americans—the San Miguel de Allende chapter of Democrats Abroad—were meeting in the mountains of Central Mexico. Their political buttons were in Spanish ("Pinche Bush," which translates as "Fucking Bush"), though few actually speak the language; and their guest speaker was U.S. consul for San Miguel, Ed Clancy, who was on hand to answer questions about the importation of prescription drugs and the possibility of extending U.S. Medicare benefits to Americans living abroad. The answer to the first question was that after many years of U.S. citizens living in San Miguel being allowed to have their prescription drugs shipped from the United States directly to the local American Consulate (diplomatic packages are able to circumvent Mexican government controls and costs), the practice would cease. It was, as Clancy explained, illegal, after all; and post-9/11 security concerns had led to a greater focus on what was being shipped, where, and by whom. In response to the question of extending U.S. Medicare abroad, Clancy remarked that he considered it a good idea, but the logistics were complicated.

This display of political transnationalism on the part of U.S. citizens living in Mexico was not an isolated one. In the months preceding the 2006 U.S. midterm elections, and again in late 2007 and early 2008, in anticipation of the U.S. presidential primaries, scenes like this one played out across Mexico, as local chapters of Democrats Abroad and Republicans Abroad mobilized in support of the candidates and the party that would represent them—thousands of miles away and on the other side of an increasingly militarized international border. In February 2008, on Super Tuesday, U.S. Democrats Abroad sponsored the first-ever global primary. While their conationals in the United States lined up at polling stations in twenty-four different states, Americans living in Mexico cast votes at polling stations in Mexico City, the beach resort of Puerto Vallarta, the colonial mountain town of San Miguel de Allende, and the fishing village of Ajijic along the shores of Lake Chapala, as well as via the Internet. Bruce Rossley, vice chairperson of the San Miguel chapter of Democrats Abroad, described the scene in that town: "It looked like any polling place in America, but when you looked more clearly, you realized that you weren't in Kansas anymore. The walls and concave ceiling of the polling place were covered in vibrant colors of red and orange, with figures of ancient Aztec warriors looking down on Americans casting their votes for the first time in a foreign land" (Paterson 2008).

Ultimately, 23,105 U.S. citizens living abroad in 164 different countries participated in the global primary, and Americans living in Mexico were responsible for a total of 1,560 of the votes cast. Of all the cities in the world where overseas votes were cast, San Miguel ranked third in number, just behind London and Paris (Democrats Abroad 2008). These overseas primary voters were represented at the August 2008 Democratic National Convention in Colorado by 22 delegates—just one fewer than the state of North Dakota.

Although political and ethno-cultural boundaries have never been as congruent as many models of the nation-state assume, the increased volume and complexity of global migration have further heightened the disconnect. Residents of one nation-state are increasingly voting in the elections of another. Candidates for political office in one country are campaigning, raising money, and meeting with constituents in another. Migrants who no longer reside in their country of origin are continuing to demand rights and recognition as citizens, and the governments of these states of origin are calling upon their citizens abroad to respect and uphold their responsibilities (economic, political, and cultural) to the homeland.

In her definition of transnational political practices, Eva Ostergaard-Nielsen calls for including any or all of the following: transnational election campaigns, cross-border voting, support for political parties abroad, participation in debates in the press, migrants' rallies in opposition to or support of the home country's policies, and formation of hometown associations to support projects in the country of origin (Ostergaard-Nielsen 2003, 761–762). These political activities are transnational in that they take place in one national locale (the country of settlement) but are designed to exercise influence in another (the country of origin). Transnational or extraterritorial citizenship also takes the form of immigrants participating in the public sphere of a polity where they currently reside but do not possess formal (legal) citizenship rights (Fitzgerald 2000; Mandaville 1999). Examples might include immigrants who are not naturalized citizens attending local city council, school board, or planning meetings; participating in rallies or protests focused on host country policies; meeting with local officials; or voicing concerns in the media. Additionally, immigrants engaged in transnational political activity may mobilize in the country of settlement to promote the political and cultural interests of the country of origin—for example, lobbying for a policy that benefits their homeland (Shain 1999) or forming immigrant organizations that support and promote the national culture of the homeland (Orozco and Rouse 2007, 1).

The literature on immigrant political transnationalism is substantial, but this chapter reverses the conventional lens to apply the insights of existing literature to the case of U.S. citizens living in Mexico. In what ways do these migrants, still relatively invisible to scholars and policy makers interested in extraterritorial citizenship, fit the profile of "transnational migrants," who, as David Fitzgerald explains, "often live in a country in which they do not claim citizenship and claim citizenship in a country in which they do not live. Alternately they may claim membership in multiple polities in which they may be residents, part-time residents, or absentees" (2000, 10). To what degree do American immigrants in Mexico stay politically connected to and engaged with the United States? What types of organizations do they form in Mexico with a focus on influencing politics or policy in the United States? How do they engage, as Americans, in local Mexican politics? And what are the current and likely implications of this transnational citizenship for the United States and for Mexico? This chapter aims not only to explore what the existing literature on transnationalism can reveal about this critical and under-studied case, but also how the case itself may call for a refinement of the existing literature.

POLITICAL TRANSNATIONALISM

The activities outlined above attest to the fact that in the contemporary era of globalization we are witnessing the unbundling of territory and political authority and the emergence of postmodern forms of configuring political space (Mandaville 1999; Ruggie 1993). Political membership that was once fully determined and delimited by residency in a nation-state has transformed into "citizenship in a territorially unbounded imagined community" (Fitzgerald 2000, 10). Territorial unboundedness, however, is distinct from deterritoriality, as discussed in the previous chapter. People's relationship to territory is now arguably more complex, more layered, less bounded, but it is no less tangible (Biswas 2005, 62). In order to make this fluid array of political identities and belongings more tangible, analysts have focused on the institutional patterns that undergird political transnationalism, or what José Itzigsohn defines as immigrants' political transnational field: "the recurrent and institutionalized interactions and exchanges between, on the one hand, immigrants and their social and political organizations and, on the other hand, the political institutions and the state apparatus of the country of origin" (2000, 1130).

Itzigsohn identifies three main actors in an immigrant political transnational field: the state apparatus of the country of origin; the political parties of the country of origin; and migrant organizations in the country of reception. Others have correctly added to this mix of variables the activities of political authorities and the cultural-societal context in the country of settlement (Faist 2000; Ostergaard-Nielsen 2003; M. P. Smith 2007). In recent decades, many sending states—the Dominican Republic, El Salvador, Haiti, and Mexico prominent among them—have increasingly sought and facilitated ties with their emigrants abroad. These sending states are motivated by economic and political factors—whether the flow of remittances and investments, the capacity of emigrants abroad to act as lobbyists in the host country on behalf of the home country, or, as Levitt explains, the fact that "states can exert greater control over migrants' political activities if they are channelled through official mechanisms" (2001a, 205). The reaching out may take the form of extending dual citizenship to emigrants, establishing ministerial departments to address the needs of nationals abroad, or even granting emigrants formal political representation within the governing bodies of the home country (Itzigsohn 2000). Equally important to the forging and maintenance of a political transnational field are political parties in the sending state that work to mobilize political and financial support from nationals abroad (Levitt 2001a, 2001b; R. Smith 2006). These parties are courting votes and campaign contributions, hoping migrants will have influence over nonmigrants' votes, and, in some cases, promoting political integration into the host society while continuing to encourage migrant commitment to homeland politics (Levitt 2001a; Shain 1999).

Once settled in the country of destination, immigrants are forming hometown associations (HTAs) designed to encourage immigrants from the same homeland region to maintain ties with and materially support their places of origin. The number of Mexican HTAs is estimated at more than three thousand. In addition to forging a sense of community among immigrants in their new land, these HTAs "represent a transnational identity rooted as much in the migrant's country of origin as in the migrant's adopted home" (Orozco and Rouse 2007, 1).

Finally, in the receiving state, systems of immigrant incorporation and particular political opportunity structures will influence the scope and agency of immigrant transnational political practices (Ostergaard-Nielsen 2003, 769). The precise nature of this influence, however, is difficult to gauge. Thomas Faist makes the point that when a receiving state grants to immigrants political opportunities such as multicultural rights, this may advance transnational ties (2000, 191). If Mexican immigrants in the United States, for example, are permitted or encouraged to maintain Spanish, they may stay more attached to their Mexican identity and be less likely to acculturate in the United States (Huntington 2004; Renshon 2005). Other scholars emphasize, however, that it is a hostile or exclusionary reception in the receiving society, not a tolerant one, which will foster greater transnational ties. If immigrants are not embraced by the host society and government, and not permitted or encouraged to become participants, they will be less likely to integrate into the host society and more likely to retain strong ties to their native land (Joppke and Morawska 2003; Portes 1999). In addition to negotiating cultural belonging in the new land, migrants are also engaging politically. Michael Peter Smith (2007) refers to this political engagement in the receiving context as a largely overlooked "second face" of transnational citizenship.

Mexicans living in the United States figure prominently into the scholarship on immigrant political transnationalism. In the mid- to late 1990s, Mexico, as a sending state, and one that had grown well aware of the importance of remittances and the potential benefit of a lobby abroad, altered its previously negative attitude toward emigrants and began to reach out to Mexicans in the United States. In 1998, Mexico ratified a constitutional amendment granting dual nationality to its emigrants, and in 2006, Mexicans living abroad were able to vote from abroad in the country's presidential election. The federal government in Mexico maintains an office dedicated to serving Mexicans abroad, and several states in Mexico that export large numbers of migrants to the United States also maintain offices to assist their constituents abroad. Candidates for Mexican political offices campaign abroad, and Mexican residents of the United States have even won mayoral offices in their Mexican hometowns (Puente 2001). Numerous studies focus on topics such as the extent to which Mexicans in the United States retain their Mexican citizenship or pursue dual citizenship; whether and how they continue participating in Mexican politics; the types of organizations Mexicans form in the United States with the aim of influencing political, social, or economic circumstances in Mexico; and the manner in which Mexicans in the United States may act as spokespersons for their country of origin (Fitzgerald 2000; Jones-Correa 2000; Shain 1999; Smith and Guarnizo 1998; Suro and Escobar 2006). Mexicans immigrants and the transnational ties they maintain are also primary targets of political punditry in the United States—whether from the bombastic CNN anchor Lou Dobbs, conservative media commentator and former presidential candidate Patrick Buchanan, or congressman and 2008 presidential candidate Tom Tancredo.

Meanwhile, U.S. politicians are either unaware of or seemingly indifferent to the movement of their compatriots southward—even though some of that migration is also undocumented and the immigrants also engage in cross-border political behavior that mirrors that of Mexicans living in the United States. As expansive as the scholarship of immigrant political transnationalism is, it has yet to be applied to the case of U.S. citizens living in Mexico, but many American immigrants in Mexico engage in activities consistent with the models of transmigrant politics and the exercise of extraterritorial citizenship. Similar to the Mexican migrants in David Fitzgerald's study on extraterritorial citizenship, American migrants are claiming "membership in multiple polities in which they may be residents, part-time residents, or absentees" (2000, 10). There are differences, to be sure, from the majority of the cases discussed in the literature on transnational politics (differences that are discussed at the end of this chapter), but U.S. citizens in Mexico are voting across borders, raising money in Mexico for political candidates in the United States, organizing and attending rallies and participating in public debates in support of or in opposition to U.S. policies, and forming and participating in associations in Mexico that are focused on preserving and promoting the political and cultural values of the United States and on building community among Americans residing in Mexico. U.S. migrants are also engaging in the public sphere in the Mexican towns and cities where they live—practicing, in other words, forms of substantive citizenship in Mexico (without securing formal membership). *Formal* citizenship generally refers to direct participation in formal state institutions, such as voting, while *substantive* citizenship, or what some simply label "membership," "describes the broader relations and practices of belonging and participation in a political community" (R. Smith 2003, 303).

AMERICAN POLITICAL PARTICIPATION FROM ABROAD

The population of Americans living abroad and their potential to influence U.S. electoral outcomes first captured widespread attention during the 2000 and 2004 U.S. presidential elections. In the aftermath of the ambiguous election results of November 7, 2000, Americans—and many would argue, the world—sat waiting, literally, for the arrival in Florida of overseas absentee ballots which would decide the election outcome in that state, and ultimately for the country. "Indeed, when the final results in Florida were certified," political scientist Taylor Dark explains, "it was clear that the late overseas vote had been crucial. . . . If all the late overseas ballots had been put aside, Al Gore would now be president" (2003a, 735–736).

After officials finally certified the 2000 Florida vote, interest in the role of American voters living abroad faded from the media and public view; nor did the scholarly community pursue the topic with any vigor. Politicians, political parties, and politically mobilized Americans abroad, on the other hand, had clearly taken note. In preparation for the 2004 U.S. presidential elections, candidates Bush and Kerry both extended their campaigns across the U.S. border; newly energized chapters of the Democrats

Abroad and Republicans Abroad geared up for another close race, and U.S. citizens living in Mexico and elsewhere outside of the United States requested absentee ballots in record numbers. A news story coming out of Chapala, Mexico, on September 13, 2004, began as follows:

> George P. Bush looked like a man on a mission. . . . Dark, handsome and flashing a brilliant smile, the 28-year-old son of Florida Governor Jeb Bush had come straight from his honeymoon to this lakeside community outside Guadalajara to ask U.S. expatriates to vote for President Bush, the man he calls Uncle George. (Walker 2004)

President Bush's nephew called on Americans at Lakeside to "Please help us out," explaining that American expatriates in Mexico comprise a "huge untapped market" (Walker 2004). During his four-day swing through Mexico, the president's nephew also met with Americans living in San Miguel de Allende and with U.S. businesspeople in Mexico City. The Kerry campaign had representatives in Mexico as well. In July 2004, John Kerry's sister, Diana, visited loyal Democrats in Mexico City; and a former Defense Department official in the Clinton administration, Ana Maria Salazar, formed and chaired an organization called Americans Overseas for Kerry. At one point, Salazar and Larry Rubin, then president of U.S. Republicans Abroad in Mexico and current CEO of the American Chamber of Commerce in Mexico, debated the upcoming U.S. presidential election on Mexican television.

Besides attending to their constituents at home, both the Democratic and Republican parties in the United States maintain contact with and work to mobilize their partisans abroad; their commitment to doing so, particularly in the case of U.S. voters in Mexico, has intensified in recent years. The Democrats Abroad and the Republicans Abroad both have headquarters in Washington, D.C., that maintain contact with and work to coordinate the efforts of chapters located throughout the world. The Democrats Abroad was officially established in 1964, although some of its early members were active in Mexico as early as the 1950s, and now has seventy-six overseas chapters. The U.S. Democratic National Committee (DNC) officially recognizes Democrats Abroad as a "state," and Democrats Abroad is represented on the DNC by eight voting members. Democrats Abroad in Mexico has a country-level chairperson and four regional chapters: Mexico City, Young Democrats in Mexico City, Lake Chapala, and San Miguel de Allende. The organization describes its mission as follows:

> Democrats Abroad is the official Democratic Party organiza-
> tion for more than six million US citizens living overseas. We
> work to advance the principles of our Party by spreading the
> Democratic message to Americans abroad and encouraging
> them to vote for Democratic candidates back home. Over
> seventy countries throughout the world organize local events
> and activities to encourage participation in the American
> political process. (http://www.democratsabroad.org)

In March 2000, Democrats Abroad listed for its Mexico country committee
104 certified members (Dark 2003b, 246). By January 30, 2007, the membership total for Mexico, according to Democrats Abroad International
Secretary Robert Checkoway, had climbed to 1,500 members (e-mail correspondence with Leo Pérez Minaya, March 23, 2007).

Republicans Abroad was founded in 1978 and now has chapters in over
fifty countries. The organization is registered as a 527 nonprofit fund-
raising group, not as an official GOP entity. Republicans Abroad in Mexico
has a country chairperson and regional chapters in both Lake Chapala and
San Miguel. The official Web site explains that

> Membership in Republicans Abroad provides a unique
> opportunity for Americans living overseas to communicate
> their concerns to Republican leaders in Washington. Repub-
> licans Abroad has fought for issues of concern to Americans
> abroad like repatriation issues, strong support of Section 911
> foreign earned income exemption, anti-terrorism legisla-
> tion, fair trade policies, and the inclusion of the expatriate
> population in the United States Census. Republicans Abroad
> members are vital to representing the concerns of Americans
> abroad to our nation's leaders while helping the Party to win
> close elections with the absentee ballots. (http://www
> .republicansabroad.org)

Despite repeated attempts, I was unable to get official Republicans Abroad
membership data for Mexico as a whole, but Norm Pfifer, former president
of the Lake Chapala chapter, did recount that the local chapter was founded
in August 2004 and by December 2004 had at least 200 paid members (field
interview, January 30, 2007).

In different towns and cities throughout Mexico—Ajijic and San Miguel
prominent among them—both the Republicans Abroad and Democrats

Abroad kicked into high gear in the months preceding the 2004 election, registering voters, raising money, and purchasing political advertisements in English-language media. While the Republicans Abroad helped support the visit by President Bush's nephew, Democrats Abroad in Chapala met in private homes to participate in international conference calls with Democratic hopefuls (including Wesley Clark, Howard Dean, John Kerry [twice], and Dennis Kucinich) (Chaussee 2004c). In an interview with a CNN reporter covering the expatriate vote in Mexico in 2004, many American voters and longtime residents of the Lake Chapala area agreed that never before had their votes been so vigorously courted (Chaussee 2004e). Americans living in Mexico responded to these mobilization efforts with unprecedented enthusiasm. The U.S. Embassy in Mexico City and the Consulates in San Miguel de Allende and Merida ran out of ballots as early as June 2004 and had to make additional, and in some cases repeated, requests for more. Then–Consular Agent Philip Maher, who represented the U.S. government in San Miguel for twenty years, remarked: "It's far more active than I've seen before. There's more discussion about the election at cocktail parties. There's more discussion at dinners" (Walker 2004). Reports from Lakeside showed similar energy on the part of Americans abroad. On August 27, 2004, "still reeling from the success of their local press conference with presidential nephew, George Prescott Bush," the Republicans Abroad Lake Chapala chapter met at the Hotel Real de Chapala to elect officers and solidify the presence of the first-ever chapter of Republicans Abroad at Lakeside (Chaussee 2004d). The next week in another part of town, U.S. Democrats living in the Lake Chapala area gathered to signal their support for U.S. presidential candidate John Kerry and to protest the war in Iraq (Chaussee 2004b).

By July 9, 2004, the number of federal post card applications for absentee ballots sent in response to requests from U.S. voters abroad reached 340,000—which exceeded by 90,000 the number of requests for the entire 2000 presidential election. In the 2000 presidential election, absentee ballots comprised 15 percent of the total votes cast—which was double the figure in the 1992 presidential race. For reasons not unlike those that confound efforts to determine the number of Americans living in Mexico, data on overseas voting are notoriously difficult to gather. Nevertheless, the Foreign Voter Assistance Program, within the U.S. Department of Defense, estimates that among nongovernment American civilians living abroad, voter turnout in U.S. presidential elections ranges between 31 and 38 percent of eligible voters. Voter turnout among U.S. military personnel abroad ranges between 64 and 69 percent; and between 64 and 79 percent among government-employed civilians (PR *Newswire* 2004). Some sources report that in 2004, overseas registration for both parties increased by 400 percent over the year 2000 ("Suppressing the Overseas Vote" 2005); and a *Newsweek* reporter covering the overseas vote in 2004 noted: "Ironically, the real battleground states of this [U.S. presidential] election could end up being countries like Canada, France and Mexico" (Conant 2004).

Ultimately, the overseas vote played a less pivotal role in the 2004 U.S. presidential election than in the previous one, but neither the political party organizations abroad nor the emigrants grew less sanguine about the role they could play in American politics or the rights they could demand as U.S. citizens—regardless of their country of residence. In 2005, Democratic Party Chairman Howard Dean visited Mexico and met with Americans Overseas for Kerry Chairperson Ana Maria Salazar, Young Democrats Abroad Chair Steve Lucero, and various other officers from different chapters of Democrats Abroad in Mexico to hear their concerns as American citizens and Democrats abroad. From March 2 through 5, 2006, five members of Democrats Abroad Mexico (three from Lakeside and two from San Miguel) joined one hundred members of Democrats Abroad from around the world at the organization's international meeting in Washington, D.C. These U.S. citizens and loyal Democrats, traveling from their homes in Mexico and other parts of the world, passed a resolution calling for the U.S. Congress to investigate whether President Bush and Vice President Cheney committed impeachable offenses. The Democrats Abroad international chairperson, Michael Cuervorst, remarked: "Whether it's denying our constitutional rights through illegal domestic spying or criminally outing CIA operative Valerie Plame, credible evidence implicates the highest levels of this administration. . . . The American people deserve to know the truth" (Chaussee 2006b). Months later, Democrats Abroad from Mexico and elsewhere traveled again to the United States, this time to Chicago, to join their compatriots stateside for the meeting of the Democratic National Committee. At this meeting, officers and members of Democrats Abroad helped sponsor a resolution against the use of torture: "The use of torture and the utter disregard of human rights constitute an affront to basic American values" (Chaussee 2006a).

In June 2007, Democrats Abroad and Republicans Abroad joined organizations like American Citizens Abroad (ACA), Federation of American Women's Clubs Overseas (FAWCO), and Association of Americans Resident Overseas (AARO) for "Overseas Americans Week" in Washington, D.C. Seeking changes to legislation and regulations that adversely affect Americans overseas, including tax laws and Medicare guidelines, these delegates held eighty-four meetings with U.S. congressional offices and research institutes, including the recently formed Americans Abroad Congressional Caucus. Democrats and Republicans Abroad and others make the case that, in terms of numbers, U.S. citizens living abroad comprise a constituency at least as large as the state of Colorado, with its 4.7 million people. "We're a rather powerful state in numbers," said one American delegate who was on Capitol Hill during Overseas Americans Week. "We are probably the 20th largest state" (Abruzzese 2007).

This constituency of Americans living abroad has felt slighted in the past, but there is evidence that some members of the U.S. Congress and aspiring politicians are beginning to take notice. The bipartisan Americans Abroad Caucus, formed in March 2007 by Representatives Carolyn Maloney, Democrat of New York, and Joe Wilson, Republican of South Carolina, now counts eleven members and is making inroads. Representatives Maloney and Wilson have changed their Web sites to accept comments from Americans overseas and on February 22, 2007, wrote a joint letter asking fellow lawmakers to follow suit in embracing this overlooked constituency (Maloney and Wilson 2007):

> We are writing to invite you to join the Americans Abroad
> Caucus, dedicated to the estimated four to six million American citizens living and working overseas. Although they live
> overseas, many of these Americans continue to vote and
> pay taxes in the United States. Whether or not they work
> for American businesses overseas, they help increase exports
> of American goods and services because they traditionally
> buy American goods, sell American goods, and create business
> opportunities for U.S. companies and workers. Their role in
> strengthening the U.S. economy, creating jobs in the United
> States, and extending American influence around the globe
> is vital to the well-being of our nation. Moreover, they are
> unofficial ambassadors, often the first contact many people
> around the world have with "America" and are our very
> informed "antennae" on the world.

Some analysts, such as Susan MacManus, a political science professor at the University of South Florida, believe that with the 2008 presidential and congressional elections approaching and the overseas vote having been an important factor in recent ballots, the timing might be ideal for the formation of this caucus. Americans Abroad can be influential, in her view, both because of the numbers they represent and the noise they are willing to make (Abruzzese 2007).

As the 2008 primary season began, U.S. Democrats in Mexico were optimistic, but not yet ready to commit to a particular candidate. In late October 2007, the Democrats Abroad held their regional meetings in Mexico City, and members of the local chapters in Lake Chapala and San Miguel traveled to the Mexican capital to participate in the event. The main agenda item was "the first ever global presidential primary," promoted to U.S. Democrats living abroad as a "surefire means of making their choice known and their voices heard" (*Roundup,* October 2007, 3). The U.S. Republicans in Mexico whom I was able to interview were less optimistic than their Democratic counterparts. One member and lifelong Republican living in Mexico City told me that morale was low due to the war in Iraq and President Bush's low approval ratings and that the organization was without countrywide leadership at the moment. As of November 2007, the official Web site of the Republicans Abroad indicated little activity, and the link to "Election News 2008" was dead (http://www.republicansabroad .org/election2008_news.htm [accessed November 15, 2007]). By May 2008, the site was posting some articles about the U.S. presidential primaries.

An additional indicator of the mobilization of Americans abroad lies in their financial contributions to candidates for U.S. political office. As a group, Americans abroad gave $908,000 toward the 2004 general election; by February 2008, they had given $1.4 million toward the primary races alone. Figures provided by the Federal Election Commission showed that the candidates had made from foreign sources more than seventeen times what they had made by the same point in the campaign four years previously (Quinlan 2008).

In addition to voting and fund-raising for candidates, Americans in Mexico also regularly publish political commentary regarding U.S. politics and policies in local English-language outlets and organize local rallies or protests focused on the United States. In the Lake Chapala area, for example, Americans have access to the English-language *Guadalajara Reporter* (published weekly), the *Ojo del Lago* and *Lake Chapala Review* (published monthly), and, more recently, an English-language section in the back of the local Mexican newspaper, *El Charal*. In San Miguel, American immigrants rely heavily on the English-language weekly *Atención,* founded in 1975, and many line up outside the public library each Friday morning to collect their copies, or mill around the *jardín* until the Mexican vendor arrives with the truckload of papers. Since 2006, Americans in Mexico can also enjoy a new publication, *Inside Mexico: The English Speaker's Guide to*

Living in Mexico, with a distribution of fifty thousand. These publications announce an array of cultural and social events, but also provide space for Americans to debate U.S. foreign policy and to weigh in on U.S. presidential candidates.

In 2001, a longtime American resident of San Miguel, Georgeann Johnson, wrote an editorial for *Atención* expressing opposition to a bill before the U.S. House of Representatives that would grant the U.S. president fast-track authority to negotiate global trade deals (HR Bill 2149). It was a bill that, in her words, could have a "serious impact on our chosen country of residence." She called on her conationals living in Mexico to contact their congressional representatives in the United States: "This bill is certainly something U.S. citizens living in Mexico should be aware of. There are potentially disastrous consequences, both economic and ecological, to the country [read: Mexico]" (Johnson 2001). This American's political activism offers an interesting twist on what political scientist Yossi Shain (1999) has described as "marketing the American creed." Immigrants living within the United States, Shain argues, should be recognized as an asset rather than a threat because through their transnational activities and networks, they typically "market" to their homelands the political, cultural, and economic values that are highly regarded in the United States (1999). Ms. Johnson, an American living in San Miguel, was attempting to effect change in her homeland, the United States, for the benefit of her country of settlement, Mexico.

Over the years, American immigrants in San Miguel and Ajijic have also used the pages of local English-language papers and cyberspace to respond to the U.S. wars in Iraq and politics in the Middle East. As with other "diasporas" living outside of their country of origin, Americans in Mexico carry with them political and cultural divisions from their homeland. The vitriol does not typically reach the level of some other diasporic groups, but is significant nonetheless. One officer of Republicans Abroad in San Miguel told me that he and his conservative colleagues grew so tired of the "liberal, anti-American rhetoric being spewed in the local English-language weekly *[Atención]*," that when Iraqis went to the polls in December 2005, the San Miguel Republicans Abroad decided to write a letter to the paper expressing congratulations to the Iraqi people and wishing them well in their newly established democracy. After that, he reported receiving "death threats from the liberals in town." When I must have appeared shocked, he clarified that he actually received "an angry phone call" (field interview, June 29, 2006). On August 25, 2006, San Miguel's left-leaning Center for Global Justice used its regular column in *Atención* to publish an editorial entitled "Report from Palestine." The author of the editorial character-ized the situation in the Middle East as follows: "Vastly out-gunned, peace loving Palestinian Arabs find themselves under attack by land-hungry Jewish Israeli terrorists" (Rivage-Seul 2006). In the weeks that followed, the newspaper was deluged with letters to the editor. Many came from insulted and angry members of the town's "sizable" Jewish community, and many accused the author, the newspaper, and the foreign-run public library (which publishes the paper) of anti-Semitism. The paper responded by temporarily suspending the Center's regular column ("Controversy over . . ." 2006). Scenarios like this one are not uncommon in the United States, but these Americans were fighting out their ethnic, ideological, political, and religious differences about the Middle East and the U.S. role in this and other conflicts from their homes and favorite gringo hangouts in the mountains of Central Mexico.

In addition to debating U.S. foreign policy from Mexico, American im-migrants also use their local English-language periodicals to dissect the candidates for U.S. political office. *Inside Mexico* devoted its September issue to the 2008 U.S. elections, publishing a "Voter's Guide '08," an article on "expat voting," and editorials by a representative of both Democrats and Republicans Abroad. In Lake Chapala, the local Spanish-language news-paper *El Charal* included on its English-language page an editorial warning Americans that presidential candidate Barack Obama is attempting to con-ceal his identification with Islam. Edited by a longtime American immi-grant to Ajijic, Tod Jonson, the column noted ("We Have Made Too Many Mistakes" 2007):

> Obama takes great care to conceal the fact that he is a Mus-lim while admitting that he was once a Muslim, mitigating that damning information by saying that, for two years, he also attended a Catholic school. . . . Obama joined the United Church of Christ which helps to purge any notion that he is still a Muslim, which, ideologically, he remains today. . . . More information MUST be gathered about Obama before he is considered for election to our highest office. Who is he? What does he really believe? Where did he come from?

The pen is mighty among Americans in Mexico seeking to influence U.S. politics and policy from abroad, but so too is the public square. U.S. citizens living in Ajijic and San Miguel have held peace marches over the years protesting U.S. military adventures, sponsored vigils in support of or opposition to U.S. presidents or presidential candidates, and organized marches focused on U.S. policies such as immigration. On January 15, 1991, in San Miguel, a crowd of over two hundred, "in the main, Americans," held a candlelight vigil to protest the pending war against Iraq. Fifteen years later in Ajijic, as war once again raged in Iraq (and the United States prepared to hold midterm elections), "close to 50 foreigners, and a healthy sprinkling of Mexicans," gathered in Ajijic for a "non-partisan, non-sectarian" rally in support of world peace. They sang "Give Peace a Chance" and closed with a peace circle. According to one participant, the rally had plenty of moral support from passing drivers: "Lots of people honked and gave us 'thumbs up' or the peace sign and only one or two gringos gave us the finger" (Chaussee 2006c).

In addition to expressing concern or support for U.S. military adventures, American immigrants in Mexico stay informed and voice opinions about U.S. immigration policy. In March 1981, San Miguel's *Atención* published an editorial sharply criticizing proposals regarding the U.S. border fence (March 17, 1981). Twenty-five years later, on May 1, 2006, between six hundred and one thousand foreigners and Mexicans filled the streets of San Miguel to protest the U.S. Border and Immigration Enforcement Act. The protesters showed their solidarity with the Mexican workers— family members, friends, and neighbors—with signs bearing the slogan "No human being is illegal" (Noriz and Ibarra 2006). Perhaps not surprisingly, Mexican immigration to the United States is the issue around which American immigrants in Mexico have found the most common ground. Regardless of their U.S. partisan affiliations, the Americans I met in Ajijic and San Miguel displayed nuanced views of the complexities of the immigration situation—at least in terms of the flow that moves in the direction opposite of their own. A large number of the immigrants I interviewed had personal knowledge of or a connection to Mexican migrants and their families who were harmed by U.S. immigration policies. One American immigrant couple in Lake Chapala empathically shared, "Our maid is in jail right now in the U.S. for trying to visit her dying father there" (field interview, February 9, 2007). This couple's maid and many other Mexicans have a very difficult time securing official and legal permission to travel to the United States, however legitimate their reasons for travel may be. I repeatedly heard stories from Americans who had learned from their Mexican workers just how expensive and laborious is the process for legally securing a travel visa from the U.S. government. Several of these American immigrants, including one of the members of the Daughters of the American Revolution in Lake Chapala, explained how they have worked to intervene at the local U.S. Consulate on behalf of their Mexican employees seeking a visa—whether by vouching for the person's integrity and financial solvency or assisting financially (field interview, February 3, 2007).

PROMOTING THE CREED

Casting ballots from abroad, meeting in a foreign country with political candidates from the homeland, raising campaign funds, writing editorials, and participating in public protests are poignant examples of the practice of extraterritorial citizenship. Additionally, however, Americans in Mexico have formed and actively participate in a range of organizations that have as their purpose, or founding goals, the promotion of American political values and cultural ideals and that seek to unite Americans on the basis of their shared nationality regardless of their residence outside of the United States. The American Society of Mexico (AMSOC) offers one early example. Founded on August 26, 1942, and still active today, the AMSOC aims to "support activities that promote U.S. culture and foster a sense of community to benefit U.S. citizens living in Mexico" (American Society of Mexico 2007). In September 2007, Greg Ritchie, current AMSOC president, used *Inside Mexico*'s electronic publication to announce that AMSOC was celebrating sixty-five years in Mexico and to encourage new members to sign up now: "We Want You!" (Ritchie 2007).

Thirteen American Legion posts are also active throughout Mexico—including two in the Lake Chapala area and two in San Miguel de Allende. The Legion's preamble reads as follows:

> For God and Country we associate ourselves together for the following purposes: To uphold and defend the Constitution of the United States of America; To maintain law and order; To foster and perpetuate a one hundred percent Americanism; To preserve the memories and incidents of our association in the great wars; To inculcate a sense of individual obligation to the community, state, and nation. (http://www.amlegion-mexico.org)

The Daughters of the American Revolution (DAR), stalwarts of American patriotism, maintain four active chapters in Mexico: Baja, Chapala, Guadalajara, and Mexico City. Headquartered in Washington, D.C., the DAR was founded in 1890 and describes itself as "a volunteer women's service organization dedicated to promoting patriotism, preserving American history, and securing America's future through better education for children" (http://www.dar.org/natsociety/whoweare.cfm). The group in Ajijic, christened the Thomas Paine Chapter, was formed in April 1999 and describes its mission as serving DAR members in Ajijic, Chapala, and neighboring communities in Jalisco, Mexico, and promoting American history, education, and patriotism (http://www.geocities.com/thomaspainedar/about_our_chapter.htm). In interviews with members of the Thomas Paine Chapter of DAR in Ajijic, one of the regents responded to my curiosity about a DAR chapter located in Mexico by explaining: "Our ancestors gave the world a great gift—the American Revolution. Those ideals are universal" (field interview, February 3, 2007). Meanwhile, the Sons of the American Revolution (SAR) founded its first Mexican chapter, in Ajijic, in 2002, with seventy founding members. The SAR hopes to establish at least four more chapters in Mexico in the near future. In an interesting twist on the nation as an "imagined community" (Anderson 1991), the SAR in Mexico decided to recognize descendants of New Spain (read: Mexicans) as American Patriots. The related resolution read as follows (SAR 2003):

> WHEREAS, Spain was a valuable ally of the colonists during the American Revolutionary War—even before July 4, 1776; her soldiers and militia men fighting the English in what is now Louisiana, Mississippi, Alabama and Florida; and because there were incursions along the Texas Gulf Coast by the British; and Spanish Galleons searched for Captain Cook, along the California coast; and because Spanish soldiers and militia were required to remain vigilant against attack by both the British and the Indians being supplied by the British, and specifically were required to guard the Camino Real, lifeline between Mexico City and Galvez' army in Louisiana.

The resolution goes on to offer a list of specific guidelines relating to the inclusion of residents of New Spain into the SAR.

Members of the SAR, DAR, and American Legion chapters in Mexico, and other immigrants from the United States, may be living in Mexico, but they continue to actively honor and identify with their national brethren. Annually, since September 11, 2001, members of the Ladies' Auxiliary of American Legion Post Seven in Lake Chapala have created patriotic wreaths in memory of first-responders who lost their lives in the attacks on the United States ("Remembering Sept 11, 2001" 2005). On September 12,

2005, after Hurricane Katrina devastated New Orleans, nearly two hundred foreign residents of Lakeside packed into Ajijic's "Old Posada" for a fundraiser for Katrina's victims. The event was organized by New Orleans native and Lakeside resident Ginger Martin and raised almost $2,000 USD for the American Red Cross relief fund. The *Guadalajara Reporter* also noted that many animal lovers at Lakeside made generous donations to the Society for the Prevention of Cruelty to Animals for the rescue and care of pets left behind during the Katrina evacuation ("Lakeside Community Raises Money" 2005). And on November 11, 2006, in a scene that repeats itself each year on U.S. Veterans Day, a large crowd of Americans gathered at the municipal cemetery in Chapala, Mexico, to honor the U.S. veterans buried there (105 as of 2006). The president of the local SAR led the group in the Pledge of Allegiance to the United States; a regent of the local chapter of the DAR gave the official welcome; one longtime American resident recited the poem "All My Sons," and another read "Freedom Is Not Free." Present in the crowd were an American couple (former residents of Lakeside) who had returned from Kansas to take part in the ceremony in Mexico, which they indicated had special meaning for them (Chaussee 2006f).

PRACTICING CITIZENSHIP
IN THE NEW LAND

Residing in Mexico does not prevent Americans from exercising their formal citizenship rights in the United States; nor does it preclude the exercise of substantive citizenship in Mexico. I met no American immigrant in Mexico who had obtained Mexican citizenship (even among those who had been living south of the border for thirty years or more) and met only a handful who were in the process of applying for Mexican citizenship. That small minority was motivated mainly by practical reasons, listing work-related benefits or other instrumental advantages. As one American immigrant in Ajijic observed: "Hey, you can never have too many passports, right?" (field interview, February 7, 2007). In two cases, immigrants from the United States identified as their motivation for pursuing dual citizenship fear of a backlash against Americans in Mexico as a result of U.S. immigration policy. In only one case did an immigrant who was actually in the process of pursuing Mexican citizenship identify political disenchantment with the United States as her reason for seeking formal membership in the Mexican state, which she now called "home"—but she proclaimed it loudly. Regardless of their general lack of interest in Mexican citizenship, Americans do engage in the public sphere in their host country—practicing, in other words, a form of citizenship not delimited by official state membership.

The context for immigrant political transnationalism in Mexico is somewhat unique in that the country has written into its Constitution Article 33, which expressly prohibits foreigners from involving themselves in Mexican politics.

> Foreigners are those who do not possess the qualities determined in Article 30. They have the right to the guarantees of Chapter I of the first title of this Constitution, but the Executive of the Union has the exclusive right to expel from the national territory, immediately and without necessity of judicial proceedings, all foreigners whose stay it judges inconvenient. Foreigners may not, in any manner, involve themselves in the political affairs of the country.

U.S. citizens and the Mexican government both profess to take this prohibition seriously, but Americans in Mexico have nevertheless found countless ways to exercise influence and make their voices heard regarding issues that affect their social, political, and economic well-being. Moreover, accounts of U.S. citizens being sanctioned for political activities in Mexico are rare. More common are examples of the Mexican government reaching out to the American immigrant population.

In both San Miguel and the Lake Chapala area, local governments maintain offices dedicated to serving the foreign community. Mayors and other local Mexican officials meet with the American community, appoint leaders within the community to their advisory councils, and provide services to the immigrants in English. In 1991, the newly elected mayor of San Miguel held a meeting with the "foreign colony" at which he emphasized that he does not look upon them as strangers, but "as residents of San Miguel on par with everyone else" ("New Mayor Meets" 1991). That same year, sixty Mexican police officers in San Miguel completed intensive English training to assist them in their work with the foreign community. *Atención* praised the program: "In view of the makeup of the population of this town, this should not be a one-shot effort, but lead to a continuation and elaboration of this type of on the job education" ("San Miguel Police Learn English" 1991). By 2004, the mayor's office in San Miguel had established an Office of International Relations and appointed Cristobal Finkelstein Franyuti the coordinator of foreign affairs. Finkelstein—sharp, young, and perfectly bilingual—was hired to manage the city's international relations and, in particular, the foreign community. Then-mayor Luis Alberto Villarreal García actively sought to "build a bridge" between the city and the foreign community, including administering an Internet survey among foreigners to seek input on how the city could improve communications, accountability, and public services. A letter from the mayor introduced the survey, noting: "We recognize the importance of the positive influence the foreign community has in San Miguel. Your participation through the years has resulted in a very special and cosmopolitan city" ("Mayor Seeks to Build a Bridge" 2004). When law enforcement in San Miguel struggled to capture a rapist in 2006, local officials established a special security task force to meet regularly with the American community to hear their concerns and keep them apprised of the investigation and the city's efforts to improve security.

Mexican officials in the Lake Chapala area reach out to the foreign community in similar ways. When a new Chapala mayor was sworn in on December 31, 2006, the *Guadalajara Reporter* noted that "a significant number of leading members of the expatriate community were on hand as special guests" (Palfrey 2007). Prior to that ceremony, Mayor-Elect Gerardo Degollado and his administration had met several times with the foreign community. During one meeting with a group of American residents at the Chapala Country Club, Degollado announced: "If we all get together, we can do it. Can I count on your help?" (Palfrey 2006a). He also met with an association of foreigners who own condominiums along the lake and expressed a commitment to having open and continuous dialogue with the foreign community (Campo 2006). In an interview with the local paper *El Charal,* one member of the Chapala municipal council, Héctor del Muro, explained that the city was going to form a link with the foreign community to help attend to their concerns: "The problems of the foreigners are very simple, principally they want better security, phone service that is good, electricity. We are going to treat them like neighbors, like friends" (del Muro 2006).

Finally, not all Americans in Mexico passively accept the prohibitions against their involvement in Mexican politics. On June 16, 2006, just weeks before Mexico's 2006 elections, foreigners in San Miguel hosted an elaborate $100 USD dinner and dance. The dress code was "Evening Festive," and the theme was "Shooting for the Stars." Elaborate parties are commonplace among the foreign community in San Miguel, but at this event, the "special guests" were Jesús Correa Ramírez and Luis Alberto Villarreal García— Mexican candidates from the conservative National Action Party (PAN) running for mayor of San Miguel and the state governorship of Guanajuato (*Atención,* June 2, 2006, 32). In January 2007, when Americans in San Miguel joined in a local effort to stop a multistory condo project, a Mexican specialist on national patrimony was present to clarify that foreigners were constitutionally permitted to participate in the effort (Ibarra 2007). On July 2, 2006, as millions of Mexicans went to the polls to choose their country's next president, some foreigners living in Mexico (Americans among them) participated in a mock election to challenge Mexico's prohibition against political participation by foreigners, or, in one organizer's terms, to "test those limits." Eighty-five mock voters stuffed ballots into a cardboard box designed by visual artist Daniel Knorr. The curator of the project, George Springer, remarked: "The candidates said that July 2 should be a day of celebrating democracy. If that's true, then why should we shut out the opinions of foreigners living in Mexico?" (Flores 2006).

Like Mexicans, Colombians, Dominicans, El Salvadorans, and Haitians, U.S. citizens, it is clear, are moving across borders and leading transnational lives. Americans in Mexico practice and promote their national culture and maintain close contact with their homeland; and, as with all migrants, technology facilitates this transnational existence for Americans in ways that would have been unimaginable even twenty years ago. The transnational ties they sustain are social, cultural, and economic, but also political. In what ways is the political transnationalism of Americans in Mexico similar to and different from the other cases that fill the pages of scholarly journals and capture the headlines in the United States?

POWER IMBALANCE IN REVERSE

If all identifying labels were omitted from the discussion above, the activities and relationships described would read like so many of the existing case studies on immigrant political transnationalism. Americans living in Mexico vote in U.S. elections, hold political rallies in Mexico focused on U.S. politicians and U.S. policies, and meet in Mexico with political candidates and party representatives from the United States. U.S. political parties are also reaching out to constituencies abroad. In fact, the emergent global organizing of Democrats and Republicans Abroad constitutes a form of extraterritorial representation and an example of transnational citizenship remarkably similar to those that capture the attention of analysts and observers of political transnationalism of Mexicans in the United States (Dark 2003a). Nonetheless, differences do exist. In fact, two of the most prominent explanations for immigrant political transnation-alism—the proactive role of the sending state in reaching out to its emigrants and an unwelcoming reception extended to the immigrants on the part of the host society and government—do not apply in the case of U.S. migration to Mexico.

Unlike Mexico and many other countries in Latin America, the United States, as a sending state, has been relatively uninterested in its conationals abroad. George Bush's nephew and John Kerry's sister campaigned in Mexico in 2004. Some of the large crop of candidates in 2008 made fund-raising trips to London (Doran 2007); but, as of June 2008, no presidential hopeful had campaigned in Mexico or referenced directly this constituency of Americans abroad in any campaign speech. Unlike former president of Mexico Vicente Fox and other prominent Mexican politicians, who now routinely reach out to Mexicans abroad, no U.S. president or candidate for president has made a promise to represent Americans living south of the border a part of his or her platform. No executive cabinet post dedicated to Americans abroad has been established, although some Americans abroad have asked for formal representation in the U.S. Congress. As noted in Chapter One, the United States has expressed little interest in and devoted limited energy to keeping track of how many of its citizens live abroad. These Americans abroad are expected to pay taxes to the U.S. government and on occasion are seen as politically expendable targets for tax increases ("Costing More . . ." 2006). Whatever their tax burden, however, these Americans are not entitled to collect social service payments such as Medicare from the U.S. government unless they are willing to return to the United States to do so. Organizations of Americans abroad complain that the hoops they must jump through to register to vote and securely cast an absentee ballot are onerous (Overseas Vote Foundation 2007). In 2006 and 2007, the Web site of the Overseas Vote Foundation featured a political cartoon of an American citizen living outside the United States shouting through a megaphone into the back of an oblivious Uncle Sam's head (http://www.overseasvotefoundation.org/overseas/home.htm). The newly formed Americans Abroad Congressional Caucus suggests a grow-ing willingness on the part of some representatives in Congress to attend to constituents abroad, but this and related initiatives have originated pri-marily from the migrants themselves, not their home government.

Second, unlike the neglect and often hostility that greet Mexican im-migrants in the United States, the reception extended to American immi-grants in Mexico is largely welcoming. There is nothing similar, either on the part of the Mexican government or society, to the nativism and xenophobia that exist in the United States and have escalated in recent years. Mexicans in Ajijic and San Miguel are not passing Spanish-only laws or monitoring who flies what kind of flag where. In no case did I witness or hear tales of Mexicans expressing outrage at Americans celebrating their culture in Mexico—whether in the form of large Fourth of July parties, Thanksgiving extravaganzas, Super Bowl bashes, or public commemorations of the deaths of American soldiers. Ultimately, these variations—a relatively passive sending state and generally welcoming receiving state—can be explained by accepting one of the guiding assumptions in the literature on transnationalism—power imbalances in the international system—but turning it on its head.

Running throughout the analyses of transnationalism is the notion of inequality—between sending states and receiving states and between immigrants and members of their host society. Transnationalism is portrayed overwhelmingly in terms of migrants moving from poorer countries to richer ones, receiving states that are more powerfully positioned in the world economy than sending states, and migrants who find themselves marginalized relative to the "natives" in the host society. Alejandro Portes et al. begin their introduction to the study of transnationalism by noting: "The events in question pertain to the creation of a transnational community linking immigrant groups in the *advanced countries* with their respective sending nations" (1999, 217; emphasis added). They also characterize transnationalism as a "set of responses and strategies by people in a condition of *disadvantage* to its [the world economy's] dominant logic" (1999, 227; emphasis added). And in the conclusion to a special issue of *Ethnic and Racial Studies,* Portes writes: "It is clear that the sending governments do not want their immigrants to return, but rather to achieve a secure status in the *wealthy nations* to which they have moved" (1999, 467; emphasis added). Faist, in his discussion of dual citizenship, contends: "Given the *asymmetric* relationships between countries of emigration and immigration, the position of the latter proves decisive" (2000, 209; emphasis added). In their recent analysis of transnationalism, Roger Waldinger and David Fitzgerald identify as a central component of twenty-first-century globalization "international migration bringing the alien 'other' from third world to first" (2004, 1177); and in distinguishing present-day transnationalism from its historical precedents, Levitt notes: "Many of today's migrants arrive already partially socialized into aspects of Western, if not North American, culture" (2001a, 203). Other scholars have identified transnationalism as a site of potential resistance against the hegemony of global capitalism and racial discrimination (Basch et al. 1994; Glick Schiller et al. 1992).

This assumption of a power imbalance as it pertains to international migration generally holds true. Overwhelmingly, immigrants are leaving less wealthy and less powerful states to establish lives in wealthier and more powerful states. The willingness of these sending states to reach out to and accommodate conationals abroad (by extending dual citizenship and other forms of political and economic rights) can be attributed to their current form of insertion in the world economy. Specifically, the strategy of promoting exports, pursued over the past two decades by many countries on the periphery of the world economy, has left these countries heavily dependent on the influx of foreign capital. Accordingly, migrant remittances become key to securing hard currency and providing subsistence to low-income households (Itzigsohn 1995; Portes, Dore-Cabral, and Landolt 1997). In the case of Mexico, remittances constitute the third-highest source of foreign exchange, just behind the maquiladora industry and oil. During 2006, Mexicans living abroad sent $23.05 billion back to their homeland. During the first quarter of 2007, the amount of those remittances was up 3.4 percent from the same period in 2006 ("Remittances from U.S." 2007). As Ostergaard-Nielsen maintains, migration provides sending countries, particularly those peripherally positioned in the global economy, "with new options for reconfiguring the reach of the nation-state through transnational economic, social and political ties with nationals abroad" (2003, 767).

If the incentive for sending state participation in, and encouragement of, transnational politics is the state's current form of insertion in the world economy, then the relative lack of interest or involvement of the United States with its citizens abroad can be explained by the fact that the United States does not occupy a peripheral or dependent position in the world economy. The United States is not reliant upon remittances from its emigrants; nor are American expatriates sending remittances. The U.S. government does require citizens living outside the country to pay U.S. income tax, which might be viewed as a type of mandatory remittance, but as discussed in Chapter Two, many Americans living abroad resent the requirement (some so much so that they renounce their U.S. citizenship) and a smaller number try hard to avoid it (Carvajal 2006).

A power imbalance, albeit in reverse, can also help explain the second distinction of the case of American migrants in Mexico: the tolerant reception of American immigrants by the Mexican host society and state, or at least the absence of public vilification. A variety of complex factors likely explains not only nativism in the United States and its recent rise, but also the relative lack of a nativist reaction in Mexico toward the influx of immigrants. For example, inverting the perception of many Americans that Mexican immigrants are harming the U.S. economy, many Mexicans may perceive American immigration as an economic enhancement. Empirically documenting the net cost or benefit of either migration flow is an incredibly complicated task, but to the extent that Mexicans in Mexico and their government officials perceive themselves as dependent in some way on the influx of U.S. capital, they are not likely to express, at least openly, hostility or resentment toward American immigrants. In reality, the United States may be as economically reliant upon Mexican migrants to the United States as Mexico is upon the capital influx and development that are believed to accompany U.S. immigration to Mexico. However, Mexico is now, and historically has been, economically and politically disempowered relative to the United States. This power imbalance influences: (1) the nature of transnationalism on the part of American migrants to Mexico and their general sense of entitlement, (2) the host country's tolerant embrace of them, and (3) their wealthy sending state's seeming disinterest in them.

The discussion above begs, however, an important question. If the United States as a sending state is not actively promoting transnational ties with Americans in Mexico, and if the migrants themselves are not marginalized or excluded in Mexico in a way that fuels their persistent attachment to the U.S. homeland (two prominent explanations for immigrants' political transnationalism), then what does explain transnationalism and the practice of extraterritorial citizenship on the part of Americans in Mexico? Several factors appear significant and are consistent with the general literature on transnationalism. First, the increasing interest of U.S. political parties in their constituencies abroad, and vice versa, certainly plays a factor in forging a transnational political field. As Itzigsohn maintains, the incentives for political parties in the country of origin to participate in transnational politics include the presence of large constituencies residing abroad and the consolidation of competitive party politics. Although the precise numbers are elusive, both the Democratic and Republican Parties in the United States have become aware of the growing numbers of U.S. voters residing outside of the United States; and the increased competition between the parties has intensified the search for party faithful. Dark makes the insightful observation that the absence of hard data on the numbers of Americans abroad and their partisan preferences may actually fuel the efforts of the parties to organize globally: "in the absence of data, hope springs eternal" (2003b, 244).

A second explanation for why American migrants practice political transnationalism in the absence of an activist sending state or hostility in the state of settlement is that the presumptions that underlie conceptualization of transnationalism have led to an overly restrictive conceptualization of the phenomenon. Transnational migration and transnational ties constitute forms of adaptation to globalization, but not necessarily resistance, and not only among the marginalized. As migrants of privilege, Americans in Mexico have the ability to transcend nation-states when it serves their interests to do so and to make claims on multiple nation-states when they stand to benefit from doing so. Their circumstances might be characterized in terms of what Linda Kerber (2006) calls state*full*ness, in contrast to statelessness: "For these people, a destabilized citizenship is an enriched citizenship. . . . Such people speak cheerfully of multiplied citizenships, a comfortable cosmopolitanism, being a citizen of the world—an empowered status, an enlargement of the traditional relationship of subject to king, citizen to nation" (2006, 138).

CONCLUSION

The case of Americans' political transnationalism confirms several common patterns discussed in the literature and suggests minor refinements in others. Globalization and migration are altering existing opportunities and constraints for political participation. As scholars of transnationalism have correctly argued, we are witnessing the birth, perhaps now the adolescence, of plural forms of political belonging that extend beyond the confines of membership in a single state. Citizenship, once defined as formal membership in one and only one state and determined largely by residency in that state, is now being stretched and reconfigured. American migrants, like others, are continuing to exercise formal citizenship rights in a state of origin where they no longer reside (the United States); they are practicing substantive forms of political belonging in a host society (Mexico) where they do not possess formal membership; and a small minority is officially pursuing dual citizenship in both states. The political transnationalism of American migrants also confirms that transnationalism, although related to globalization, is distinct from it in that the former is characterized by "highly particularistic attachments," typically to two nation-states (Waldinger and Fitzgerald 2004). Migration may give rise to a multiplicity of belongings, but "here" and "there," however defined, and the significance attached to these sites and sources of belonging, have not been thoroughly transcended. Nor have states faded from view as institutions that manage human movement and shape human identity.

Chapter Two discussed some of the ways states persist as powerful actors, domestically and internationally, in spite of globalization and deterritorialization. This chapter builds on that view, confirming Robert Smith's claim that "possession of state-given citizenship rights still matters so much. It is for this reason that migrants are fighting so hard—via membership practices—to expand these citizenship rights" (2003, 303).

The case of Americans in Mexico differs slightly from other cases in that the sending state has, compared to most, been minimally involved in fostering transnational ties with its emigrants; and, although the migrants themselves are largely responsible for forging transnational networks, they are not motivated by an experience of marginalization in the host society. These variations contradict predominant explanations for immigrants' political transnationalism, but can be explained by reference to the role of power in the international system. Because the bulk of the scholarship on transnationalism presumes migrants and sending states that are disadvantaged relative to host societies and receiving states, a case that reverses that presumption reveals a different dynamic. As a global superpower, the United States is not reliant upon its emigrants for an influx of foreign capital. American migrants are capitalizing on the benefits of life south of the border, but are cognizant of and motivated to retain the benefits of their membership in a politically and economically powerful state of origin. As a receiving state, Mexico reacts to the immigrants on the basis of a perceived dependence upon both them and the powerful state from which they hail. This case argues for the need to expand the recognition and analysis of transnationalism to include the less familiar, but no less significant, cases that illustrate, albeit in alternative ways, the implications of inequalities in the international system.

Chapter Two explored how technology allows migrants to transcend borders and boundaries, but emphasized that this transcendence does not occur totally unencumbered by the control that states continue to exert over citizens, residents, and sojourners under their jurisdiction. This chapter continued with the analysis of transnational lives by focusing on how Americans in Mexico practice extraterritorial citizenship. Chapter Four turns to look more closely at the issue of identity formation among transmigrants in North America. Specifically, the chapter will explore how the proliferation and intensification of transnational ties affect the way U.S. citizens living in Mexico negotiate a sense of belonging in the world.

Four   "THEY LOVE US HERE!"

Privileged Belonging in a Global World

Forty new Americans here means forty new maid jobs.
— AMERICAN RESIDENT OF SAN MIGUEL DE ALLENDE

*Mexican immigrants in the U.S. have an inferiority complex,
but the Americans here have a superiority complex.*
— AMERICAN RESIDENT OF SAN MIGUEL DE ALLENDE

One February morning, along the shores of Mexico's Lake Chapala, I was having breakfast with members of the local Thomas Paine Chapter of the Daughters of the American Revolution. After discussing the apparent peculiarity of a patriotic U.S. organization with chapters located throughout Mexico, and the reasons these particular Daughters decided to cross the border, I asked about the reaction of local Mexicans to the American presence along Lake Chapala. One of my breakfast companions replied, without hesitation, "We are a national treasure." Given that multiple, transnational belongings were a central theme of my study, I needed to clarify which, or whose, nation she believed treasured her. "We are a national treasure to Mexico because of all the money we bring into this country," she explained. Her response echoed that of the American woman I met on a bench in the *jardín* the first time I visited San Miguel in June of 2005. When I asked that American how Mexicans responded to the influx of immigrants from the United States, she assured me: "They love us here!"

The confidence these immigrants feel at being warmly welcomed in a foreign land stands in stark contrast to the sense of alienation and marginalization that many Mexicans and Mexican Americans, regardless of their legal status, experience in the United States. In fact, the conventional North American migration story is one of immigrants who cross the border from south to north under varying degrees of duress; experience hostility or at the very least neglect from the host society and government; and lack, at least initially, sufficient financial, political, and cultural capital to live securely in their settlement destination. Oscar Handlin, in his classic text *The Uprooted* (1951), focused on how this migration experience affected the migrants. The story, he explained, is one of "broken homes, interruptions of a familiar life, separation from known surroundings, the becoming of a foreigner and ceasing to belong" (quoted in Deux 2006, 11).

Exceptions to this portrayal of the immigrant experience have always existed, and recent research suggests a less bleak reality for migrants, at least with regard to acculturation. In fact, transnationalism—and the practices, processes, and social fields to which it gives rise—have been credited with improving the lives of some immigrants (Deux 2006). From this perspective, transnationalism, although closely associated with globalization, is recognized as an effective and affective strategy for coping with the turbulence of global change. The instrumental underpinnings of transnationalism involve, for example, migrants who cross borders for economic gain and sending states strapped for capital that reach out to migrants abroad for millions of dollars annually in needed remittances. But beyond its role as a strategy for coping with the vagaries of global capitalism, transnationalism also has an affective dimension. Maintaining ties with the homeland and forging social fields that span the place of origin and the place of settlement eases the migration process and the challenges of coping with strangeness, marginalization, and even hostility in the receiving state (Abdelhady 2006; Viruell-Fuentes 2006). Transnationalism, in other words, is an increasingly common form of negotiating belonging in a turbulent global world.

As noted in previous chapters, Americans in Mexico generally fit well the models of immigrant transnationalism, with the exception of their relative wealth and power. This exception is significant, however, in the ways it influences the array of opportunities and constraints that undergird the daily transnational existence of American migrants, the specific contours of their political transnationalism, and the way these migrants negotiate a sense of identity across borders. This chapter will explore how U.S. citizens living in Mexico sort through the ambiguities of belonging associated with residing in one country while remaining formally and informally tied to another and how they live amidst a new and somewhat distinct set of cultural practices while never straying far from the familiarity of their own. Claims like "they love us here" and "we are a national treasure" reflect a peculiar confidence, and perhaps an arrogance, to which power and privilege give rise; but they also highlight an additional theme of import—the ambiguity of identity and belonging in an increasingly globalized world. Who exactly are the cherished "we" to whom the respondents above are referring? Who are "they," perceived to be bestowing love? What is the nature of the interaction between these imagined social formations; and what is their relationship to notions of "here" and "there" and the spaces that emerge in between?

These questions are reminders that globalization in all of its dimensions—economic, cultural, political—not only unsettles people's material lives, but their emotional and psychological ones as well (and the two are, of course, related). Changing notions of identity and belonging affect, albeit differently, nonmigrants as well as migrants, immigrant-receiving societies as well as sending ones, small communities as well as continents. As goods, services, people, and ideas move frequently, rapidly, and farther in a world characterized by the compression of time and space, individuals increasingly question: "Who am I, and where do I fit?" Neither human migration nor the ambiguities of identity and belonging are new, but both have intensified in an era of globalization. How, exactly, globalization influences migrant belongings depends heavily upon context; and for Americans in Mexico, the context is one of relative privilege. This privilege shapes the stories Americans tell about their lives in Mexico, the identities they construct for themselves, and those that they assign to others.

THE NATURE OF BELONGING

Amin Maalouf, a writer and Lebanese-born, Arab Christian immigrant to France, opens his book *In the Name of Identity* with this statement:

> A life spent writing has taught me to be wary of words.
> Those that seem clearest are often the most treacherous.
> "Identity" is one of those false friends. We all think we know
> what the word means and go on trusting it, even when it's
> slyly starting to say the opposite. (2003, 10)

Since the early 1990s, references to identity have filled the headlines of major newspapers, the speeches by politicians, and the pages of journals and books. The term "belonging," although with somewhat less frequency, has also entered into the public discourse (Croucher 2003; Fortier 2000; Geddes and Favell 1999; Migdal 2004). These terms aim to capture a reality that caught many observers by surprise—namely, the persistent power of ethnicity, race, religion, gender, and nationhood as bases for sociocultural unification and political mobilization. Scholars and policy makers alike had presumed that these forms of attachment would become anachronisms in a post–Cold War "new world order," or an economically developed and politically advanced global village. The tragic events in Bosnia provided one of the early indicators of the inadequacy of this worldview. Countless other examples have followed those in the former Yugoslavia, and the events of 9/11 and since seem to have silenced any remaining celebratory utterances about the advent of a postnational, postmodern world (Fish 2002). More commonplace, as we begin a new millennium, are references to civilizations clashing, the "West" locked in battle against "the rest," and the need for "us" (composed of some combination of freedom-loving, Western, Christian, white, Anglo-Saxon, Protestant heterosexuals) to stand strong against "them" (the evildoing, backward-thinking, brown, Muslim, Arab, women-hating sissies) (Croucher 2006).

Given the troubling exclamations and explanations that now circulate in reference to contemporary world events, Maalouf's quotation about identity is a useful reminder of the need to be cautious about invoking the term, or the concept, without interrogating its meaning. His analysis joins countless others in illuminating important and often misunderstood aspects of identity and belonging. Perhaps the most significant insight stemming from this literature is that identity is made, not born. As Vikki Bell explains with respect to "belonging": "One does not simply or ontologically 'belong' to the world or to any group within it. Belonging is an achievement at several levels of abstraction" (1999, 3). The constructed and achieved nature of identity and belonging is evinced by their multiplicity and fluidity. All humans possess multiple identities, some of which may overlap, intersect, or collide; and these identities shift over time and across space as the circumstances of our lives change.

Scholars working from this constructivist perspective do not deny the very real power and potency of identity. In other words, terms like construction, definition, imagination, and invention are not intended to imply ethereality or delusion. Nor do analysts of identity construction perceive the process as arbitrary. Identities are not constructed out of thin air, and the scholarship on this topic has focused on how such constructions and imaginings occur (Cornell and Hartmann 1998; Marx 1998; Migdal 2004). In doing so, it has revealed that identity and belonging are relational and contextual. Who we are is shaped in relation to who we are not, and the boundaries of belonging are forged and maintained not simply on the basis of who is contained within those boundaries, but who is excluded by them. Specific, though not static, historical, sociocultural, and economic factors influence which formations of belonging emerge as prominent, and which do not, as well as among which individuals and groups, where and when. Finally, and perhaps most importantly, the process is deeply and thoroughly infused with power and politics, and the tug and pull of vested interests. As anthropologist Kevin Yelvington explained, paraphrasing Karl Marx: "People invent their [identities] as they invent their history, but not exactly in ways which they please" (1992, 3).

Immigrants and immigration have always provided valuable foci for the study of identity construction and negotiated belonging. Heavily influenced by U.S. scholars and the U.S. context, the assimilationist framework long offered descriptions and prescriptions regarding the processes by which immigrants shed one identity and adopt another. University of Chicago sociologist Robert Park famously theorized that after an initial stage of *contact,* immigrants would experience *competition and conflict* within the host society, then *accommodation,* and finally *assimilation.* In the ultimate stage of assimilation, they would "acquire the memories, sentiments, and attitudes of other persons or groups [in the society], and, by sharing their experience and history, [be] incorporated with them in a common cultural life" (Park and Burgess 1921, 735). Years later, Milton Gordon (1964) famously added to this approach a model of assimilation as comprising seven sequential stages from cultural to civic assimilation. Over time, however, it became clear that these descriptions, and perhaps the prescriptions underlying them, were flawed, and scholars turned their attention to how and why some groups maintained their cultural ties and what might explain the variation in identity formation within and across groups. This shift in focus generated valuable insights regarding the significance of power and politics in the shaping of identity. It helped explain, for example, why some immigrant groups in the United States became "white," while others did not; and why access to certain resources—symbolic and otherwise—could facilitate the construction of one type of group identity versus another (Cornell and Hartmann 1998; Deux 2006). Cuban immigrants, for example, arrived in the United States beginning in the 1960s in the midst of a Cold War political context that celebrated them as heroes escaping Communism. A U.S. racial context granted them the enviable status of "whiteness," and the economic context, particularly in South Florida, was ripe for the type of ethnic enclave development for which they became well known. These were also immigrants who, at least in the initial waves, possessed high levels of human and social capital (Croucher 1996). Other immigrant groups who have arrived prior to and since then, Haitians notable among them, have not been privy to the same context for identity formation.

The contexts in which immigrant identity and belonging are negotiated have shifted profoundly in recent decades as a result of the increasing interconnectedness of the globe. Globalization in its various guises has influenced both the mechanisms and resources with which individuals and groups define their identities and has altered economic and political landscapes in ways that affect the perceived need, and opportunities available, for belonging (Croucher 2003). Scholars of transnationalism seek to make sense of this reconfigured context and how it affects migrant belongings. In its earliest iterations, scholarship on transnationalism pointed to fundamental shifts, even ruptures, in how migrants make their place in the world. Instead of leaving behind one society and culture to integrate into a new one, transnational migrants move back and forth between worlds and carve out alternative social fields that transcend the geopolitical and cultural boundaries of nation-states (Glick Schiller et al. 1992; Basch et al. 1994; Appadurai 1996; Mountz and Wright 1996). Implicit and sometimes explicit in these accounts is the notion that either immigrant assimilation into the host society is a relic of the past or assimilation and transnationalism are juxtaposed positions. Other scholars, however, have insisted that assimilation and transnationalism are not mutually exclusive processes. Continuing to belong to one's homeland is not incompatible with aspiring to or achieving simultaneous belonging in a new land (Joppke and Morawska 2003; Kivisto 2001; Levitt 2001a). Today, analysts of transnationalism agree widely that migrant belongings are best characterized in terms of multiplicity and fluidity. General agreement also exists with regard to how territory and place figure into migrants' notions of identity and attachment. Portrayals of globalization tend to emphasize a world of decentered, deterritorialized, and denationalized processes and flows. Alternatively, analysts of transnationalism emphasize various forms of transcendence and reconfiguration, but do so without ever losing track of the fact that transnational belonging remains rooted in specific places, namely two or more nation-states (Faist 2000; Smith 2007; Waldinger and Fitzgerald 2004).

The literature on identity formation and the related implications of globalization offer valuable insights into the case of American migrants in Mexico. Like all individuals and groups, immigrant and otherwise, Americans in Mexico maintain multiple attachments. These attachments are shaped and maintained in relation to others and are influenced by specific configurations of opportunities and constraints. Chapter Two illustrated how technology allows American migrants to transcend, albeit not entirely, the conventional confines of territory, place, and space. Chapter Three discussed the persistent, although reconfigured, significance of citizenship. This chapter looks more closely at the nature of transnational belonging, particularly when practiced by migrants with relatively unique access to political, economic, and cultural power.

"I'M AN AMERICAN LIVING IN MEXICO"

In general, U.S. citizens living in Mexico do not spend a great deal of time pondering questions of identity and belonging, at least not in the manner and via the jargon that academics might. Nevertheless, many of the immigrants I interviewed were willing to engage the theme when asked to, and some did so quite thoughtfully. On occasion, an immigrant would express a particularly confident sense of who or what he or she was or was not: "I will always be an American"; or, "It's not like I'll ever be Mexican." On other occasions, immigrants acknowledged that their sense of identity and belonging had been altered in some way by their transborder existence. In several instances, my discussions of belonging with American immigrants concluded with a statement similar to this one made by a U.S. citizen in his late sixties who had been living in San Miguel for five years: "Well, I guess I'm an American living in Mexico" (field interview, June 7, 2006).

The question of how "Americanness," or the United States, figures into these immigrants' sense of being in the world provided interesting examples of the contemporary ambivalence that surrounds nation-state attachments, particularly for individuals or groups who have transcended them in some way. It is important to point out that because I was specifically interested in political transnationalism as one aspect of this study, my sample of respondents likely overrepresents migrants who are politically engaged. An unknown number of U.S. citizens is certain to be living throughout Mexico, maintaining minimal attachments to, or at least no strong cultural or psychological identification with, the United States or other U.S. nationals who move to Mexico. These American migrants are much less likely to surface as research participants for a study such as this one. Among the immigrants I did interview, their U.S. origins tended to be central to their sense of identity, but not in predictable or static ways. Chapter Three documents the many ways that U.S. citizens abroad continue to engage politically with the government of their homeland: voting, raising money for favored candidates and parties, lobbying for advantageous tax regimes and citizenship regulations, and the extension of benefits such as Medicare. On one level, these activities confirm the pervasive power of states to control lives and regulate the distribution of resources. But beyond the more instrumental ties that continue to bind citizens to their states, the discourse of Americans living in Mexico also attests to the persistence of affective ties to an imagined national community—albeit a community whose contours are in flux.

During my meetings in February 2007 with the Daughters of the American Revolution in Ajijic, one of the women went out of her way to clarify for me that the DAR was not a political organization: "But I want to make sure of one thing—that you know that DAR is a strictly nonpolitical organization. With ladies of all political persuasions as members, but with their patriotism in common, it has to be that way" (field interview, February 3, 2007). My questions about the local chapters of Democrats and Republicans Abroad had prompted her to emphasize that the DAR was nonpartisan (and indeed the DAR regent sitting to my left that morning was active in the local Democrats Abroad chapter and the woman to my right was an avowed Republican). I also gathered that her clarification about the "nonpolitical" nature of her organization was prompted, in part, by hurt feelings and social tensions as a result of intense partisanship within the American immigrant community in Lake Chapala during the 2004 and 2006 U.S. elections. In any event, the fact that she and other Americans who had made the decision to live their lives in Mexico were emphasizing patriotism toward the United States as the glue that bound them seemed to strike only me as odd. This same and seemingly peculiar patriotism was evident when *Inside Mexico,* the monthly periodical that bills itself as "the English speaker's guide to living in Mexico," devoted its September 2007 issue to the upcoming U.S. presidential primaries. In addition to publishing a voting guide that provided U.S. voters in Mexico with background information on all of the candidates in the 2008 U.S. presidential primaries, the magazine gave Republicans and Democrats Abroad a column each to make the case for their party. Beyond the predictable partisan jabs, both immigrant editorialists, writing from their adopted land south of the Rio Grande on behalf of their fellow party constituents abroad, sang the praises of the United States of America.

U.S. citizens living in Mexico have moved to a foreign land, but continue to express deep attachment to their nation-state of origin; and, for the most part, they do so unapologetically and with little sense of irony. In an interview in January 2007, one officer of the Mexico chapter of Young Democrats Abroad who has lived in Mexico for ten years discussed with me his enduring identity as "American" and his deep commitment to mobilizing (from within Mexico) for political change in the United States. Another officer of a different chapter of Democrats Abroad has lived in Mexico for eight years and insists that he has no plans to ever leave. Nevertheless, he remains attached to, and strongly committed to effecting political change in, the United States. During the intense mobilization of Americans abroad in 2004, one lifelong Republican living in Chapala summarized the point of the Republicans Abroad international campaign as "simple": "Be an expatriate. Vote" (Walker 2004). For him, not only was residency in Mexico compatible with political engagement with the United States, they were synonymous.

When I pushed each of these and other respondents to explain their enduring political ties and commitments to the United States, despite many years of living in Mexico and no plans to leave, their reported motivations included a deep sense of civic responsibility (even strident nationalism in rare cases), practical calculations, and, occasionally, a cosmopolitan desire to use their influence as voters registered in the United States for the betterment of the world. One officer and founding member of Young Democrats Abroad in Mexico (young, in this context, meant forty) explained that in addition to registering voters and raising money for the Democrats, his organization was truly committed to building community among the Americans in Mexico: "It really bothers me to see Americans leaving the U.S. and forgetting all about it. They move to Mexico and live with a vacation mentality the rest of their lives" (field interview, January 20, 2007). In Ajijic, a member of the local chapter of Democrats Abroad explained: "I plan to get my dual citizenship here in Mexico. . . . Hey, you can never have too many passports, right? But I will never *not* be an American" (field interview, February 7, 2007). Another American immigrant who had lived in Mexico more than thirty years and was active in Republicans Abroad remarked: "It is a good thing to be an American. We are proud of that and want to stay on top of things and not let China become the superpower" (field interview, April 12, 2007). One officer of Democrats Abroad who lives in Mexico and holds citizenship in both the United States and Britain offered this remark, the sentiments of which were echoed by some other politically active Americans abroad as well: "It is powerful a thing to have a say in what happens in the most powerful country in the world. . . . a U.S. election is a world election" (field interview, March 27, 2007).

I regularly felt somewhat disoriented during interviews such as one with an American couple in San Miguel who sat comfortably ensconced in their colonial Mexican home, sharing with me over coffee their love for Mexico and their loyalty to the U.S. Republican Party. All the while, the sounds of Fox News filtered into the perfectly manicured Mexican courtyard from a flat-screen television in the adjacent room. In another interview in Lake Chapala, I listened to a Texan couple, also avid viewers of Fox News, who, while lounging beneath their large, glass-encased American flag, told me they would never leave Mexico, although they wanted to leave Ajijic due to the growing number of Americans in town. Curiously, the migrants themselves rarely expressed any sense of incongruity resulting from their border-transcending existences. Some of their comments, however, did reveal a certain ambiguity with regard to identity and belonging. Many migrants confidently proclaimed themselves Americans, while others seemed to fall back on their national origin as a default identity: "I guess I think of myself mostly as American, I mean it is not like I could ever be Mexican. . . . I doubt I will ever pursue dual citizenship" (field interview, June 7, 2006). An officer of Young Democrats Abroad expressed his deep commitment to U.S. politics, but when I asked him to identify his most central sense of identity, he chose "Chilango"—the Spanish term for residents of Mexico City (field interview, January 20, 2007). His comment reminded me of one made by Alexandr Manin, an immigrant from Kazakhstan, and not a U.S. citizen, who nevertheless joined the U.S. military after 9/11, explaining, "It doesn't matter that America is not my country. New York is my city" ("War on Terror" 2001).

Other American migrants also expressed sentiments of attachment toward Mexico. Judy King, who edits the online magazine *Living at Lake Chapala,* writes on her Web site about her first visit to Lake Chapala in 1990: "I felt like I had come home. I knew I had to live in Mexico—to learn, to teach, and to be complete" (http://www.mexico-insights.com/gen/Editors.aspx [accessed June 2007]). She also described returning to Ajijic after a visit to the States: "When I crossed the border and saw the Mexican flag I felt something that might be described as patriotism—at least it was a feeling of attachment to and some pride in Mexico" (field interview, February 6, 2007). Another American woman living in San Miguel spoke nostalgically about a summer trip to Mexico with her grandfather when she was an adolescent:

> I did not want to go at first. I thought Mexico was dirty, but I really fell in love with the country. People actually looked you in the eye here, like they cared. I brought back a fifty-

cent coin and carried it in my pocket. I knew I would go back to live in Mexico someday. Here I am, and I feel very much like I belong here. (field interview, June 17, 2007)

In San Miguel, another American woman who had been living in Mexico less than a year was quickly swept up in her adopted country's enthusiasm for soccer. Referring to a match between Mexico and Argentina during the 2006 World Cup tournament, she exclaimed: "We almost snuck one by them there at the end" (field interview, June 18, 2006). "We," for this newly arrived American immigrant, referred to Mexico.

Discussing the role of technology in her daily life, one American in San Miguel revealed how some immigrants feel simultaneously at home in Mexico and closely connected to the rhythms of life in the United States:

> Many of us are registered for Google Alerts and get notices of articles that appear anywhere on the Web about San Miguel, Mexico, *our home town,* favorite candidates, etc., and we send them around to our friends. Many of us check in on YouTube daily to find out what is "hot" in the U.S. that day, too. (e-mail correspondence, June 19, 2007; emphasis added)

An interview respondent who understood and shared my interest in fluid belongings reported with amusement that in the recent past, the local chapter of the Daughters of the American Revolution in Ajijic chose a Jewish Canadian as its "Woman of the Year." At a Rotary meeting in Ajijic in February 2007, another American, who had just moved inland from Mexico's Pacific coast, told me that he travels frequently, but always feels American: "Look, I am Jewish. I have this argument a lot with friends about Israel. Of course I belong to Israel. But if there was ever a conflict, I am American first and foremost" (field interview, February 6, 2007). Some of these immigrants were more conscious of and interested in the fluidity or multiplicity of their belonging than others, but none expressed any discomfort with the ambiguity.

In addition to having fluid and multiple imaginings of community and identity, Americans in Mexico are also negotiating who they are in relation to other groups. In *Blood and Belonging: Journeys into the New Nationalism,* author Michael Ignatieff (1993) emphasizes the central role "they" play in giving shape to "we." In doing so, he also invokes Sigmund Freud's notion of the "narcissism of small differences" to illustrate that the degree of distinction between individuals and groups, and the intensity that surrounds it, can be manufactured rapidly and along the most arbitrary and previously insignificant dimensions of difference. Ignatieff is referring to locations like Bosnia and Northern Ireland, where groups who share more commonalities than differences have been literally at each other's throats. American immigrants in Mexico are not now, nor likely to be, caught up in conflicts of this sort. Nevertheless, various discourses through which Americans in Mexico differentiate themselves from others become central to defining who these migrants are and carving out a sense of belonging in their new land south of the border.

Particularly intriguing to me, and much more prominent in the Lake Chapala area than in San Miguel, is a differentiation that is widely drawn between immigrants from the United States and immigrants from Canada. This differentiation is largely self-referential, since local Mexicans do not seem to notice or take interest in the cultural differences that Seymour Martin Lipset (1989) once characterized in terms of "The Continental Divide" between North Americans who reside north of the 49th parallel and those who reside to the south. For the Mexicans in Ajijic and San Miguel, these immigrants are simply lumped together as either "*norteamericanos*," "*la comunidad extranjera*" (the foreign community), or "gringos." Nevertheless, U.S. migrants, who prior to moving to Mexico shared with most Americans the tendency to ignore their Canadian neighbors to the north, now interact closely with them as fellow foreigners in Mexico. Despite what might seem like overwhelming similarities of language, culture, race, and immigration status, many members of both groups of North Americans maintain an awareness of notable differences between the two. This topic was never an intended focus of my study, and the references to it were always unsolicited. Still, and in spite of its seemingly trivial nature, it was repeated often enough to warrant mention.

Many U.S. migrants to Mexico hold fast to a stereotype of Canadians as "cheap." Time and again immigrants from the United States worked into our conversations references to Canadians in town who don't tip well, or order only one buffet plate and share it between two people. At one of the town's infamous fund-raisers sponsored by the foreign community, an auctioneer anxious for an opening bid on a cocktail party for twenty-five quipped: "Come on. Do we have a bunch of Canadians here tonight, or what?!" (February 1, 2007). He was forced to apologize when a table of Canadians seated near the stage took offense and started to leave. For their part, many Canadians living along Lake Chapala perceive Americans as loud and brash and resent that partisan disagreements over U.S. politics take up so much space in the social life of the Mexican town. One Canadian, who coincidentally made his living loaning money to Americans who wanted to buy homes in Mexico, where bank mortgages don't exist, told me: "They [Mexicans] don't like the Americans here . . . for political reasons." He went on to invoke a famous line from former Canadian Prime Minister Pierre Trudeau: "They like us Canadians because both of us are just 'mice hoping not to get stepped on by the big elephant'" (field interview, January 20, 2007). I also had more than one Canadian (aware of the tipping stereotype) tell me, defensively and unsolicited, that Americans needed to remember that the Canadian dollar is worth less and does not stretch as far in Mexico as the U.S. currency.

Nor are the immigrants the only ones using Mexico as a stage for drawing distinctions between the U.S. citizens and Canadians. In January 2007, a former deputy prime minister of Canada, Sheila Copps, addressed a meeting of the Canadian Club of Lake Chapala. A record turnout of three hundred Canadians and "a few strays from Mexico and the United States" reportedly "paid rapt attention" as Copps spoke to the expatriates about their roles as ambassadors to Mexico. She emphasized the similarities of the two nations, Canada and Mexico, straddling the superpower between them. She also opined that Canadians, because they are accustomed to dealing with diversity in their own country, are particularly well suited to adjust to living in a culture into which they weren't born (Chaussee 2007). While I doubt that any foreigner living in Ajijic would deny that these national stereotypes circulate widely, many would want to, and in fact did, clarify that not all Canadians conform to any one stereotype, nor do Americans. Several also shared that they had formed meaningful cross-national (as in U.S./Canadian) friendships since moving to Mexico. The Lake Chapala Society, for example, in its outreach to and mobilization of foreigners living along Mexico's largest lake, makes a concerted effort to recognize and respect the national variation among the immigrant population. Although 71 percent of the organization's membership hails from the United States, twenty-four different nationalities make up the Society's global membership (Lake Chapala Society 2006, 39).

Another way in which American immigrants in Mexico define and situate themselves is in opposition to their compatriots who have not migrated south, but remain "north of the border," or "NOB." I first encountered the acronyms "NOB" and "SOB" on Web-based discussion forums populated by English speakers living in Mexico. Beyond providing a shorthand way to refer to the United States versus Mexico, these abbreviations conveyed a reconfigured sense of belonging. Americans living in Mexico are conscious of the border as a marker of difference and aware of themselves as migrants who live their lives across that border. For many, the fact that they do so attests to an adventurous spirit prevalent among Americans who live SOB and absent among those who remain NOB. After a Rotary meeting in Ajijic in February 2007, one American immigrant expressed interest in my study and asked excitedly: "Don't you find that we expats tend to be more adventurous than most Americans?" (field interview, February 6, 2007). Another chimed in, sounding a note of pride: "This [Mexico] is the most foreign country I've been in. If you can't adjust, you won't make it" (field interview, February 6, 2007). Migrants who define themselves as having embraced life SOB, in spite of its foreignness, see this as something that distinguishes them from the tourists, who visit only occasionally and interact with the local culture only superficially. Living year-round in Ajijic or San Miguel, and/or having committed to an indefinite period of residency there, unites many migrants who make it a pastime to bemoan the arrival of the seasonal migrants and the newcomers, who don't understand "how we do things here." One immigrant living in San Miguel, an artist from New York, explained: "We all dread the tourists. The ones from Texas are the worst. They are so loud and only care about shopping" (field interview, June 11, 2006). In another interview, an American immigrant from California remarked: "Things are fine until the Texans get down here. If you need to cross the street and the car coming has Mexican plates, you're fine; but if the plates are from Texas, you better watch out. They will run you dead over" (field interview, June 5, 2006). Another American, a real estate agent who had been living and working in San Miguel for almost sixty years, noted: "Even by the late 1980s and early 1990s, when things were really starting to change, we joked about putting up gates and requiring a pass to get in" (field interview, June 26, 2006).

Beyond these mechanisms that immigrants use to differentiate between "us versus them"—country of origin, state of origin, or residency status—foreigners living in Mexico also define themselves in relation to their preferred town of settlement, and in opposition to those who have chosen to settle in a different Mexican town. When I mentioned to immigrants in San Miguel that I was headed next to Lake Chapala, or to those in the lakeside village of Ajijic that I had spent time in San Miguel, I was often regaled with tales of how "that town" or "those people" are snobby and cliquish or are "rednecks who drink too much." One American in San Miguel told me: "Don't even bother with Lake Chapala. The only thing you're going to find there is bridge and booze" (field interview, June 2, 2006). Another prominent member of the foreign community in San Miguel boasted that it is his chosen Mexican town that attracts "the cultured people who really care about the arts and philanthropy" (field interview, June 27, 2006). Earlier research on expatriate communities suggests that this tendency is a common one (Cohen 1977).

Curiously, Mexicans, the native inhabitants of Ajijic and San Miguel and the group who would seem to offer the most obvious "other" to the American immigrants' "us," are not necessarily the most frequently invoked. Yet, despite the energy the immigrants expend defining themselves in relation to tourists, Canadians, or Americans who have chosen to settle in a different Mexican town, they cannot escape the fact that they are, as a phrase widely circulated there has it, "living like kings and queens" in a foreign land where many of the native-born around them are living like paupers. Whether they ignore this reality, seek to justify it, or react defensively to portrayals of it, many Americans make claims that echo colonial discourses of an earlier era.

GRINGO'S BURDEN

In one of the most extensive academic analyses of expatriates, sociologist Erik Cohen maintains that "Though their contribution to those countries should not be belittled, they [expatriates] are still a neo-colonial or imperialist phenomenon" (1977, 5). The literature on neocolonialism and neoimperialism is immense and complex. The history of U.S.–Mexico relations is equally complex and riddled with evidence and overtones of imperialism and neocolonialism. American citizens who reside in Mexico have historically been implicated in this dynamic—whether as settlers and soldiers furthering U.S. expansionism in the nineteenth century, businesspeople and investors spreading U.S. capitalism southward throughout the twentieth century, or overseas defenders and promoters of the United States during wartime. The American Society of Mexico, founded in 1942, was inspired explicitly by the threat of World War II. The founders and other Americans living in Mexico at the time gathered together "with a view toward preparation for war work" ("Dollars and Sense of Community" 1974, 5). Sam Bollings Wright, American industrialist and resident of Mexico, tells of being called upon by Nelson Rockefeller to help keep Latin America pro-Ally:

> Mr. Rockefeller came here and he turned Mexico over to
> me. I had 37 movie projectors going all over Mexico trying to
> keep Mexico pro-Ally. We showed pictures (*The News Parade*)

to over 3 million people. (quoted in "Dollars and Sense of Community" 1974, 5)

Americans who are migrating to Mexico today do so under distinct circumstances, but they, too, carry with them and aim to propagate the economic, cultural, and political values of their homeland. This is evident in their actions, but most notably in their narratives about life SOB. As news of their settlement in Mexico spreads, some American immigrants are confronted with a need, or an opportunity, to justify, to themselves and others, their privileged status in Mexico. In doing so, they not only draw upon familiar themes that invoke the virtues of capitalism and neoliberal economic principles, but some simultaneously resurrect a discourse akin to that of the "white man's burden." The phrase itself comes from Rudyard Kipling's famous poem exhorting the United States to assume its imperial responsibilities in the Philippines in the late 1800s, but has been broadly used to refer to the presumed responsibility of white people to govern and impart their culture to less civilized nonwhite people. In pointing to various advantages that allegedly accrue from their migration to Mexico, Americans in Ajijic and San Miguel regularly mention jobs, education, and a leg up for local Mexicans in the universal drive for modernization, but many also justify their presence SOB by reference to the superior cultural values they are imparting to the natives.

As discussed in Chapter One, when asked about which factors pulled them to Mexico, most American immigrants mention the sunny climate, some invoke the warmth of the Mexican people, and they all describe the incredible financial benefits of living south of the border. For decades, U.S. leisure and financial magazines, travel sections in major newspapers, tour companies, and Web sites have promoted paradise at bargain prices south of the border. The specifics of the bargain change, but the message remains the same: Americans who move to Mexico can afford bigger and better houses and more luxury services than would ever be the case were they to remain in the United States. Even a quick perusal of the articles that have been written in recent years on gringo life in Mexico reveals their capacity to capture the attention of the most reticent American bargain hunter. A report in the *Dallas Morning News* in 2001 begins with this scenario:

> Suppose you've never saved a lot of money, that you've had one or another disaster, and that you find yourself at the brink of old age or downsized into early retirement. . . . Suppose none of your employers ever heard of 401k plans or pensions.

> Suppose what you've got is a funky little house, an aging
> Oldsmobile, and the prospect of Social Security as your pri-
> mary source of support? What can you do? Where can you
> live? Mexico. (Burns 2001)

Mike Nelson, author of *Live Better South of the Border in Mexico,* explains:

> As a general rule, you can live on about two-thirds of what
> you live on at home. Most foreigners have incomes of $800–
> $1,200 a month. You can live on less if you are willing to
> be very frugal or choose a small town. No matter what you
> spend, your quality of life will be better. (quoted in Burns
> 2001)

AARP Magazine gushes, "For 600 bucks a month, retirees in Mexico can live
in a three-bedroom home, with a gardener. For a cool thousand . . . well,
you won't believe it" (Golson 2004).

Because these advertisements have as their primary audience U.S. seniors, they pay particular attention to whether American migrants can live
"comfortably" in Mexico on their Social Security checks. The answer, according to AARP, "is an unqualified yes." Karen Blue, who with Judy King
cofounded the popular Web site Living at Lake Chapala, explains: "Truth
is, . . . there are lots of respectable homes you can rent for about $600, and
then you add maybe $100 for a gardener and maid." King adds: "I actually
know a fair number of people who do it on less than that. They've looked
around, gotten a decent little place for $350. They may not go out to eat
much, they eat more tacos than steak, but they have a very nice life here.
So, yes, you can live here on your Social Security check" (Golson 2004). In
San Miguel, Carol Schmidt's popular Web site and book, *Falling in Love with
San Miguel,* focus specifically on "retiring to Mexico on Social Security."
She regularly dispenses advice about price fluctuations in San Miguel and
where to get the most for your converted U.S. dollars (www.fallinginlove
withsanmiguel.com).

American migrants are unabashed about taking advantage of the deals to
be had in Mexico. Yet neither the immigrants themselves nor the countless
publications that tout the bargains spend much time pondering the implications for Mexico and Mexicans of this American trek southward. When
asked, the immigrants typically respond with a list of benefits they are bestowing upon their adopted land: jobs, education, charitable contributions
that run the gamut from eyeglasses to pet vaccinations, and the opportu-

nity for Mexicans to acquire uniquely "American" values of hard work, efficiency, and civic responsibility. A majority of Americans are quite confident that they are helpful and generous to Mexicans (Bloom 2006, 199), and some share stories designed to demonstrate that their Mexican hosts recognize and appreciate the contributions. A smaller number of American respondents offer more nuanced assessments, acknowledging the potential downsides of the foreign influx into Ajijic and San Miguel, not only for themselves as settlers who want to preserve their "authentic" Mexican towns, but for the Mexicans who were born and raised there. One Texan and owner of a bed and breakfast who lives in Ajijic mused: "Well, there's bound to be some resentment [on the part of the local Mexicans]" (field interview, January 25, 2007). Nevertheless, a larger group is confident they are bringing progress to Mexico, and many have also developed rejoinders to the potential and actual criticisms about their presence.

In June of 2006, when I was systematically interviewing migrants in San Miguel, Mexico, one American and seven-year resident of the town explained confidently: "Forty new Americans here means forty new maid jobs." Another recent American immigrant sitting in the room concurred: "Right. And when we build and remodel homes here, we are hiring Mexican plumbers, electricians, bricklayers" (field interviews, June 18, 2006). Several Americans also maintained that towns like Ajijic or San Miguel, thanks to their sizable foreign populations, tend to weather Mexico's infamous economic crises better than the rest of the country: "When the peso was devalued in '94 and '95, this town [Ajijic] did not suffer like the rest of Mexico. Because everything was cheaper, more tourists came. There was a construction boom. More restaurants opened, more people bought houses, hired maids, and so forth" (field interview, February 6, 2007). Another American migrant who seemed to have given this issue more thought than most, told me emphatically:

> Look, let's just say there are half a million gringos in Mexico, a low estimate, . . . and, say, each has an income of $1,000 a month, the average Social Security check, and also a low-ball estimate, that amounts to $500 million being pumped into Mexico every year by us gringos. (field interview, June 2, 2007)

Americans living in Mexico are equally quick to share details of the charitable activities and organizations they oversee in their adopted towns. The examples the migrants offer of the important contributions they make to Mexicans are sometimes ones with communitywide effects. One American in Ajijic explained: "Unemployment is practically nil here. We have built a new high school and a university college so their kids no longer have to go into Guad [Guadalajara] for a higher education. Our Mexican neighbors tell us we are very welcome here" (Russell 2005). Frequently, however, Americans share examples of the informal, individual help they have offered to their Mexican maids or gardeners and their families. Unsolicited, they recount stories of purchasing a new roof for their maid's house, buying braces for a maid's son or daughter, or footing the bill for a significant celebration such as a wedding for one of their Mexican workers or the worker's child. Some do so with what appears to be humility: "It was really not a big deal for us to do it, you know, in terms of finances" (field interview, June 8, 2006). Another demurred, "It is hard to say who helps who more. We have done a lot for [the maid's] family, but they are loving people. They give us back so much" (field interview, June 7, 2006). Claims about Mexican workers being "just like family" are commonplace: "She is a dear tiny lady. She has become like family. We give her keys to our house" (field interview, February 1, 2007); or, "We adore our maid, we really want to support her" (field interview, February 6, 2007).

Migrants to Mexico also perceive themselves as helping the locals by imparting certain cultural values, such as those associated with the American work ethic. Discussions among Americans in Mexico regarding their ability to market to Mexicans the American creed of hard work, efficiency, and dependability typically coincide with complaints about Mexicans, or "the Mexican culture." The immigrants' characterizations of local culture belie a peculiar ambivalence. What they claim to admire in one breath, they often criticize in the next. Cultural characteristics attributed to Mexicans that are in one instance endearing become in another annoying to Americans and a sign of the inferiority of Mexico and the Mexican people. This ambivalence is most evident when Americans complain, which they do frequently, about the so-called "mañana" syndrome in Mexico.

One American woman, who had lived in San Miguel for over eight years and seemed to have a sincere appreciation for the culture and even spoke ample Spanish, described to me how the different sense of time in Mexico was "very frustrating" (field interview, June 12, 2006):

> One day I had to get my car worked on. I arrived at the shop first thing in the morning. Not a soul was there, no lights on, nothing. People started to trickle in around 9:20; but then they have to start the whole greeting and kissing each other

thing while I am standing outside waiting. I can see them inside there just going on and on. I mean, come on, these people see each other every single day.

Over and over, Americans in Mexico explained to me that "mañana" in Mexico does not mean "tomorrow"; in fact, they insist, it really just means "maybe." Nor does "*ahorita*," which in Spanish translates technically to "right now," mean "right now," or even "this week" for that matter. One American respondent commented about Mexican workers: "You have to keep after them. You'll find them just sitting around talking doing nothing, they might disappear for days and then show up again" (Banks 2004, 370).

Even Doug Bower, travel writer and long-term American resident of Mexico who prides himself on blending in with the local flavor of Mexico (and is pointedly critical of Americans who do not), succumbs to the frustration. In an Internet essay posted on December 21, 2006, Bower recounts an experience with a bank in Mexico (where he was attempting to access the U.S. royalty checks he receives for writing books about how to retire in Mexico) that left him ready to "murder someone," and hence more sympathetic toward the complaining gringos:

> They [Mexican bank employees] will look you straight in the eye and tell you whatever comes to their minds, whether it is the truth or not. What I do not get is just why no bank employee knows how anything works! This brings me to a conversation with an American expat who has lived in Mexico much longer than I have. She said once that what Mexico needs is a *Business Manager*. . . .
>
> Trying to do banking in Guanajuato is not the only thing that doesn't work. I would love to tell you that this is so but I would be lying. Once we tried going to the movies. The theater manager was at a party and was having too good of a time to show up with the keys to the box office to sell tickets. She sent word that someone was welcome to come and get the keys and sell tickets, otherwise we would all have to wait. Can you begin to imagine what would have happened in America when this movie theater manager finally showed up? She or he would have been lynched by the crowd. (Bower 2006)

Another American migrant blogged about a particularly trying trip to the grocery in San Miguel, and then explained:

> Traditionally a customer who goes into a store often needs to
> walk around the person sweeping the floors, or wait for the
> cashier to finish talking to a friend or eating a snack. . . . More
> stores are switching to US marketing values, which I think is a
> good thing, especially in a global economy. Waiters and other
> employees are being trained in the US businesses, and in those
> Mexican businesses where the owners have lived in the States
> or studied in US colleges, to put the customer's needs first.
> (Schmidt 2007b)

Curiously, when some American immigrants find themselves pleased by
the service they receive in Mexico, they quickly assume that it is foreigners
who deserve the credit. In her article "Moving to Mexico's a Breeze," American immigrant Jennifer Rose praises the immigration office in San Miguel
de Allende as "the most helpful of any," and goes on to note: "I suspect it's
really staffed by English agents working undercover!" (Rose 1996).

Americans publish essays devoted to their frustration with "Mexican
culture," write blog entries about it, gripe about it at social events, and
report with an air of pride and accomplishment their ability to come to
terms with it. In doing so, they reveal the ongoing struggle of American
immigrants in Mexico to let go of the same cultural tendencies they claim
to be escaping when they leave the United States—a hurried uptightness
about time, a readiness to judge others, a fixation with material consumption. They also reveal how privilege allows those who possess it to embrace
certain attitudes or behaviors when convenient and pass judgment on them
when not. One morning, an American man and longtime resident of Ajijic, who had just days before explained to me his version of and frustration
with the "mañana" syndrome, turned up wearing a T-shirt that said in bold
letters "Get Er Done . . . ," while at the bottom, in smaller print, appeared
the word "tomorrow." The shirt's slogan expresses, as do many Americans
in Mexico, a commitment to a life of laid-back leisure. But Mexican maids
who don't arrive on time or car mechanics that take extra time to greet
their coworkers disrupt the lifestyle Americans in Mexico aim to achieve.

Also disruptive, or at least puzzling, to Americans in Mexico is an apparent indifference on the part of some Mexicans toward turning a profit.
I heard various and repeated versions of this story, but the following two
examples stand out. An American man who had been living in Ajijic for ten
years was selling in the United States Mexican handicrafts and artwork he
bought and exported from Mexico. He encountered a Mexican man on a
pier weaving baskets made from fishing nets and purchased three to use as

hanging lampshades in his Ajijic home. He paid 30 pesos each for the shades (the equivalent then of slightly less than $3 USD). The American then decided to sell the baskets in his U.S. store, and he returned to ask the artisan what the cost would be were he to purchase one hundred baskets instead of three. The American respondent tells me that the Mexican man thought for a moment, appeared to be doing some calculations in his head, and then said "40 pesos apiece." At this point in his story, the American chuckled, flashed me an expression of "can you believe it?" and then explained: "The guy figured out that he would have to work a lot more to make that many baskets, and so he was going to charge me more. It was kind of crazy, but it didn't really matter because we would charge at least twenty bucks apiece for those things in the States" (field interview, February 7, 2007). From the American's perspective, purchasing a higher quantity of a good should guarantee a lower unit price. The Mexican artisan, although he had most likely not read Karl Marx, wanted to be fully compensated for the value of his labor. He also, as the American telling the story surmised, calculated as a cost the time he would not be able to spend with his family if he were busy weaving one hundred baskets.

A similar story circulates in both Ajijic and San Miguel regarding how Mexican grocery store owners choose to stock their shelves. As the story goes, Americans in Ajijic or San Miguel try to persuade a local Mexican grocer to stock a particular item of interest. The product in question changes depending on who is telling the story, but in at least a few of the renditions I heard it was some special form of rye bread (not a staple in the Mexican diet). The Mexican grocer agrees to stock the product, and the Americans recount to me their glee at being able to secure yet one more comfort from home while living across the border in a Mexican paradise. The next time one of these Americans heads to the store, however, he or she cannot find the product on the shelves. The grocer then explains that too many people were buying it; it was hard to keep in stock, and the people who kept asking for it were disappointed when the store had run out. Americans were incredulous that a seller would for any of these reasons eliminate a popular product. Mexican store owners apparently decided that the payoff was not worth the hassle. It is not at all clear that these accounts (or any of the others above) accurately characterize any aspect of Mexican culture. In fact, many Mexicans in Ajijic and San Miguel have been quite adept at recognizing and profiting from the growing market of American consumers living in their hometowns. One enterprising Mexican businessman owns a store in Lake Chapala that brings in from Southern California two forty-eight-foot trailer loads of American groceries every month. Nevertheless, for Americans, the lesser degree of materialism in Mexico is seen as both a draw and a fundamental flaw.

Americans' ambivalence and sense of superiority toward Mexican culture (or the characteristics they attribute to it) emerge in other realms as well. Americans describe their Mexican maids as warm and attentive, but also shared with me patronizing descriptions of their employees: "not too sharp," "a little slow," or "just doesn't get it." In fact, echoes of colonialism in Ajijic and San Miguel are most pronounced when American migrants discuss their Mexican "help." Frequent declarations of "love" for the maid, and assurances that she is "just like family," resonate with historical claims made by white Americans in reference to their African American house slaves and, later, maids; by British colonists in Africa and India; and, more recently, by American expatriates in countries throughout the global south (Hill Collins 2001; Backer 2001). One Mexican maid in San Miguel was annoyingly prone to put away her employers' laundry while it was still damp; another in Ajijic allegedly snuck beer from the refrigerator; and they all seem to have a knack, according to their American bosses, for putting things away in places where no "reasonable" person would think to look. Equally common were whispers about a maid's problematic husband or wayward child and the American boss's steadfast willingness to offer moral and financial support. Some Americans living in Mexico also passed adverse cultural judgment on the same close-knit family structure in Mexico that they at other moments envied and admired. Mexican families are, according to a small number of Americans I interviewed, "too close." The allegation was that large Mexican families live together, work together, and socialize in insular ways that can perpetuate long-standing feuds and prevent women from escaping abusive relationships. In frequent cases, the Mexican servants whom Americans employ—the maid, the cook, and the gardener—are related. In this way, Americans have minimal exposure to Mexican extended family relationships, but just enough for some immigrants to feel confident issuing a broad verdict.

This ambivalent and patronizing attitude toward Mexicans extends in other directions as well. In spite of the portrayals of Mexicans as warm and generous, I was also told repeatedly not to trust the directions Mexicans gave me when I stopped to ask in the street: "They will tell you anything just because they don't want to disappoint you." When I asked one U.S. citizen who had been residing in Ajijic for fifteen years about the impact of immigration on the Lake Chapala region, he replied: "These kids used to run around naked. They ate mangoes on a stick. Now they have clean, packaged foods" (field interview, February 2, 2007). This, in his mind, was a sign of progress (as was apparently for Bower the American compunction to lynch a remiss service provider), although he went on to complain that all the packaging had contributed to a new problem: "We do have more trash in town now." I often saw the "mangoes on a stick" to which he was referring, but they were now being gobbled up not by naked Mexican children, but by North American tourists who were awestruck by the selection of fresh, colorful, and cheap fruit available at Ajijic's Wednesday open market, or *tianguis*. Another American's view of the benefits of immigration took this form:

> Take stray animals. When I got here, there was an abject neglect of dogs and cats. Now, we have an excellent pound, and animal-care groups train kids in school to care for animals. It's common to see well-fed dogs with collars and leashes out walking with families. It's been a really positive change. (Toll 2006, 76)

In addition to making remarks concerning improved notions of customer service, enhanced pet care, and perhaps an appreciation for packaged foods, some migrants commented on how the Americans' commitment to and experience with civic engagement provided a valuable model for Mexicans. One American who lives and works for a nonprofit organization in San Miguel observed: "Mexicans don't have a culture of civic involvement like Americans do; and we are doing important things for them that their government won't do" (field interview, June 21, 2006). Another maintained:

> I think the "do good" organizations are a wonderful model for Mexicans to follow. They have no idea of how to do this. The affluent Mexicans usually just build another ranchito instead of a library at a school. . . . It is a Latin or Godfather mentality. Hopefully we can be a good model for this kind of thing. A few more Margarita meetings and we can fix the world!! (http://groups.yahoo.com/group/Civil_SMA, June 17, 2006)

Studies of British expatriates in southern Spain reveal a similar tendency on the part of the migrants from the north to engage in rhetoric reminiscent of the colonial era. In the same way that agents of the British Empire believed colonization was justified in that it would bring wealth, health, happiness, and education to poor and backward peoples, Britons living in Andalusia today believe that they are developing a poor economy and educating a backward culture (O'Reilly 2000, 161; Rodriguez et al. 1998). One British man living in the coastal town of Fuengirola offered this description of his Spanish hosts: "They are so backward in so many ways . . . if only they would learn from us" (O'Reilly 2000, 161). Much like the Americans in Mexico, Britons in Spain believe they are imparting peculiarly British values of punctuality, professionalism, experience in the wider world, and respect for animal rights. For this, as well as a pathway out of poverty, they believe the locals should be grateful (O'Reilly 2000, 163; Rodriguez et al. 1998). Perhaps not surprisingly, Brits in Spain are also the immigrant group mostly likely to eschew that country's offer of government-subsidized Spanish language classes for foreigners—a forward-looking policy designed to facilitate the acculturation of newcomers (Montague 2008).

Americans in Mexico maintain a similar self-confidence about their generosity and helpfulness, and most feel themselves to be embraced by their host society. When I asked about their relations with Mexicans in Ajijic and San Miguel, close to half of the American respondents repeated stories of being invited to christenings, weddings, and, most often, baby showers. During one interview, an American woman in San Miguel pulled from her purse two different small, pink pieces of thick paper, the size and style of business cards, that had printed on them invitations to an expectant Mexican mother's baby shower. "Look," she exclaimed, "I am invited to two this week" (field interview, June 17, 2006). Additional, albeit very different, evidence of how welcome the immigrants feel in Mexico comes from several Americans (in this case, all residents of the Lake Chapala area) who pointed to the sympathy and support that poured forth from their Mexican neighbors after the September 11th terrorist attacks on the United States. One American living in Ajijic recalled:

> Mexico celebrates its independence on September 16. I remember so well, in 2001, the celebration was happening just days after 9/11 and some of us Americans went down to the plaza to watch. The Mexicans kept coming up to us and saying how sorry they were. . . . Their speeches here always end with "Viva Mexico," but that time, the mayor also said, "Viva America!" (field interview, February 6, 2007)

Other immigrants in Ajijic recollected that in the days after the terrorist attacks on New York and Washington local Mexican schoolchildren brought condolence notes and flowers to the Lake Chapala Society (LCS), the recognized headquarters of the foreign community living along Lake Chapala. Some local schools joined together, in a symbolic display of unity, the corners of the Mexican and U.S. flags. Several members of the LCS also remember that Mexican officials contacted the organization after 9/11 offering to send troops to provide protection to the American immigrant community. In fact, a Mexican attorney involved in a research project on the impact of post-9/11 security policies on Mexico shared with me his finding that the Mexican military has in place a specific plan to protect the American community living in San Miguel. Maps clearly mark which routes into and out of the mountain town are to be shut down in the event of a threat to Americans living there (field interview, March 5, 2007). It is unclear whether the latter is an indication of positive local attitudes toward American immigrants, or further evidence of the perpetual significance of states and armies in the contemporary context of heightened national security in North America, or both.

On occasion (and with growing frequency as news of American migration southward spreads), U.S. citizens living in Mexico have been faced with opposing perspectives regarding the positive impact of their presence south of the border. Sometimes the contradictory evidence or alternative assessments come from dissenters within the migrant community itself, sometimes from U.S. journalists reporting on the emerging migration trend, and sometimes from researchers. Less frequently do Americans experience disapproval from Mexicans, although a few longtime American residents in San Miguel report a growing chill in the local population's attitude toward foreigners. When confronted with skepticism or critiques regarding the impact of U.S. migration to Mexico, some migrants respond with thoughtful discussion. Others are quite defensive. Those in the latter group have crafted critiques of the critiques, or identified scapegoats more deserving of blame than themselves.

The rapidly rising prices in towns like Ajijic and San Miguel are one potentially harmful consequence of American migration southward. Forty more Americans living south of the border may translate into forty more maid jobs, as one American in San Miguel insisted, but if those Mexican maids find it increasingly difficult to afford living in their hometown, the net benefit of immigration is reduced. There is little disagreement that the cost of living is on the rise in Mexico's immigrant towns—particularly in terms of real estate. Today, the same sources that tout the affordable (for Americans) paradise south of the border describe booming real estate markets in towns like Ajijic and San Miguel. In 2001, California-born real estate agent Michael Herrera noted that San Miguel real estate has appreciated greatly in the last twenty years and that the central historical district remains the focus of attention for most people (Burns 2001). Four years later, another California-born real estate agent living and working in San Miguel reported that the number of foreigners looking for houses in town had increased "hugely" over the past year ("Go South" 2005).

Similar reports come out of the Lake Chapala region. In 2006, the *Guadalajara Reporter* noted that the influx of expatriate settlers to the area had taken a quantum leap during the past three decades. The report drew on research by a local geographer to conclude: "The heated activity seen in today's construction and real estate markets is an indicator that investors are expecting the trend to continue and intensify in the near future" (Palfrey 2006b). Many of these stories point to specific properties as evidence of dramatic price increases. As early as 1981 San Miguel's *Atención* ran an article, "Surreal Estate," reporting on a survey of five prominent real estate agencies in town that revealed that prices of houses, lots, and undeveloped land had soared in the past two to three years. "One house that sold for $55,000 USD in 1979 now sells for $125,000" ("Surreal Estate" 1981). Twenty years later, in 2003, *Money* magazine reported that in San Miguel, "Home prices have been on the rise—the Meyers, who paid $160,000 for their 2,500-square-foot home nine years ago, figure it's worth $250,000 today" (*Money* 2003). Real estate agents confirm this trend. One agent working in San Miguel said, in 2006, that housing prices in the town had generally doubled over the past three years (Migration Policy Institute 2006, 51). When I asked Americans living in Mexico about changes they had observed in their adopted towns, they regularly referred to rising prices and cited specific examples of properties that sold for one price ten years earlier and were going for another price double or triple that one today.

Prices have surged not only in the real estate markets, but in the local restaurants and stores as well (McKinley 2005; Welch 2007). One American who had moved to San Miguel in 1980, "as a young starving artist," had by 2000 begun to work in real estate, renovating and selling homes. He explained: "I worry a lot about the rising prices since all of these wealthy retirees are arriving. It is really hard for those of us who are living on the peso" (field interview, June 2, 2006). Another American who had been living in town for twenty-five years, also an artist, complained:

> I am so mad at this town. I can't even afford to live here now.
> People are just coming to make money. I don't even meet
> intelligent people anymore. And that damn paper *[Atención]*,

they are making so much on real estate ads. I sent them a
notice of my showing, and they didn't even publish it. (field
interview, June 23, 2006)

Meanwhile, Web sites maintained by American immigrants living in
Ajijic and San Miguel include glimpses into specific price increases over
time. In 2007, an American resident of San Miguel described a celebratory
night out at Harry's, a local gringo hot spot:

> We both had heaping platters of crispy fried quarter-sized
> oysters, coleslaw and fries. The dish now costs 115 pesos, about
> $11 US, and the price was 60 pesos four years ago. . . . I also
> had the huge wedge of dark chocolate truffle cake that is like
> eating a pound of fudge (70 pesos, up from 45 four years ago),
> and [my dinner companion] had a dinner-sized platter of fried
> plantains, caramel sauce, whipped cream and ice cream that
> Harry's calls Velvet Elvis, though it's similar to Bananas Foster
> (60 pesos, up from 35). (Schmidt 2007c)

American immigrants agree, and frequently complain, that prices have
increased significantly in Ajijic and San Miguel over the years, in restaurants, stores, and particularly in real estate. On very rare occasions, an immigrant or a reporter pauses to reflect on how these price increases might
be affecting local Mexicans. In pondering how rapidly escalating real estate
prices in San Miguel in the 1980s would affect "the character of this picturesque town," one immigrant worried not only about the foreign community—the "unmoneyed artists and writers"—but also the "native artisans
who have lived here for generations. Will they be pressured to sell their
long-held family properties?" ("Surreal Estate" 1981). Twenty-five years
later, an American living in San Miguel issued the following cautionary
note to the "we can save the world" discourse of many Americans who post
on a popular Internet list:

> Gringos should not be so smug about "offering jobs." While
> that is obviously a good thing, there are so many other un-
> employed people whose cost of living is negatively impacted
> by these hirings, pay, and the resultant inflation—there IS a
> trade-off here (some profit; some are hurt). And the real estate
> market (actually a bubble waiting to burst) is causing more
> and more Mexicans to live further and further away from

these jobs in Centro. (http://groups.yahoo.com/group/Civil_
SMA, May 30, 2006)

Finally, a reporter from the United States offering tips to Americans on the
financial advantages of retirement in Mexico shared this poignant observation about glaring inequalities in San Miguel. After describing his experience with the town's famous foreign-run Sunday home tours, he wrote:

> The house we've just been through, all 220 of us, is straight
> out of *Architectural Digest,* recently completed, and beautifully
> furnished. It's an investment, including artwork, of at least
> $2 million. But it would cost far more in the United States.
> What intrigues me is the inconceivable chasm between the
> value of the house and the cost of the maid. The common
> figure is that you can have a full-time maid in Mexico for less
> than $200 a month. *So this house and its contents may represent 833
> years of her work.* (Burns 2001; emphasis added)

In my interviews I specifically asked Americans residing in Mexico
about the effects of rising prices on Mexicans living in Ajijic and San
Miguel. A few immigrants responded regretfully, acknowledging the
potential harm. One American woman who had lived in San Miguel since
1986, in the heart of El Centro, the historic downtown, said nostalgically:
"These houses are all owned by foreigners now. Mexicans can't afford to
live in El Centro" (field interview, June 22, 2006). More often, however,
Americans responded to my query with justifications, or efforts to shift the
responsibility for rising prices elsewhere. The following anecdote I heard
numerous times, albeit with slight variations. "You know, I ask my Mexican gardener about prices going up here, and he told me, 'Sure, a beer in
this town used to cost less, but now I have a job and can afford to buy a lot
more beer'" (field interview, January 23, 2007). Sometimes the Mexican
informant being referred to was a roofer or the maid's son, and sometimes
the commodity in question was a shot of tequila instead of a beer, but the
message was the same: prices may be going up in Ajijic and San Miguel as
a result of American immigration, but so is the availability of jobs. As a
result, the immigrants reason, everyone wins. (Of course, also conveyed in
these anecdotes by Americans is an image of Mexicans as people who measure their quality of life in terms of the quantity of alcohol they consume.)
Another justification I heard from immigrants, on more than one occasion,
took the form of this one uttered by an American living in San Miguel: "If

a Mexican can sell his home in El Centro to foreigners for a huge profit, then he can buy a bigger house outside of town and maybe send a kid to college" (field interview, June 8, 2006).

The details of the discussion change, but American migrants on the whole perceive themselves as contributing to an economic tide that lifts all boats. If confronted with the realization that certain boats might be sinking, or are stranded on the shore, many Americans quickly shift the blame elsewhere. In response to the concern that surging real estate prices have driven Mexicans out of San Miguel's historic center, or out of the Lake Chapala village of Ajijic, one American couple insisted: "Poorer Mexicans never had these houses anyway" (field interview, February 1, 2007). Their argument was that wealthy Mexicans are to blame for social and economic inequality in Mexico, not foreigners. In San Miguel, the alleged culprits are the Chilangos from Mexico City, and in Ajijic, American immigrants like to shift blame to the wealthy Mexican families from Guadalajara. "They come in for weekends, clogging up the streets and restaurants" (field interview, January 31, 2007). Americans in both towns assured me that when it comes to the Mexicans from the big cities, "The locals can't stand 'em!" A couple of respondents also wanted me to know that Mexico is a very race- and class-conscious society and that upper-class and lighter-skin Mexicans treat their poorer and darker brethren much worse than any foreigners do. One American man who had been living in San Miguel for nine years quipped about Mexicans: "The lighter-skin ones are the worst" (field interview, June 2, 2006). When Americans living in Mexico did perceive a less than enthusiastic welcome of foreigners on the part of Mexicans (and few did), this chilly response too was attributed to other foreigners, not themselves. Longer-term American residents, for example, blamed more recent arrivals for souring the otherwise happy coexistence of Mexicans and Americans in Ajijic and San Miguel: "It's the new people that are causing us problems . . . the ones who are coming down now in big fancy cars and buying their starter castles" (field interview, June 12, 2006). When I asked one American in Ajijic about the reaction of Mexicans to the American presence, she explained: "Yes, life is better, but I know how I feel about the winter people. They must feel it even more strongly" (field interview, February 6, 2007).

The few American respondents who were more tentative in their assessment of their welcome in Mexico noted as a possible indicator of local Mexican resentment toward immigrants the practice of charging "gringo prices." The allegation is that Mexican store clerks, service providers, or ticket booth operators charge foreigners a higher price for the same items than what they charge Mexicans. During one discussion of these gringo prices, and the reaction of Mexicans to foreigners, an American immigrant living in Ajijic added: "Oh, yeah, and they make us wait longer in lines at the city offices too" (field interview, February 3, 2007). Other immigrants sitting at the table concurred. In most instances, however, conversations about gringo prices turned quickly from the theme of Mexicans' resentment of immigrants to American immigrants' frustration over rising costs. A group of foreigners in Ajijic grew so annoyed with the perceived inequity that in 2004 they formed a consumer protection group designed to "level the playing field" for foreign residents in Mexico. Founding member Sandy Bell complained: "There are many indications that certain merchants, medical staff, auto mechanics and other service personnel have one price for Mexicans and another for foreigners." The group's goal, she explained, was to "resolve conflicts amicably, but legal action is not ruled out as a last resort" (Chaussee 2004a).

Finally, because one of my trips to San Miguel took place in the summer of 2006, coinciding with the July 2, 2006, Mexican presidential election, many American immigrants were following the political drama unfolding in their adopted homeland. The election pitted National Action Party (PAN) candidate Felipe Calderón against the Democratic Revolutionary Party (PRD) candidate Andres Manuel Lopez Obrador. In a situation reminiscent of the 2000 U.S. presidential election, the race was tight, the results extremely close and contested, and Calderón, the more conservative of the two candidates, was ultimately declared the victor. While reminding me that they were abiding by all laws that restricted them from any formal involvement in Mexican politics, several Americans did comment that a Calderón presidency was more favorable to Americans living in Mexico—given his commitment to free market economics, global capitalism, and law and order. Some expressed concern that were the left-leaning, populist Obrador president, American migrants might be less welcome in Mexico.

In addition to displaying a tendency to deny the potential economic downsides of their growing presence in Mexico, many American migrants also resent what they perceive as unfair portrayals of their social and cultural integration into the host country, or lack thereof. Rarely does a researcher have the opportunity to witness reactions from participants to a work still in progress, but I had just that experience after publishing a short essay on this study in the journal *Dissent* in the winter of 2007. As yet another testament to the centrality of technology in these transmigrants' lives, within weeks after the article appeared, Americans living in Mexico had accessed it electronically, posted links to the article on their blogs, and begun assessing my portrayal of their lives in Mexico. My goal in writing the *Dissent* article, during a particularly ugly period of anti-immigrant hysteria in the United States, was to use the reverse case of Americans migrating south to expose the narrow-mindedness and hypocrisy that characterize much of the immigration debate in the United States and specifically the rage directed toward Mexican immigrants as a threat to "our" economy and culture. Among other things, my article addressed the lack of Spanish language acquisition among U.S. immigrants in San Miguel and the insular nature of the foreign community residing there. Some Americans living in Mexico reacted thoughtfully; others responded defensively. Among the former and more introspective group were several individuals who joined a discussion forum on the popular site Falling in Love with San Miguel.

> I agree with many of the interesting points the author raises in her article. It seems to me that one way Americans can make themselves useful in San Miguel is through engaging in legal activities vs. the illegal ones mentioned frequently in her article. One of the most obvious ways in which we can be productive is to register some political pressure concerning the way our host country is being treated by the U.S. (http://forumsfallinginlovewithsanmiguel.com/showthread.php?t=505&highlight=Sheila+Croucher, March 8, 2007)

Another wrote:

> Goodwill and good report. I enjoyed reading the full report. One thing that really affected me was the comments about how our country treats them and they are "polite" to us. Maybe we should try harder to be like American-Mexicans (like the Mexican-Americans in the US) rather than expats. (http://forumsfallinginlovewithsanmiguel.com/showthread.php?t=505&highlight=Sheila+Croucher, March 8, 2007)

On another popular San Miguel Internet list, an immigrant, after reading the *Dissent* article, replied simply and good-naturedly, "I think we have been outed" (http://groups.yahoo.com/group/smacoollist/message/6591, March 7, 2007).

Meanwhile, a number of other immigrants in Mexico took issue with my analysis. One American woman and frequent poster to the Mexico Connect discussion forums wrote this:

> Good grief. Who was she talking to? I lived there [San Miguel] for three years. . . . I don't know where all those English-speaking service people were hiding. We couldn't even get gas delivered without passing a note in Spanish to the counter person at their office. Obtaining a bank account involved several hours of non-English communication. . . . Most expats do their best to learn Spanish. Most do learn enough to get by. (http://mexconnected.com/perl/foros/gforum.cgi?post, July 10, 2007)

Curiously, this same woman posted the following message two months previously during a discussion about the difficulties of learning a foreign, or "non-English," language later in life: "I've noticed the Mexicans are very patient with us. If we get stuck, they usually revert to their English, which is better than our Spanish in most cases" (http://mexconnected.com/perl/foros/gforum.cgi?post, May 10, 2007).

Another American immigrant had this response to the article I had written:

> There are Americans living in Mexico who wouldn't dream of embarking upon any remunerative activity without a proper work permit. There are many who live here without VOIP, without a stateside address, who don't form relationships with the help other than an employer-employee one, who don't attend concerts and fundraisers, and who could care less whether there's a Republican, Democrat or Know-Nothing Club, and who nonetheless seem to lead fulfilling and productive lives. In fact, that group outnumbers those who live here with all of the above. (http://mexconnected.com/perl/foros/gforum.cgi?post, July 10, 2007)

This poster was concerned that the groups she describes, and characterizes as the majority of Americans living in Mexico, was not properly represented in my sample:

> If the pool is self-selected, left out are many voices, which simply don't want to be interviewed for one reason or another. . . . we have better things to do with our time. The thrill of being quoted or even being an unidentified source just no longer is there. We don't need to justify why we live

here any more. And yes, I know that makes it harder for researchers to put us under the microscope. And that does make
any researcher's conclusions skewed. (http://mexconnected
.com/perl/foros/gforum.cgi?post, July 10, 2007)

This concern as to whether or not my study would fairly represent all
Americans in Mexico was also communicated to me off the list by two
Americans, and subscribers to Mexico Connect, who, after reading the online discussion of my research project, sent private e-mails warning me that
online forums like Mexico Connect were insular groups and not representative of the whole community of Americans living in Mexico. One man
wrote: "I would say you have chosen a poor medium for your research in
Mexico Connect. That medium attracks [sic] a limited and insular audience.
Your research will be flawed. E-mail me if you are truly serious" (July 9,
2007).

In keeping with the current terminology of the academy, these Americans embraced their role as research "participants" in remarkable ways, actively rejecting what they perceived as an attempt on my part to treat them
as "subjects." It was curious, nevertheless, to witness Americans living in
Mexico use actively and at length an English-language Internet site designed for and accessed almost exclusively by North Americans (from, in
this case, the United States and Canada) to portray themselves as part of an
acculturated majority of immigrants in Mexico that does not have access
to sophisticated technology, nor the time to be bothered with discussions
of their motives for moving there. Similarly curious were the few subscribers from the Internet list who felt compelled to communicate to me
privately that they considered themselves distinct from the other members
of that "nonrepresentative" group. To invoke postcolonial theorist Gaya-
tri Spivak's (1988) seminal work "Can the Subaltern Speak?," in which she
analyzes how the marginalized social status of some groups renders them
without agency and representation, these Americans may fit, in a technical
sense, the definition of immigrants, but they are not marginalized, and
they most certainly can and do speak.

Ultimately, the experiences of Americans in Mexico with regard to
identity resonate with much that is written on the topic; but their relative
privilege results in experiences that are also quite distinct. Identity formation and negotiation among Americans in Mexico speak to the fluidity,
multiplicity, and ambiguity of sociocultural and political belonging and
to the role of "others" in giving shape to "us." Americans living in Mexico
may, for example, be simultaneously American, Texan, Democrat, Uni-

tarian, heterosexual, female, and San Miguelense—to name just a few. The salience of any of these identifications and attachments will vary depending on the context, a context that includes a shifting array of "others"— Canadians, New Yorkers, Republicans, Anglicans, tourists, newer arrivals, Americans NOB, and Lakesiders, or those in other Mexican towns—who help give shape and form to the identity at hand. Americans living in Mexico are also immigrants; but it is here that the congruence with other cases of the formation of identity and belonging begins to fade.

The context in which Americans negotiate belonging is one of power and privilege. This is the case not only in terms of the individual resources of human and financial capital that they have at their disposal, but the cultural and political resources they carry with them as migrants who have left the United States physically, but who still have access to and embody the material and symbolic resources associated with America, both as a world superpower and Mexico's dominant neighbor to the north. The migrants regularly invoke various aspects of the American creed to justify their presence in the foreign land. Many are particularly partial to a free market ideology that translates into some version of the following: Everybody wins when Americans freely cross borders. The migrants secure a better quality of life at a cost unimaginable in the United States. In the process, they create jobs for Mexicans who would not otherwise have them, and inculcate cultural values essential to the global marketplace, such as efficiency and responsibility. Notably, Mexican immigration into the United States may also bestow benefits, economic and otherwise, on the host society, but because Mexican immigrants NOB lack the privileged status of their American counterparts SOB, the effectiveness of such claims are limited—both in terms of staving off hostility and as a substantive thematic content for the formation of identity and belonging.

In spite of the fact that identity narratives of Americans in Mexico draw frequently and assuredly on economic justifications, their notions and practices of belonging still display a degree of ambivalence. Ambivalent belonging is common to the immigrant experience, but takes on a unique twist in this unique case. In his analysis of nationalism in Greater Mexico, David Gutiérrez uses the concept of a *third space* to explain how ethnic Mexicans within the territorial United States carve out social space at the "interstices between the dominant national and cultural systems of both the United States and Mexico" (1999, 488). They convey ambivalence about their relationship to the nation-state and the national "community" it supposedly represents—whether that nation-state is the Republic of Mexico or the United States of America. Gutiérrez predicts that such ambivalence will deepen as globalization and mass human migration intensify. Americans in Mexico also inhabit what might be described as a third space. They display some ambivalence with regard to their attachments to either nation-state, but in their case, the social space carved out at the interstices is a space of empowerment, not marginalization.

CONCLUSION

Albert Memmi began his seminal work *The Colonizer and the Colonized* with the following statement (1965, 3–4):

> Today, leaving for a colony is not a choice sought because of its uncertain dangers, nor is it a desire of one tempted by adventure. It is simply a voyage towards an easier life. One need only ask a European living in the colonies what general reasons induced him to expatriate and what particular forces made him persist in his exile. He may mention adventure, the picturesque surroundings or the change of environment. Why, then, does he usually seek them where his own language is spoken, where he finds a large group of his fellow countrymen, an administration to serve him, an army to protect him? The adventure would have been less predictable; but that sort of change, while more definite and of better quality, would have been of doubtful profit. The change involved in moving to a colony, if one can call it a change, must first of all bring a substantial profit. . . . Our traveler will come up with the best possible definition of a colony: a place where one earns more and spends less.

Americans in Mexico certainly do not think of themselves as colonists, nor do they tend to think of themselves as immigrants. In fact, a particularly revealing statement found in one of the quotations above, and a sentiment conveyed by other Americans living in Mexico, is the following: *"We don't need to justify why we live here."* Such confidence, perhaps self-righteousness, is peculiar for most immigrants (and even their children), who often spend their lifetimes feeling compelled to justify "why we live here," and can suffer significant stress as a result of the challenges associated with acculturation in a foreign land (Deux 2006, 203; Berry 1995). U.S. citizens who move to Mexico, in spite of the fact that they have relocated to a foreign country where many of them do not speak the language and many fewer possess formal citizenship, feel comfortable that they belong. Some feel so comfortable that it has never occurred to them to consider that they are "immigrants" or to question the impact of their presence in a foreign land. When immigrants from the north do ponder their impact on Mexico, or are asked to, they typically respond with an array of justifications that range from "we are creating jobs," and "we are inculcating important cultural values," to "we are not the problem — it's the rich Mexicans, the tourists, or the Canadians who don't tip."

An examination of the discourses of Americans in Lake Chapala and San Miguel reveals valuable insights into the dynamics of how and why they negotiate their particular form of transnational belonging. In the late 1980s, Eleanore Stokes spent eight months in Lake Chapala analyzing the collective identity that emerged among American residents there, or in what she termed "the foreign colony," and the nature of their interactions with their Mexican host community. Much of what she identified over twenty years earlier is still evident today. In reference to the relationship between Americans and their Mexican servants, Stokes (1990, 176) writes:

> Even though communication seldom extends beyond warm greetings and instructions for tasks, Lakesiders form opinions about the host culture from this personal contact. If a maid persists in washing dishes in cold water, or a yardman is frequently late, these behaviors are seen as examples of the imperfections of the culture. Conversely, satisfaction with a servant produces statements of global perfection: "Mexicans are polite, loyal, warm."

Stokes also describes the American community in Lake Chapala as confronted with two conflicting constructs: an ideology that American culture is superior to Mexican culture and the reality that the "American Colony" has limited power or authority in Mexico's political/legal structure (1990, 177). Certain attitudes and behaviors, including avoidance of or condescension toward Mexicans, constitute a strategy for dealing with this dissonance. Stokes also emphasizes the significance of a social boundary between Americans and Mexicans that helps to forge a collective identity and maintain a stable social field for Americans living in Mexico. Lakesiders codify this stratified social structure by downplaying the differences within the foreign colony and affirming their cultural distance from their Mexican host community (1990, 178). Additional research on retirement communities has found that such communities structure themselves in opposition to the larger society as a defense against the stigma of age and nonwork (Rosow 1967). Whatever status Americans may lose as a result of employment or life-cycle changes may, according to Stokes, be offset by their privileged socioeconomic and cultural status as Americans living in Ajijic and San Miguel.

Psychology professor Stephen Banks also found ambivalence on the part of U.S. citizens living along Lake Chapala, evident in the familiar commentary "Mexicans are friendly and warm, but also lazy and untrustworthy." He argues that the narratives Americans engage in about Mexicans and Mexico serve an identity formation function for the immigrants. American immigrants tell stories and offer descriptions that provide a logic for intercultural relationships in Mexico and that "position the retirees as interpersonally attractive, culturally tolerant and pragmatically adaptable" (2004, 361). So when Americans repeatedly characterize Mexicans as friendly and helpful, they safely consign Mexicans to a role of serving. The immigrants simultaneously emphasize their own capacity for appreciation and secure for themselves a position as legitimate evaluators with the moral right to assign character descriptions (Banks 2004, 374).

Finally, in a fascinating article titled "Like One of the Family," sociologist Patricia Hill Collins (2001) offers an analysis of white American women's narratives about their black maids as "one of the family" that mirror the way many Americans in Mexico discuss their Mexican maids. Hill Collins argues that claims such as "we just love her" or "she's just like one of the family" serve to mask pervasive power differentials: "Pinioning [the maid] within the framework of a beloved yet second-class family member allows [the employer] to ignore the power relations linking the two women" (2001, 4). More powerful groups use these claims to minimize the importance of social inequalities, and less powerful groups are left with limited space to advance an alternative assessment. Hill Collins's analysis draws from a cartoon series popular among African Americans in the 1950s that features Mildred, a black domestic worker, and her white employer, Mrs. C. It is on the pages of the cartoon strip that Mildred, fed up with the insincere and demeaning narratives of familial inclusion, challenges her white boss's rhetoric:

> In the first place, you do not *love* me: you may be fond of me, but that is all. . . . In the second place, I am *not* just like one of the family at all! The family eats in the dining room and I eat in the kitchen. Your mama borrows your lace tablecloth and

your son entertains his friends in your parlor, your daughter takes her afternoon nap on the living room couch and the puppy sleeps on your satin spread. . . . So you can see I am not *just* like one of the family. (2001, 24)

Mildred continues:

Now when you say, "We don't know what we'd do without her" this is a polite lie . . . because I know that if I dropped dead or had a stroke, you would get somebody to replace me. . . . You think it is a compliment when you say, "We don't think of her as a servant . . ." but after I have worked myself into a sweat cleaning the bathroom and the kitchen . . . making the beds . . . cooking the lunch . . . washing the dishes . . . I do not feel like no weekend house guest. I feel like a servant. (2001, 26)

Many Americans in Mexico portray their relationships with their Mexican help in much the same way Mrs. C. did. Whether or not Mexicans in Ajijic and San Miguel who are employed by American immigrants share Mildred's frustration remains to be seen; but as will be touched on in the next and final chapter, there are reasons to question the American immigrants' self-confidence regarding the multiple benefits they bestow on their hosts. What this chapter hopes to suggest is that by paying attention to the role of privilege in the practice of migrant transnationalism, we might improve both the study and practice of belonging in a global world.

Five

RETHINKING THE FENCE

I was finalizing the sale of my house in Dallas with my agent and we talked about my moving to Mexico. We laughed a bit when we realized that her dream as a Mexican had always been to leave Mexico and come to the United States. And now she was helping me with my dream to leave here and live in Mexico. . . . kinda strange, don't you think?
— AMERICAN RESIDENT IN AJIJIC
(QUOTED IN TRULY 2006, 188)

The American dream is becoming the Latin American dream.
— XÓCHITL CASTAÑEDA, BORDER HEALTH
POLICY INSTITUTE

Harvard political scientist Samuel Huntington begins his article "The Hispanic Challenge" with the following warning (2004, 30):

> The persistent inflow of Hispanic immigrants threatens to divide the United States into two peoples, two cultures, and two languages. Unlike past immigrant groups, Mexicans and other Latinos have not assimilated into mainstream U.S. culture, forming instead their own political and linguistic enclaves—from Los Angeles to Miami—and rejecting the Anglo-Protestant values that built the American dream. The United States ignores this challenge at its peril.

Huntington identifies six aspects of Mexican immigration that render it particularly threatening to the United States: contiguity, scale, illegality, regional concentration, persistence, and historical presence. *Contiguity* refers to the extensive land frontier shared by the United States and Mexico, marked, at least historically, by nothing more than a line in the dirt and a shallow river. The geographic proximity of these two countries "enables Mexican immigrants to remain in intimate contact with their families, friends, and home localities in Mexico as no other immigrants have been able to do" (2004, 33). *Scale* refers to the fact that Mexican immigrants comprise the largest percentage of the foreign-born population in the United States, and their percentage has increased steadily in recent decades, from 14 percent in 1970 to 27.6 percent in 2000. The *illegality* factor speaks to the claim that an increasing number of undocumented immigrants are entering the United States, and Mexicans are estimated to comprise the largest percentage of that undocumented population. *Regional concentration* is a fourth factor making Mexican immigration uniquely threatening to Americans. America's Founding Fathers, Huntington claims, considered the dispersion of immigrants essential to their assimilation. Defying the founders' preference, Mexican immigrants concentrate heavily in specific regions of the United States. *Persistence* refers to Huntington's concern that unlike some migration waves that eventually subside, the current wave of Mexican immigration to the United States shows no sign of ebbing, and the conditions that sustain it are likely to endure. The sixth factor is *historical presence*. Mexican immigrants, Huntington acknowledges, unlike any other immigrant group in U.S. history, can assert a historical claim to U.S. territory—territory that previously belonged to Mexico, but was conquered in war or annexed by the United States. He quotes political scientist Peter Skerry to lend credence to this alleged threat: "Mexican Americans enjoy a sense of being on their own turf that is not shared by other immigrants" (2004, 36). The combination of these six factors, Huntington maintains, gives rise to a large and growing population of immigrants in the United States who have little interest in or incentive for assimilation. Given that "profound cultural differences clearly separate Mexicans and Americans," he writes, this immigration trend threatens "the end of the America we have known for more than three centuries" (2004, 45).

As indicated by material presented in the preceding chapters of this book, an almost identical analysis could be written regarding the challenges that contemporary migration from the United States may pose for Mexico. Reversing the lens reveals that the same *contiguity* that enables Mexican immigrants to stay connected to their homeland prompts American immigrants to maintain close ties with the United States. As with Mexican immigrants in the United States, immigrants from the United States comprise, by far, the largest percentage of Mexico's foreign-born population—

69 percent in 2000 *(scale)*. Like some Mexicans in the United States, some Americans in Mexico live and work south of the border without securing the proper documentation *(illegality)*. Americans can be found living throughout Mexico, but as is the case with Mexicans living in the United States, immigrants from the United States tend to cluster in specific regions and locales in Mexico *(regional concentration)*. To use Huntington's words, they, too, "establish beachheads" (2004, 35). The conditions that fuel contemporary migration to Mexico are as likely to *persist* as the reverse ones. In other words, the migration wave south also shows no sign of ebbing. In fact, one source predicts that as many as 10 million North Americans will move to Mexico over the next thirty years (Shetterly 2006, 20). Finally, the same *historical* entanglements that lead Huntington to characterize Mexican immigration to the United States as a potential threat to America's territorial integrity could surely affect how Mexicans perceive the growing influx of gringos into their heartland. As Huntington correctly acknowledges: "Mexico is the only country that the United States has invaded, occupied its capital—placing the Marines in the 'halls of Montezuma'—and then annexed half its territory" (2004, 36). Huntington and others fear that as the descendants of the formerly conquered peoples return north to the land of their ancestors, there is the potential for a reconquest of what is now the southwestern United States. If even the Harvard-educated elite in the United States, the conquering nation, are capable of experiencing, or at least proffering, such fear, how must the arrival of growing numbers of Anglos who seem to "enjoy a sense of being on their own turf" be perceived in Mexico—a nation that has not only suffered military defeat at the hands of the United States, but endured persistent and often heavy-handed political and economic control?

American immigrants who now reside in Mexico feel confident that they are welcomed by the host society and that their presence is beneficial. The accuracy of these claims has yet to be systematically explored. This concluding chapter will do so only anecdotally in order to illustrate that social reality in places such as Ajijic and San Miguel may be more complicated than many settlers from the United States suggest. This anecdotal treatment also serves to identify critical questions for future research, namely: how do Mexicans themselves perceive the influx of Americans, and what is the actual economic and cultural impact on Mexico of this migration flow from the United States? Before highlighting some of the ambiguities that surround these questions, the following section summarizes the insights gained from reversing familiar analytical lenses to focus on a migration flow moving in a direction opposite of the northward flow that now captures so much scholarly and political attention in the United States.

MIGRANTS OF PRIVILEGE: "SIMILAR TO BUT BETTER THAN"

In a 1994 article, political theorist Susan Okin rejects the claims of some postcolonial scholars that feminism cannot be global because Western women cannot step outside of their own privilege to understand the marginalization suffered by women in the developing world. Okin's opposing view is that women throughout the world are oppressed in similar ways, albeit to different degrees. Her article, which focuses on documenting the universality of gender oppression, is organized around this rhetorical device: "similar to but worse than." The hardships suffered by "poor women in poor countries" are "similar to but worse than the situation of many women in richer countries" (1994, 14). I borrow from Okin's approach, albeit with a slight twist, to summarize how U.S. migration to Mexico compares to other cases. Specifically, the situation of migrants from the United States to Mexico is "similar to but better than" that of most immigrants to the United States, particularly immigrants from Mexico.[1]

The same factors that influence the flow of migrants northward across the Rio Grande also affect the movement of U.S. citizens south to Mexico. Both groups are driven by the desire to improve their quality of life. They are pulled to a new land by the promise of improved economic well-being and pushed from their homelands by the belief that the security or comfort they desire is unattainable there, or at least less easily attained. For both groups, social networks influence the decision to move and facilitate the process of doing so. Various technologies are also significant in that they ease the migration process, assist in the maintenance of transnational ties, and foster community building among immigrants in the country of settlement.

Like Mexican nationals in the United States, U.S. citizens in Mexico lead lives that challenge conventional assumptions about territory and its centrality, or lack thereof, in shaping identity, belonging, and the rhythms of daily life. They live in one locale but continue to speak the language, follow the events, practice the customs, and celebrate the holidays of another. They reside in one state, but cast their votes in the elections of another.

They meet with and raise money for political candidates of a nation-state other than the one where they reside, and voice opposition or support for political policies crafted and implemented by a government thousands of miles away and on the other side of an increasingly militarized international border. The fluidity of their lives is reflected in how they negotiate multiple and shifting senses of belonging. As is the case with Mexicans and other immigrants in the United States, Americans' migration to Mexico changes the context in which they define their identities. The meaning and relevant constituencies of "us" shift, as do the definitions of who constitutes "them." Immigrants who move to Mexico form communities based on new notions of commonality and difference that did not exist, or were not significant, "back home." The homeland continues to figure prominently into the migrants' identity, but invocations and remembrances of home take on specific forms in the land of settlement. Meanwhile, these rhythms of postmodernity are interrupted by frequent reminders of the persistent power (a power that is sometimes more fungible than at other times) of the modern nation-state—in patrolling borders, collecting taxes, dispersing benefits, granting citizenship, and counting votes.

In all of these ways, the migration of U.S. citizens to Mexico resembles Mexican migration to the United States. Yet, as emphasized throughout this book, notable differences exist—differences that relate to the privilege of U.S. migrants compared to their counterparts moving in the opposite direction and to the native inhabitants of the land where they are settling. In short, the immigration experience for Americans is similar to, but better than, that of other immigrants. U.S. citizens residing in Mexico use technology to maintain contact with family and friends in the United States, but because of their far greater access to sophisticated communications technologies and abundant leisure time, they are more likely to blog or chat with their kin via Vonage than use prepaid phone cards or await the arrival of a videotape carried across the border by a relative. Like other migrants, Americans in Mexico practice political transnationalism, but they do so with some unique twists. U.S. citizens in Mexico are not sending millions of dollars of remittances to the United States, except for compulsory taxation, although most continue to store their financial capital in U.S. banks for reasons of security or preferable economic returns. Americans abroad continue to engage with the U.S. political system, but unlike most immigrants from Latin America who now reside in the United States, politically active Americans in Mexico are not responding to or cooperating with a proactive sending state that seeks their input or eagerly cultivates their commitment to the affairs of the homeland. As a sending state, the

United States has been relatively indifferent to its nationals abroad. In recent years, and as a result of close presidential elections, the two major political parties in the United States have taken an interest in voters abroad, and some members of the U.S. Congress have recently made gestures of embrace to their constituents living outside of the United States. For the most part, however, the political transnationalism of U.S. citizens has been self-generated.

The acculturation of Americans in Mexico, or lack thereof, is another factor that reveals the uniqueness of this case. Like many Mexicans in the United States, Americans in Mexico are more comfortable speaking their native tongue. Many make some degree of effort at some point to learn some Spanish. Most confront the reality that learning a foreign language is challenging, and even more so at an older age. The culture of their homeland continues to suffuse their daily lives, and like immigrants in the United States, Americans in Mexico tend to find security in social networks composed largely of immigrants from their country of origin. The differences, however, are these. The lack of acculturation on the part of these U.S. immigrants in Mexico poses for them few challenges. They may struggle now and then with a "non-English-speaking" service provider, as posted on the Mexico Connect discussion forum by the American immigrant quoted in Chapter Four. But as that same woman noted on another occasion, and most every U.S. citizen I met in Mexico confirmed, "the Mexicans are very patient with us. If we get stuck, they usually revert to their English, which is better than our Spanish in most cases" (http://mexconnected.com/perl/foros/gforum.cgi?post, May 10, 2007). By no standard measure are Americans in Ajijic and San Miguel assimilating. Yet as they go about their days, many self-identifying simply as "Americans living in Mexico," they encounter minimal resistance, experience no hostility, and suffer little sense of loss or alienation in a foreign land. They quite comfortably and effortlessly negotiate transnational belonging—experiencing Mexico and Mexicans as warm and welcoming and feeling self-assured that their impact on the host society is a positive one. Remembering the signs, "English Spoken Here," that hung in the shops of some Anglo businesses in Miami, Florida, during that city's 1990s immigrant influx, I saw no mean-spirited signs in the windows of Mexican shops announcing "Spanish Spoken Here," nor any other not so subtle jabs at the ever-present sound of English. In contrast to the unwelcoming "For Service Speak English" signs appearing today in some small towns throughout the U.S. heartland (including in my home state of Ohio), I encountered no business establishment of any sort anywhere in Mexico that posted announcements such as "For Service Speak

Spanish" (Morse 2005). Nor did a single American living in Mexico whom I met or interviewed ever describe such a thing. Many Americans complained about having to wait too long for service providers; some complained about gringo prices. They all bemoan the "mañana" syndrome, but on the whole, these immigrants are a marvelously contented group.

These economic, political, and sociocultural variations in the case of U.S. migrants to Mexico can be explained in large part by the fact that these are migrants of privilege. As individuals, they possess financial, human, and social capital that typically exceeds that of their hosts and of their Mexican counterparts headed north; and as a group, they also have access — material and symbolic — to the cultural, economic, and political power that accompanies formal membership in the world's superpower. Both sources of privilege, individual and international, make it easier for Americans compared to most other immigrants to cross borders, stay connected to loved ones, settle into a foreign land, have a voice in a polity where they reside but do not possess formal membership, speak their native language in public and private, practice their culture without inviting resentment or retribution, and feel confident that they belong and are bettering not only their lives but the lives of those around them. Just as racial privilege blinds many white Americans in the United States to their advantages and to the very idea that notions of race or ethnicity apply to them at all (McIntosh 1988), most Americans in Mexico are comfortable with, and sometimes blissfully unaware of, their relative privilege, and accordingly, they fail to recognize any personal association with the label "immigrant." Moreover, assimilation, even if it were a goal or desire, is impeded in this case by the fact that immigrants from the United States speak a language and practice a culture that have in many respects become universal in influence and scope. At the very least, Americanization and Western homogenization have penetrated Mexico to a degree that calls into question the immigrants' portrayals of their adopted land as "foreign" or "exotic."

Americans' perceptions of a warm welcome by the host society may be accurate and a function of the sincere hospitality of the Mexican people, but it is also reasonable to assume that the relative lack of wealth and power on the part of the Mexican people and government influences the reception they extend to their gringo guests. At the same time that U.S. citizens are arriving from the north, a growing number of poor immigrants from Central America are crossing into Mexico via the country's southern border. In June 2006, while I was living in San Miguel, a seventeen-year-old undocumented immigrant from Honduras, Carlos Lorenzo Zavala, was killed on a train track just outside of town. The local English-language weekly published a feature story on the intensifying migration flow northward into Mexico from Central America and how many of these migrants, traveling as stowaways on trains, pass through San Miguel. This account and others have highlighted Mexico's less than welcoming attitude toward—and too often mistreatment of—immigrants from the south, and suggest that in Mexico it is quite unlikely that one will hear an immigrant from Honduras, Guatemala, or Nicaragua repeat the American mantra, "they love us here" (García 2006; Ibarra 2006a). Analyses of both migration flows into Mexico, from south and north, are a reminder that "To talk about the ubiquitous experience of movement is not to deny power and authority, and the differential motivations and gratifications in that experience that hierarchy might give on to" (Rapport and Dawson 1998, 24).

The literature on transnational migration has tended to assume that the patterns and behaviors associated with this border-transcending phenomenon are practiced by migrants who are disadvantaged economically, culturally, or politically in the international system and in the countries where they settle. It is in this way that transnationalism has been characterized as a form of resistance to the vagaries of global capitalism, a pattern of social networking on the part of a vulnerable population, a strategy for maintaining or regaining power within cash-strapped sending states that need the emigrants' financial investment, and a mechanism for coping with the marginalization immigrants often face in hostile receiving states (Smith and Guarnizo 1998; Portes 1999). Transnationalism, in other words, is conceptualized not merely as an aspect or indicator of globalization (the growing interconnectedness of the globe), but a response, or as some suggest, a form of resistance, to it (Glick Schiller et al. 1992; Basch et al. 1994). Americans are not immune to the vagaries of globalization, or to practicing transnational migration as a means to minimize the associated costs and maximize the benefits associated with global shifts. Retirees who flee dwindling pensions, rising health care costs, and an uncertain economic future in the United States for more affordable real estate, service provision, and pharmaceutical drugs in Mexico have much in common with the Mexican laborers who leave their homeland in pursuit of higher wages, better job opportunities, and a chance for a more secure future in the United States. But the transnational experiences of Americans living in Mexico, as migrants of privilege, are *similar to but better than* those of most other migrants.

When contrasted with Mexicans migrating to the United States, Americans migrating to Mexico clearly face far fewer constraints and have at their disposal many more opportunities. From Mexico's perspective, however, the cost/benefit calculus related to American migration is less clear. Missing from the analysis presented in this book are two important questions that should be high on the agenda for future research on U.S. migration to Mexico. The first concerns the reaction of Mexicans in towns like Ajijic and San Miguel to the influx of immigrants; and the second relates to the need to compile better empirical data on the impact of U.S. migration to Mexico. To date, neither topic has been systematically explored.

AMBIGUOUS ASSESSMENTS

This project did not seek to investigate Mexican attitudes toward immigration from the United States, or to assess empirically the impact of that migration on Ajijic and San Miguel. Both are critical topics and warrant careful future investigation. The discussion presented below intends only to problematize existing discourses that portray American immigrants as welcomed unconditionally in Mexico and as vessels of unquestioned economic and cultural good.

The Mexican Reaction

Although I did not systematically solicit the views of Mexicans in Ajijic or San Miguel, I did ask those with whom I interacted closely their views on American migration; I also read commentaries on this topic in Mexican newspapers and blogs. The American immigrants are not alone in noting the positive contributions they make to Mexico. Some Mexicans acknowledge benefits as well. As discussed in Chapter Three, Mexican officials in Chapala and San Miguel have expressed appreciation for the foreign community over the years by regularly extending official messages of welcome. In December 1991, *Atención* reported that the newly elected mayor of San Miguel had met with the "foreign colony," and wished to emphasize that he and his administration did not look upon them as strangers, but as San Miguel residents on par with everyone else ("New Mayor Meets . . ." 1991). By November of 2004, the municipal government of San Miguel had created an Office of International Relations, and its coordinator, Cristobal Finkelstein Franyuti, was scheduling a series of meetings with groups like the Unitarians and others to inform the foreign community of his responsibilities in providing them assistance. In December 2004, San Miguel

Mayor Luis Alberto Villarreal García wrote a column in *Atención,* in English, announcing his desire to improve communication with and accountability to the foreign community. Similar outreach on the part of municipal officials regularly takes place in Chapala as well. In a 2006 interview, Ajijic Mayor Ricardo Gonzalez described communication between the Mexican and foreign communities in his town as "very beautiful because each side respects the other." He credited foreigners with helping improve the area's education, environment, and economy: "We are learning many useful things from them that improve our lives" (Toll 2006, 77). Even before taking office in January 2007, the current mayor and his staff began meeting with the immigrants to promote "open and continuous dialogue with the foreign community to understand [their] problems and needs" (Campo 2006).

In addition to extending a verbal welcome, the Mexican government has also implemented concrete measures to ease the migration process; and recent research suggests that these efforts have had a direct impact on Americans' migration decisions (Migration Policy Institute 2006). Beginning in the late 1980s and through the 1990s, Mexico experienced a period of economic opening, or *apertura.* It was during the administration of Carlos Salinas de Gortari (1988–1994) that Mexico introduced the FM3 visa now popular among Americans living in Mexico. Various versions of the visa, such as one for students and another for import/export businesses, are available, but most common is the FM3 temporary residency visa, or what the Mexican Consulate terms the "Nonimmigrant Visa (FM3) for Retirees." This visa requires simply that the applicant demonstrate solvency in the form of a guaranteed monthly income of $1,000 USD, and does not entitle the holder to work in Mexico (http://www.consulmexny.org/eng/visas_fm3_retirees_all.htm). Judy King, editor of *Living at Lake Chapala,* explained that even the process of securing this visa has been greatly improved in recent years: "It used to take nine months and $1,000 to even get an FM3, but now it is all so much smoother. Currently newcomers using the services of a facilitator can obtain an FM3 in two to four weeks and at a total cost just over $200" (field interview, February 6, 2007).

It was also during this period of economic opening that Mexico made it easier for foreigners to own businesses and residential properties in Mexico. As CBS News reported in 2005: "Fearing they would frighten off the goose laying the golden egg—Americans with money—the Mexican government scrambled to tighten up real estate laws, make transactions transparent and extend into perpetuity the terms of the bank trusts Americans must use to buy land here" (CBS News 2005). In 2008, the Mexican government, under the direction of the Secretary of Housing and Public Credit (SHCP), conducted a national survey of U.S. and Canadian citizens living in Mexico. Its goal was to identify the major obstacles this group faces in the migration process, and based on the findings, to simplify the requirements and enact public policies that would facilitate a smoother migration of North Americans into Mexico (Secretaría de Hacienda y Crédito Público 2008).

In addition to recognizing the potential benefit of a capital infusion from immigrants, Mexican government officials and entrepreneurs also see an opportunity in the field of health care for U.S. seniors. Mexican government and business officials are aware of benefits to be had and are preparing for and anticipating the possibility that Medicare may one day be extended to Americans living within their borders. The Mexican government, through its National Institute for Public Health and nongovernmental organizations such as the Mexican Health Foundation (FUNSALUD) and the Inter-American Development Bank, is studying the potential implications of the U.S. retirement migration for the country's health care industry.[2] Meanwhile, Mexican and multinational hospitals are preparing by seeking accreditation from the International Joint Commission on Accreditation of Healthcare Organizations in hopes that U.S. policy makers will eventually enroll these institutions in the Medicare program (Connolly 2007a, 17). Mexican billionaire Carlos Slim and other entrepreneurs have moved quickly to capitalize on the migration of U.S. baby boomers to Mexico and are lobbying private U.S. insurance companies to pay for medical treatment in Mexico ("Carlos Slim's Medical Maquiladoras" 2008).

Some Mexican officials and commentators, such as Dr. Jorge Castañeda, have spoken publicly about the potential benefits of migration from the United States. In 2006, Castañeda, Mexico's foreign minister under former President Vicente Fox, sat down for an interview with the English-language monthly *Inside Mexico*. Asked whether Mexico should encourage the immigration of American retirees, Castañeda (2006) remarked, "For Mexico, it's a very important opportunity. We are one of the few countries in the world positioned to take advantage of this phenomenon. . . . They [the retirees] have high disposable incomes. They bring in hard currency. They will demand services that will create jobs."

In terms of what Mexico can do to prepare for the influx, Castañeda pointed to the need for health care facilities (as well as the provision of payment by Medicare and other U.S. insurance companies) and for golf courses, movie theaters, and satellite television. Ultimately, he acknowledged, "There will be a cultural impact, certainly, as there has been in the United States with all the Mexicans living there. However, I think this will be in the best interests of both countries" (Castañeda 2006).

In March 2007, in anticipation of U.S. President Bush's trip to Cancún, political commentator Juan Ignacio Morales Castañeda published an editorial in Guanajuato's *El Correo* proposing the following:

> Like all gringo presidents, George Bush does not go to other countries to offer friendship but rather business. In the case of Mexico, it would be a very interesting offer to extend the benefits of a less severe climate than that in the north, and lodging in nursing homes and middle-class subdivisions, to the thousands of pensioners who will retire in the next 30 years. This is a lucrative possibility that would generate much investment and, fundamentally, minimum guarantees of security.[3] (Morales Castañeda 2007)

My capacity to assess the Mexican reaction to foreigners living in Ajijic and San Miguel was limited by the fact that I am a foreigner, but when possible, I posed the question to Mexicans with whom I interacted. A Mexican woman in her late fifties, born and raised in San Miguel, who works closely with the foreign community, said this of the foreigners in her town: "They are good for San Miguel, and generous. They have started many charities" (field interview, June 23, 2006). Similarly, a high-level official in charge of international relations for the municipal government in San Miguel pointed out: "Their [the foreign community's] presence does great things for the city" (field interview, June 20, 2006). Others were less optimistic, and their responses tended to fall along a spectrum between mild frustration and acquiescence to a situation over which they perceive themselves as having little control. I myself never heard from a Mexican resident of Ajijic or San Miguel the point that some Americans made about locals now being able to buy more beer or tequila, in spite of rising prices. Several Mexicans did, however, express to me concern about the rising cost of living in their towns. One Mexican flower seller in Ajijic told me that the increasing prices in the village were making it difficult for her and her family to make ends meet, and that local wages had not kept pace with the surge in prices (field notes, February 9, 2007). And among the few Mexicans I got to know comfortably, I heard comments similar to this one from a woman in real estate who works closely with the foreign community in San Miguel. Sitting in a popular restaurant one evening, she pointed out, "Look around. I am the only Mexican in here" (June 30, 2006). Ultimately, one of the most poignant assessments of U.S. migration came from a Mexican woman, age 46, born and raised in San Miguel, who teaches Spanish at one of the local language schools. She said, simply, "De ellos comemos"—meaning, "from them we eat" (field notes, June 24, 2006).

Commentary by some Mexicans in newspapers and on blogs revealed a somewhat harsher assessment. In March 2007, *El Correo,* the daily newspaper of the Mexican state of Guanajuato (home to San Miguel), published, in Spanish, a lengthy editorial titled "San Miguel de Allende 'For Sale.'" The author, Eliazar Velázquez Benavides, described the report as a compilation of many voices and testimonials, but chose not to reveal the names of those interviewed. The article opens with the claim that "San Miguel de Allende, like other places in Mexico and Latin America, has experienced a slow appropriation of its physical and symbolic spaces" and that "its original inhabitants are being expelled from their own homes." Velázquez Benavides goes on to recount growing concerns over the "interminable colonization" of San Miguel, including the loss of the town's main garden to English-speaking gringos and the sale of the town's prime real estate to foreigners. In addition to buying up properties surrounding the city, gringos are described as now owning 80 percent of the city's central zone. One notable example of how local Mexicans are feeling "overwhelmed" by foreigners concerns San Miguel's popular central garden, or *el jardín:*

> The main garden used to be for everybody, it was a space to come to the city and do fun activities, or rest, or meet people; we used to say "see you in the garden" . . . This is no longer the case, now English is spoken there. Before, one could go and buy a soft drink at whatever little store around the center of town, now there are not little stores and if you want a water or coffee you have to go to a restaurant and pay many times more than the normal price.[4] (Velázquez Benavides 2007)

A section subtitled "Gringo Viejo" [Old Gringo] notes that retired gringos who began settling in San Miguel in the 1970s did not cause too many problems, although their presence eventually contributed to additional waves of immigrants from the United States. The Americans who began arriving in the 1990s, however, are characterized as viewing San Miguel primarily in terms of a good business opportunity.

> [They] take advantage of the production of art works, of the land, to construct their hotels (their disguised houses that really function as hotels), and they began also to insert themselves into the economy, the food products, into everything. We actually have gringos who work as plumbers and electricians contracting with other gringos, so that even this labor is not left for the Mexicans. They are overwhelming everything.[5] (Velázquez Benavides 2007)

The town's various mayors are accused of subordinating themselves to the gringos, and local Mexican authorities are blamed for contributing to the gringo takeover by not charging foreigners the proper taxes and offering them numerous privileges for living in San Miguel. Additionally, the contemporary colonization of Mexico by U.S. citizens is likened to that by the Spaniards in earlier centuries, but described as even more problematic. Whereas during the era of the Spanish invasion, the natives, some Mexicans claim, could at least find common ground with the colonists in the area of religion, "the gringo does not have religion. He does not have anything, for the gringo everything is money. Here then there are already problems with tradition and culture because how can you interrelate with someone who has no religion and to whom all that matters is the game of money?" (Velázquez Benavides 2007).[6]

Similar indications of resentment on the part of at least some locals are evident in Lake Chapala as well. In 2005, the local Mexican newspaper, *El Charal,* began featuring an English-language section at the back of each issue, presumably attempting to reach out to the large and growing number of Americans and Canadians residing at Lakeside. In the December 23, 2006, issue, an American immigrant contributed a column, in English, called "New Things in the City Hall." North American Mike Campo praised the new Chapala municipal administration's outreach to the foreign community and noted many positive changes taking place in Ajijic and surrounding areas as a result of the city's work with an American consultant, Dr. Todd Strong. On January 6, 2007, the paper published an anonymous reply to Mike Campo's editorial, written in Spanish by a local Mexican resident: "It appears that this foreign gentleman wants to reconquer Mexico and establish a little United States or Canada in our very Mexican shore of Chapala" ("Sobre el articulo . . ." 2007). This Mexican reader was particularly bothered by the proposal, promoted by the Americans, to build booths with video cameras on the main roads to allow police to monitor people coming in and out of town and catch criminals:

> The booths are perfect for international highways, like those that go toward the US, where drugs are consumed by the tons. But to put them at the entrance of a town like Ajijic would be an insult. . . . If Mr. Strong and many other foreigners do not like our system, however primitive or backward, it is ours, we invite them to return to their countries of origin.

The author goes on to suggest, "It would be good, Mr. Campo, to translate the article to Spanish and listen to the opinion of the Ajijic community" ("Sobre el artículo . . ." 2007).

Two months earlier, the same Chapala newspaper did a story on the local restaurants raising their prices in anticipation of the annual arrival of Americans who reside along the lake during the winter months: "As soon as the snowbirds arrive (the foreigners that come to spend the winter on the shore), the restaurant owners raise their prices" ("Los Restaurantes Suben" 2006). Meanwhile, a Mexican living in Mexico City wrote this on his travel blog after a weekend trip to Ajijic and the shores of Lake Chapala in 2006:

> Something that appeared odd to me was that Ajijic is full of gringos, practically half of the people that I saw were gringas. The town is full of five things: dental care, attorneys at law, galleries, real estate agencies, and bars. The first four are businesses for the older gringos who came to live in Ajijic, and the last seemed to me to be for the children of the retired gringos. Thus, all the signs in town are in English and Spanish, which never ceased to surprise me. (http://kad.gulags.org.mx/index .php/blog/show/145.kad)[7]

The reaction of Mexicans to the presence of American immigrants in their homeland tends to assume heightened significance during episodes of resurgent immigration tensions NOB (north of the border), in the United States. One such episode occurred over a decade ago, in April 1996, when video cameras captured a brutal scene of U.S. sheriffs in Riverside County, California, beating undocumented Mexicans. The video subsequently aired widely on Mexican television, and in June 1996, reporter Sam Quiñones traveled to San Miguel to cover brewing tensions in the town.

> America's crackdown on illegal immigrants is finding an odd echo in this sleepy town in central Mexico. Townspeople are up in arms over the growing number of illegal Americans living here. . . . Last month, just after the videotape of Riverside County sheriffs beating Mexican immigrants aired nationwide, the town vented its feelings in an anti–U.S. immigrant march. About 150 residents—mainly farmworkers and people with relatives in the United States—demanded the ouster of illegal American immigrants. They claimed that Americans buy homes and rent them out without paying taxes on the proceeds, as required by law. Others, they say, work without visas or exploit Mexican workers by not paying them overtime.

The report went on to detail a list of complaints issued by Mexican residents in San Miguel. For example, Americans own some of the nicest, oldest homes in San Miguel. The buying power of the Americans has made life in San Miguel expensive by Mexican standards. Many landlords rent only to Americans. Prices for real estate and cars are in dollars. Signs announcing their sale are always in English. Eduardo Lera, Mexican owner of a computer store and a member of the San Miguel Citizens Forum, which sponsored the anti–U.S. immigrant march, remarked: "Some people have been here 20, 25 years and still don't speak Spanish." Eric Ramirez, another of the march's organizers, explained: "People are truly mad. . . . But we also know that we need [the Americans]." Ultimately, Ramirez offered this: "They're treated well here. . . . What we'd like is that our people be treated the same way over there" (Quiñones 1996).

Ten years later, when anti-immigrant sentiment in the United States had again reached a fever pitch, *Atención,* San Miguel's English-language weekly, surveyed San Miguel residents about proposals in the United States to build a wall and deploy troops along the U.S.-Mexico border. Responses were varied, but included concerns similar to those expressed in 1996. "They know we Mexicans and other Latinos do the hardest jobs gringos would never do," exclaimed Ana María Sánchez, a forty-four-year-old merchant. "Here in San Miguel, there are plenty of gringos, and we treat them politely. They should do the same with Mexicans." Sandra Galicia, a flower seller, suggested the following: "We should forbid gringos from coming into Mexico, just as they do with us. Mexico is a mediocre country for allowing this kind of thing to happen." Raquel Matehuala, a sixty-two-year-old merchant, said: "We are neighbors, and they should not take such measures against us. I feel bad when I hear of any Mexican killed in the US. Why do we Mexicans allow them to come to our country and treat them politely, and they instead treat us like that?" (Ibarra 2006b).

As discussed in Chapter One, the Americans in Mexico are a generally charitable crowd, and many Mexicans acknowledge and express gratitude for the foreigners' generosity. Nevertheless, there is actually a potential downside to these good works. On July 29, 2006, the *Guadalajara Reporter* ran a story on the plight of Mexican professional language teachers in the Lakeside area who perceived that the plethora of free or inexpensive language classes offered by volunteer groups within the foreign community was negatively affecting their businesses (Chaussee 2006d). As to the alleged practice of merchants charging foreigners higher prices than Mexicans, or "gringo prices," this was not something I personally experienced or attempted to validate. If it is the case, however, that such a practice occurs, it might reasonably be interpreted as an enactment of resentment on the part of Mexicans, or what James Scott (1985) termed, in another context, a "weapon of the weak," to refer to the myriad, often quite subtle ways that oppressed peoples resist domination.

Because neither this study, nor any other that I am aware of, addresses directly the Mexican reaction to American immigration, speculating about how relations between the host society and the foreigners might evolve is just that—speculation. Nevertheless, an episode from almost thirty years ago is a reminder that there may be limits to the tolerance of some Mexicans. In 1980, in Puerto Vallarta, a magnificent villa owned by Americans reportedly experienced a servant rebellion. A maid, cook, and houseboy, who had worked for the American immigrants for eleven years, suddenly walked out. Reportedly having become members of, and indoctrinated by, a Communist-controlled union, these Mexicans lashed out at their American employers: "We slave all of our lives, and you live here in Mexico in luxury and leisure, without doing anything. This is our country, not yours!" (Davis 1980, 86). The American journalist writing about this event interpreted it as follows:

> Barring a revolution, which is an unlikely event, . . . the Mexican poor still have a long way to go before they can make their presence felt in a way that would endanger the good life for Americans. . . . Most people feel that the Mexi-

can rich, the Europeans and the Americans have at least ten good years left. That brings us to 1990, when experts predict Mexico will be an oil superpower, with all the problems and possibilities that entails. (Davis 1980, 86)

The year 1990 has come and long gone. The author's predictions regarding Mexico's superpower status have not been borne out, nor do the Mexican poor seem any closer to endangering the good life that Americans and other immigrants from wealthy countries continue to enjoy in Mexico. One thing is for certain: a clearer understanding of the empirical impact this migration trend has on Mexico and Mexicans would facilitate efforts to predict the future for foreigners headed south of the border.

The Data

Questions regarding the impact of U.S. immigration to Mexico should be empirical ones; yet, even when the questions themselves seem straightforward, the answers rarely are. For example, do immigrants to the United States take jobs away from "native" workers, or do they create more jobs by stimulating the economy through low-wage labor and the demand for consumer goods? Few countries have devoted more time and money to assessing the costs and benefits of immigration than the United States. Yet, after decades of research, reams of reports, and millions of dollars spent, experts still disagree over the economic and cultural impact of immigration to the United States, Mexican or otherwise. Proponents on one side of the ongoing debate claim that immigrants displace American workers, depress wages, and drain national coffers. Those on the opposing side insist that immigrants do the jobs no one else will do; act as complements to U.S. workers in the labor market, not substitutes; and pay taxes in excess of any services they use.[8] Assessments of the cultural implications of immigration to the United States are similarly polarized. An increasingly vocal group of politicians, pundits, and U.S. citizens contend that the growing number of foreigners in the United States threatens "our" culture and "our" way of life (Renshon 2005; Huntington 2004; Buchanan 2002). Opponents of this view counter those claims, pointing, for example, to evidence of high rates of assimilation among immigrants in the United States, particularly those in the second generation (Waldinger 2007; Hakimzadeh and Cohn 2007).

Mexico, widely and historically known as an immigrant-sending state, now faces a situation that may warrant assessments more familiar to immigrant-receiving states. Specifically, what are the costs and benefits to Mexico of the growing number of U.S. citizens settling in towns and cities throughout the country? Many of the claims American immigrants make regarding their impact on local Mexicans are, at least theoretically, open to empirical examination. Take, for example, the issue of increased prices and decreased purchasing power. Even though a beer today costs more in Ajijic and San Miguel, is it indeed the case, as some American immigrants claim, that local Mexicans now have the resources to buy more beer? (I use the example of alcohol here only because it is the one that many Americans used. The Mexicans whom I met in 2006 and 2007 were more likely to express concern about the price of tortillas than tequila.) Few observers disagree that the real estate booms in San Miguel and along Lake Chapala have forced many Mexicans out of the housing market; but whether Mexicans who have sold their homes to foreigners are now using that money to send more children to college, as some American immigrants suggest, has not been assessed. Analysts interested in these questions regarding the impact of U.S. migration to Mexico face challenges similar to, if not greater than, those faced by analysts studying the reverse flow. Gathering the appropriate data, particularly at the municipal level, and isolating specific cause-and-effect relationships between American migration and socioeconomic conditions in Mexico can be daunting. Below I briefly summarize data from other studies that report on the social and economic conditions in municipalities throughout Mexico, including Chapala and San Miguel, and may shed some light on questions concerning the quality of life for Mexicans in immigrant towns.

In 2000, the United Nations Development Program's Office for Human Development in Mexico constructed an index of human development and applied it to the 2,442 municipalities in Mexico. The index was constructed on the basis of factors such as infant mortality, literacy, level of education, and gross domestic product per capita. The human development scores ranged from a high of .930 for the wealthy municipality of Benito Juárez in the Mexican capital (Distrito Federal) to a low of .362 in the very poor municipality of Coicoyaán de los Flores in the state of Oaxaca. The municipality of Chapala, which includes the Lakeside village of Ajijic, scored "high" on the UNDP's human development index and was ranked 195th out of the 2,442 municipalities in the country. Chapala's development score placed it 10th-highest out of the 124 municipalities in the state of Jalisco. San Miguel de Allende scored "medium high" on the human development index, ranking 775th out of the 2,442 municipalities in the country and 13th out of the 46 municipalities in Guanajuato (UNDP

TABLE 5.1. QUALITY OF LIFE RANKINGS IN CHAPALA AND SAN MIGUEL
DE ALLENDE, 2006

| | Rank within the State | |
# of dwellings in municipality with:	Chapala, Jalisco (out of 124)	San Miguel, Guanajuato (out of 46)
Electricity	20th	8th
Running water	19th	7th
Sanitation service	20th	10th
Television	21st	9th
Refrigerator	20th	9th
Washing machine	21st	13th
Computer	13th	6th

Source: INEGI 2006.

2000). Five years later, in 2005, Mexico's National Council on Population (CONAPO) constructed an index of marginalization. This index draws upon measures similar to those in the UNDP study, such as literacy and education, but also includes data on the number of dwellings in the municipality with sanitation, electricity, sewage, and running water. In contrast to the UNDP study, which ranks human development, this study measures marginalization—the further down the list a city ranks, the lower the level of marginalization. Chapala scored "very low" in terms of marginalization and was ranked 2,298 out of 2,442 municipalities in the country, and 118th out of 124 municipalities in the state of Jalisco. San Miguel scored a "medium" in terms of marginalization, ranking 1,549 out of 2,442 in the country and 25 out of 46 municipalities in the state of Guanajuato (CONAPO 2005).

Mexico's National Institute of Statistics, Geography and Information (INEGI) also publishes an annual statistical yearbook that contains information on certain social and economic indicators by municipality. Using census data, INEGI reports on quality of life measures such as the number of residences with running water, electricity, or computers. Table 5.1 shows where Chapala and San Miguel ranked in 2006 within their respective states of Jalisco and Guanajuato. INEGI and the UNDP also provide information on gross domestic product (GDP) per capita, or the equivalent, for Mexican municipalities. Data available between 1999 and 2004 show that the GDP per capita in both Chapala and San Miguel regularly fell below the national average for Mexico.[9]

Finally, in 2006, the Migration Policy Institute published a report on U.S. seniors in Mexico that contrasted their socioeconomic conditions to those of Mexicans. The data revealed that U.S. seniors in Mexico have higher monthly incomes (on average four times higher) than Mexicans. They live in larger houses with fewer residents. On average, immigrants from the United States live in houses with 5.7 rooms for 2.6 people, while Mexican seniors lived in houses with an average of 4.6 rooms for 3.9 people. Seventy percent of U.S.-born seniors in Mexico lived in households with access to a car, compared to 28.9 percent of Mexican seniors. On average, 29.7 percent of U.S. seniors living in Mexico had a computer in their home, while only 7.1 percent of Mexican seniors did. In the state of Jalisco, home to Lake Chapala, the percentage of U.S. seniors with computers was 51.4 (Migration Policy Institute 2006, 32–39).

It is difficult to draw any firm conclusions from these sporadic data. For example, to tie levels of human development or marginalization in Chapala and San Miguel to the influx of American immigrants would require a longitudinal approach and more systematic efforts to isolate a causal relationship between the factors. Similarly, evidence that American seniors live much more affluently in Mexico than do Mexican seniors may indicate reasons for resentment on the part of Mexicans, but does not prove that one condition leads to the other. Two preliminary conclusions can be safely drawn from these studies. First is that the quality of life for Mexicans in towns heavily populated by American immigrants is far from the worst in the country, but is also not the best. This is most notably the case in San Miguel, which achieved neither a high score on human development nor a low ranking in terms of human marginalization. The second, and perhaps most important, insight to be gleaned from these sources is that further analysis of the impact of immigration on Mexico is warranted and could benefit both Mexico and the United States.

Because a bulk of the international migration flow southward now consists of retirees, such analysis could borrow in meaningful ways from existing literature on retirement migration (Sunil, Rojas, and Bradley 2007). Much of that scholarship has focused on domestic migration—U.S. retirees settling in Florida, Arizona, and other parts of the U.S. sunbelt. In general, popular retirement destinations in the United States have benefited economically from the related capital influx, but "saturation"—manifesting in overcrowding, environmental degradation, and social fragmentation—is a serious concern (Reeder 1998; Sunil, Rojas, and Bradley 2007). Mexican officials must be cognizant of similar effects in popular American settlements throughout the country. For example, data compiled by the Oakland-based think tank Redefining Progress suggest that the ecological footprint of the average U.S. resident is five times as heavy as that of the average Mexican. As more Americans move south, the environmental weight of those large feet is being felt in towns such as those that surround Lake Chapala. Writing for the monthly periodical *Inside Mexico,* Stan Cox acknowledges that Lake Chapala would be threatened even without the foreign presence, but he goes on to insist that "there is no doubt a greater ecological price to pay from the growing collection of big houses on the north shore slopes, with their acres of pavement, swimming pools (always full in spite of frequent water shortages), well-watered lawns and dryers running full blast despite the hot sun and availability of clotheslines" (Cox 2007).

As Mexico weighs the costs and benefits of U.S. migration southward, some in the United States are doing the same. In his book *Power, Terror, Peace & War* (2004), Walter Russell Mead proposes that the United States enlist the help of Mexico "in solving one of our major social problems"—namely, the millions of U.S. seniors set to retire in the next decades and unable to afford the quality of life they expect. Mead writes: "Why not allow—encourage—U.S. citizens to retire where costs are lower and where their consumer spending can encourage local economic development?" The logic of this question becomes even clearer when considering that health care and other industries in the United States that cater to the elderly are part of the job magnet that pulls Mexican immigrants northward (Mead 2004).

INTO THE FUTURE

On October 15, 2007, Kathleen Casey-Kirschling, the United States's first baby boomer, filed for Social Security retirement benefits. Casey-Kirschling is at the front of a "silver tsunami" that over the next two decades will carry 80 million aging Americans, more than 10,000 a day, into Social Security eligibility (Lassiter 2007) (see Table 5.2). The approach of this tsunami coincides with growing concerns regarding the solvency of the U.S. Social Security system and America's pensions more generally, an ailing health care system, a decline in private savings, and a growing number of Americans who are uninsured.[10] Notably, just one month before this baby boomer milestone was reached in the United States, another headline

TABLE 5.2. U.S. POPULATION OF OLDER ADULTS AND SENIORS 2005–2025
(AS A PERCENTAGE OF THE TOTAL POPULATION)

	2005	2010	2015	2020	2025
Older adults (ages 50–64)	17.0	18.9	19.5	18.9	17.6
Seniors (ages 65+)	12.4	13.0	14.5	16.3	18.2
Older adults and Seniors	29.4	31.9	34.0	35.1	35.7

Source: EMarketer 2005.

appeared announcing that in 2007, Mexico had moved up four spots to number one on International Living's annual list of the world's top retirement havens. International Living's Laura Sheridan explained:

> Moving to Mexico means you can still have all of the amenities you grew accustomed to north of the border: cable TV, high-speed Internet, and modern home appliances. And if you prefer, when you move to Mexico you can even bring all of your favorite things with you without paying import taxes. . . . Goods and services cost less, so you can afford the kinds of luxuries only the very wealthy enjoy up north: a maid, a cook, and a gardener for example. If health care is a concern, you should know that . . . medical care and prescription drugs will cost you only a fraction of what you would pay in the States. (Sheridan 2007)

Both of these news flashes support the predictions that the migration flow discussed in this book shows no signs of ebbing and, barring some unforeseen economic or political circumstances, is likely to intensify. This likelihood poses potential challenges and opportunities for both the United States and Mexico and for scholars who study transnational migration. From the U.S. perspective, the growing number of U.S. citizens residing outside the sovereign borders of the United States can affect domestic policies and politics in various ways. Many Americans abroad are now engaged in concerted efforts to have Medicare extended outside of the United States. Through organizations such as American Citizens Abroad, the Association of Americans Resident Overseas, Democrats Abroad, and Republicans Abroad, U.S. citizens living outside of the United States are lobbying their elected officials to grant them a benefit that they have earned and to which they feel entitled. Patricia Harris is an American who chose to retire in Mexico and recently underwent an emergency appendectomy at a Mexican hospital. She and her husband paid for the $7,000 USD procedure in advance and with a credit card. Harris asks a question increasingly being posed by Americans moving abroad: "Why should a U.S. senior citizen forfeit the medical benefits they are entitled to and contributed to their entire working life? We're still subject to all the obligations of citizenship. Why should we not carry those medical benefits?" (Connolly 2007a, 16). Adele Goldschmied, another American immigrant to Mexico, agrees: "Populations are moving frequently between the States and Mexico. Eventually [Medicare] is going to have to change" (Connolly 2007a, 18). Professor David Warner at the University of Texas's LBJ School of Public Policy has studied this issue for years. His recent study of Americans in Mexico revealed that a large number (86 percent) of the immigrants he surveyed intend to live south of the border permanently and are quite pleased with the quality of health care available in Mexico. Warner is confident that the numbers of Americans moving to Mexico will "grow very rapidly" (Connolly 2007a, 18); and he notes: "As medicine is increasingly practiced through telemedicine and the Internet, limitations on coverage determined by place of residence should become less relevant" (1999, 1).

Political parties in the United States will likely continue to increase their engagement with the American electorate abroad in Mexico and elsewhere. Not only is this constituency growing, it comprises a demographic known in the United States to be particularly politically active—seniors. The relative indifference of the United States, as a sending state, to Americans abroad may change as both the size and the political mobilization of this population increase. In addition to confronting continued demands that Medicare be extended across the border and that U.S. citizens abroad be included in the U.S. Census counts, the United States will also face tough questions about how campaign finance law and voting procedures should be adjusted, debates about overseas taxation, and concerns over the proper role in American politics of citizens who have lived many years abroad (Dark 2003b).

This latter question raises intriguing philosophical issues, as well as practical and political ones. The growing presence and political transnationalism of Mexican immigrants in the United States have led many analysts and observers to warn of the dangers of dual allegiances. In 2005, John Fonte, senior fellow at the Hudson Institute in Washington, D.C., published a report entitled "A Challenge to Immigration Reform and Patriotic Assimilation." Newt Gingrich wrote the foreword, in which he characterizes dual allegiance as an "insidious challenge . . . to our national unity and to American exceptionalism" (Fonte 2005, 2). Thomas Bock, national commander of the American Legion, penned an introduction to the report that warns: "In today's dangerous post-9/11 world the question of whether we as a people still believe in undivided national loyalty . . . is a serious one" (Fonte 2005, 3). It is not clear whether Commander Bock is aware that hundreds of his fellow Legionnaires have chosen to practice their national loyalty to the United States south of the border from within the territory of another sovereign state. Fonte's report focuses primarily on the practice of dual citizenship, but the use of the more general phrase, "dual allegiance," seems intentionally designed to cover an even broader set of concerns.

The concerns Gingrich and others express about the dangers of dual allegiances when held by Mexicans and other immigrants in the United States could arguably extend to Americans abroad. If political and philosophical consistency were at issue, they would. In an article entitled "Should Expatriates Vote?" philosopher Claudio López-Guerra argues: "If we accept — as perhaps all contemporary democratic theorists do — that long-term residency in a democratic state is what should entitle people to full political rights . . . then we must also endorse the idea that permanent non-residents should be disenfranchised" (López-Guerra 2005, 217). No commentators in the United States are now calling, or are soon likely to call, for the disenfranchisement of Americans abroad or to question their allegiances to the homeland. Some observers in the United States have, however, supported extending membership rights to noncitizens in the United States on the basis of their long-term residency — accepting the premise invoked by López-Guerra that long-term residency in a democratic state is what should entitle people to full political rights. Such efforts, however, are frequently met with political and public hostility, as New York Governor Eliot Spitzer learned in 2007 after proposing to grant driver's licenses to undocumented immigrants. In other words, preserving membership rights in the U.S. nation-state for Americans who voluntarily leave the United States raises few objections, but granting those rights to Mexican immigrants who choose to reside in the United States raises many.

In keeping with the theme of political and philosophical consistency, a caveat is warranted here. To the extent that this book is not merely examining, but also problematizing, the growing presence of Americans in Mexico, it risks tacitly accepting, even privileging, a static nation-state-centric framework. If, for example, social and economic inequality in Mexico is one of the concerns at stake, why should American immigrants, by sheer virtue of their national birthright, be held any more accountable for that inequality than wealthy Mexicans? Mexico, after all, is a country notoriously divided by class inequalities. By the same token, should the widespread and growing inequality within the United States be rendered any less problematic or significant than that between Americans and Mexicans living in San Miguel merely because the former festers within the cultural and geographic confines of the imagined national community? In other words, the ideology of nationhood should neither excuse injustices within national boundaries nor allow blame to be directed only toward those outside the boundaries.

As Benedict Anderson (1991) explained, the imagining of a national community relies heavily on the belief in horizontal comradeship among members. This fiction has never been fact, in the United States or elsewhere, but it contributes significantly to the power and perpetuation of nationhood as an ideological formation. Cosmopolitan critics have challenged many of the unquestioned assumptions upon which loyalty to a nation-state is based. Martha Nussbaum, for example, maintains that as a source or site of allegiance, the nation-state is morally irrelevant: "The accident of where one is born is just that, an accident" (1996, 7). She agrees that the values Americans hold dear—respect for human dignity and the opportunity for each person to pursue happiness—are of great moral significance, but on what basis do we allow the values that bind us as Americans to "lose steam" at the morally arbitrary borders of a nation? If Americans, she writes, "really do believe that all human beings are created equal and endowed with certain inalienable rights, we are morally required to think about what that conception requires us to do with and for the rest of the world" (1996, 13). When applied to migration, cosmopolitanism calls for a more humane view and approach toward immigration into the United States. Yet, and in the spirit of philosophical and political consistency, if I, or anyone else, wish to defend the rights of Mexicans to cross state borders in pursuit of life, liberty, and happiness, then Americans pursuing those same dreams south of the border must be afforded the same sympathies. Notably, however, cosmopolitanism is not simply a call for the rights of world citizenship, but also a recognition of the associated responsibilities. Americans who move to Mexico cannot escape the fact that they do so with entitlements that flow directly from the accident of their births.

Beyond considering philosophical and political consistencies, policy makers in the United States could benefit from considering how migration to Mexico reflects flaws in the current systems and structures of the sending state. On a humane note, for example, it might behoove U.S. officials, service providers, and the public at large to consider the number of

American emigrants to Mexico who identified social and cultural factors as something that pushed them from the United States and pulled them to Mexico. Cultural preferences are obviously as varied as the people who possess them, but consistent themes among the Americans I interviewed in Ajijic and San Miguel were the longing for community and connectedness with neighbors, the comfort of a health care system that leaves patients feeling listened to and valued, and the security of living out their later years of life in a culture that respects older people. In some sense, emigration from the United States may now be acting as a sort of safety valve for brewing tensions around health care and retirement woes. Whether this safety valve will remain open depends, at least in part, on Mexico's response to the immigration influx. Moreover, the United States has certainly taken many opportunities to hold the Mexican government accountable for what is perceived as a problematic exodus to the north. Mexico, too, might legitimately require accountability as the migration flow southward from the United States intensifies.

In the near future, official Mexico's generally positive attitude toward American immigrants seems unlikely to change, and the resentment on the part of some Mexican citizens will likely remain muted. Although the precise economic impact on Mexico of U.S. migration is not clear and likely depends on whose interests are in question, where, and what is being valued, Mexico could continue to take steps to maximize the benefits and minimize the liabilities. Anticipating and preparing to capitalize on retirement migration from the United States by building and certifying hospitals, nursing homes, and retirement subdivisions are ways to maximize benefits. Cracking down on undocumented American workers who are violating employment regulations and tax laws in towns like Ajijic and San Miguel is a strategy for minimizing costs. Given the magnitude of the bargain for Americans moving south of the border, it is also probable that Mexico could levy additional fees on foreigners, in real estate, for example, without frightening off "the goose that lays the golden eggs." In fact, a tax on real-estate transactions by foreigners was one of the specific solutions proposed during a series of meetings on the foreign presence in San Miguel, sponsored in 2005 by the Center for Global Justice in San Miguel (Yasui 2005).

From the academic perspective, scholars of transnationalism are a vibrant group and continue to contribute new empirical material on their subject matter and refine existing analytical insights. Currently, a general consensus has emerged among these scholars around at least two key issues. One concerns the need for additional case studies to allow for broader comparative analysis of transnational phenomena. The second involves a belief in the benign nature of transnationalism and its compatibility with integration of immigrants into the host society. This book responds to the first call, including moving beyond what Roger Waldinger and David Fitzgerald describe as the preoccupation with the single case of the United States (meaning immigration into the United States) (2004, 1179). In doing so, it calls into question some of the assumptions that underlie the second claim.

As the field of transnational studies advances, scholars are emphasizing the need to explore more systematically the causes and consequences of, and variations in, immigrants' transnational practices. Some analyses have focused on characteristics, at the level of individuals and groups, that affect transnational behaviors. Factors such as language fluency (Rumbaut 2003), perceived likelihood of return to the homeland (Morawska 2004), length of time in the society of settlement (Waldinger 2007), and socioeconomic status (Levitt 2001a) have been shown to influence immigrants' transnational practices. Institutional factors are significant as well—sending and receiving states, political parties, and civil society organizations (Faist 2000; Itzigsohn 2000; Levitt 2001b; M. P. Smith 2007). Nevertheless, key voices in the study of transnationalism are in agreement with this observation from Levitt (2001a, 197): "Few studies compare how transnational practices vary between different kinds of sending and receiving-country communities." "How," she asks, "do the activities of strong states compare with those of weak ones?" (2001a, 211). Waldinger and Fitzgerald (2004, 1179) also emphasize the need for "sustained comparisons across time and place [in order to] illuminate the sources of variation in migrant trans-state politics." These latter two scholars are particularly interested in how political constraints and variations in political culture shape the practice of transnationalism; and they add to the standard focus on individual states and political parties an important recognition of how "the relationship *among* states affects the conditions under which international migrants and their descendants can pursue homeland interests" (2004, 1185; emphasis added).

This study of Americans in Mexico adds an important and under-studied case to the body of empirical material that informs theorizing about transnationalism. As a strong and wealthy democratic state, the United States is less interested in reaching out to its emigrants than the other sending states on which much of the existing literature focuses. As a less wealthy and less powerful receiving state, Mexico is more welcoming to immigrants, at least those arriving from the United States. The power differential between these states influences, in other words, the practice of immigrant transnationalism. As to the widespread agreement that the maintenance of transnational ties need not impede, and may in fact facilitate, assimilation into the host society (Deux 2006; Joppke and Morawska 2003; Levitt 2001a; Portes 1999; Shain 1999; M. P. Smith 2007; Waldinger 2007), the case of Americans in Mexico suggests the opposite. For these particular migrants of privilege, the ease with which they practice transnationalism, the power of their sending state and culture, and their individual privilege relative to their hosts appear to discourage their integration into the society of settlement. This finding mirrors Kenneth Thompson's (2002) study of South Asian diasporas in the West, which concluded that new media technologies, rather than being corrosive of immigrants' ethno-cultural differences, act to strengthen them. Middle-class and professional immigrants, he argues, often have access to resources that facilitate the preservation of an identity distinct from that of the host society.

Although addressing a different context, Peggy Levitt identifies a related factor that may impede Americans' integration into Mexico. In identifying historical variations in the nature and practice of transnationalism, Levitt makes the point that heightened global interconnectedness influences contemporary transnationalism in that "today's migrants arrive already partially socialized into aspects of Western, if not North American, culture. Often, they already strongly identify with U.S. values because they have been thoroughly exposed to them through the media" (2001a, 203). If the migrants in question are Americans, and the societies where they settle have already been permeated by aspects of U.S. culture, then the options for adopting a new or hybrid sense of cultural identity, even if desired, are limited.

Scholars who view transnationalism as compatible with assimilation have also insisted that dual allegiances need not be viewed as threatening to the host society. Whether or not this presumption holds in the case of wealthier immigrants from more politically and economically powerful states who are exercising plural citizenships across borders and in multiple locales remains to be seen. As noted at the outset of this chapter, if dual allegiances on the part of Mexicans residing in the United States threaten the American superpower, how is it that a similar if not greater threat would not result from the migration of that superpower's citizenry into Mexico? At the very least, this case and others suggest that analysts should take seriously Ostergaard-Nielsen's (2003) call that immigrants' transnational networks everywhere be subjected to greater democratic transparency and accountability.

CONCLUSION

On October 26, 2006, U.S. President George W. Bush signed into law the Secure Fence Act of 2006, authorizing the construction of seven hundred miles of fence along the U.S.-Mexico border. His support for this measure was designed, in part, to appease Republicans in the House of Representatives, like House majority leader John Boehner, who deemed such an apparatus as essential to U.S. national security and hailed the bill's passage as "a major victory." Democrats tended to view the legislation as pointless: "an empty gesture," in the words of Texas Representative Silvestre Reyes, or "the worst in election year politics." Meanwhile, then–Mexican President Vicente Fox made it clear that he wanted the bill vetoed, and joined twenty-seven other Organization of American States members in signing a statement that called the bill "a unilateral measure that goes against the spirit of understanding that should characterize how shared problems between neighboring countries are handled and that affects cooperation in the hemisphere" (Fletcher and Weisman 2006). Analysts questioned the effectiveness of the fence, and opinion polls suggested that in neither country, the United States or Mexico, does a majority of the population support the construction of a border fence (Stephens 2006).

Just prior to a meeting in Cancún between Presidents Bush and Fox (and Canadian Prime Minister Steven Harper) in March 2006, a Zogby poll explored how individuals on both sides of the border view the U.S.-Mexican relationship. The results of that poll offer reasons for both hope and concern with regard to the continental "spirit of understanding" envisioned by Fox. Ninety percent of Mexicans and 69 percent of Americans surveyed disagreed with the idea of building a fence. Very small percentages in both countries believed that their nation perceived the other as a threat (Americans 6 percent and Mexicans 18 percent). And 55 percent of Mexicans considered it in their country's best interest to adopt a "look North" attitude. These results suggest a foundation for cooperation between North American neighbors, and the potential for fence-mending of a sort quite unlike that proposed in the 2006 Secure Fence Act. Other findings, however, highlight the challenges that remain. Sixty-one percent of Americans support more restrictive immigration regulations. Seventy-nine percent of Mexicans believe Mexicans are discriminated against in the United States. Fifty-two percent of Mexicans have an unfavorable view of Americans; only 36 percent view Americans favorably. Only 25 percent of Mexicans view Americans as hardworking. A mere 22 percent see Americans as honest; and a troubling 72 percent of Mexicans view Americans as racist (Stephens 2006).

In the fall of 2007, the former Mexican president, Vicente Fox, was traveling through the United States to promote the release of his book *Revolution of Hope* (Fox and Allyn 2007), written in English. Fox used the book and the related speaking engagements to express his continued disappointment with the tone and content of the immigration debate in the United States: "To be so repressive isn't democratic or free . . . to be putting up fences, chasing Mexicans, that isn't right . . . The U.S. needs better answers than repression, weapons and violence." Fox went on to attribute blame to "[t]he xenophobics, the racists, those who feel they are a superior race . . . [T]hey are deciding the future of this nation" (Santos 2007). Fox hoped his book would help the United States better understand Mexico's view in the immigration debate. Moreover, and in addressing the complexity and ubiquity of migration and the deep historical ties between the United States and Mexico, he shared a personal experience that speaks directly to the themes of this book. Fox's grandfather, Joseph L. Fox, was born in Cincinnati, Ohio, on April 14, 1865, and lived there for thirty-two years before migrating to Guanajuato, Mexico, in 1897 (Hispanic Chamber 2007, 40). He never learned Spanish, but worked his way up from a job as a night watchman at a carriage factory to a prosperous plantation owner. Vicente Fox remarked, "My grandfather embodied the dream of many Latin Americans and Americans who believe the American dream exists, whether in the United States, Mexico, or other parts of Latin America. That says something about the universality of immigration" (Corchado 2007).

I write this book now from the same Midwestern U.S. city that Vicente Fox's grandfather left over a hundred years ago en route to the state of Guanajuato, which sits in Mexico's heartland. During my time in San Miguel, a town nestled in the mountains of that same state, I met Americans who, many decades after Fox's grandfather, had also migrated to Mexico from Cincinnati, Ohio, and various other parts of the American heartland. In working with the local Latino immigrant community in southwest Ohio, I regularly meet Mexican immigrants from Guanajuato who have chosen to settle in or near Cincinnati. Ultimately, we all migrate, from one place to some other place in some fashion at some point during our lifetimes. Sometimes we move from house to house, neighborhood to neighborhood, school to school, job to job, town to town, or state to state, and sometimes from country to country. The motivation to improve our lives and those of our loved ones is a largely universal one. Migrants of all sorts have experienced some discomfort or unease at being somewhere new and unfamiliar, being "away from home"; and they tend to respond by seeking out familiar sounds, sights, smells, and symbols. When it comes to migration, then, various commonalities of experience transcend borders, cultures, and time; but these commonalities are powerfully disrupted by variations in how, why, and with what degree of facility and security we move.

For some migrants, globalization will facilitate their movement across borders. For other migrants, globalization will necessitate their movement. Some migrants will sustain transnational ties by traveling via commercial, or even private, airplanes. They will communicate across borders effortlessly and inexpensively with the help of the Internet, Vonage, and Skype; and they will stay abreast of the happenings in their homeland via satellite television and radio. Other migrants will spend large portions of their earnings, and wait in long lines, to apply (often unsuccessfully) for visas. Some will pay exorbitant fees to unscrupulous coyotes for help in crossing the border. They will swim rivers, climb mountains, jump on and off moving trains, crawl through rat-infested sewage pipes, and trek through vast deserts in an effort (often unsuccessful and often deadly) to cross borders. A large majority of migrants today maintain transborder ties. Some do so via sophisticated communications technology; some by purchasing long-distance phone cards from Wal-Mart or a local convenience store and calling what may be one of few phones in a small village where they have prearranged for their loved one to wait; or still others by watching videos of birthdays, weddings, and other celebrations that travel back and forth across borders with the transmigrants themselves. Some migrants endure a state of statelessness, and others, as Linda Kerber (2006) reminds us, enjoy an experience of *statefullness*—noting nonchalantly, as do some American immigrants in Mexico, "Hey, you can never have too many passports," or declaring confidently, "We don't have to justify why we live here."

This case study of Americans in Mexico tells the little-known story of migrants who move from north to south, exiting a wealthy state to resettle in a less developed one. The uniqueness of the case helps diversify the empirical material that informs current theorizing on transnationalism. This case also confirms what many scholars have written about the seeming paradoxes of the contemporary world—a world characterized, on the one hand, by mobility, transcendence, and fluidity, and, on the other hand, by (1) the pervasive power of states to control their borders and their citizens; (2) the significance, however reconfigured, of place; and (3) the perpetual appeal of membership in a nation even if this form of imagined community is only one among many to which we belong. In the final instance, this study is motivated by the hope that the political and policy debates surrounding the remarkably divisive issue of immigration can be engaged in a more expansive and humane way. This portrait of U.S. citizens living in Mexico speaks to an often overlooked aspect of global interconnectedness and reminds Americans, in particular, that we are migrants too.

NOTES

INTRODUCTION

1. Notable books on these topics are too numerous to mention. Reputable journals include *Identities: Global Studies in Culture and Power, Diaspora,* and *Global Society,* and influential think tanks include the Migration Policy Institute ⟨http://www.migrationpolicy.org/⟩ and the Center for Immigration Studies ⟨http://www.cis.org/⟩.

2. Cubans arriving in South Florida between 1960 and 1980 were able to benefit from the context of racial politics in the South and Cold War politics. As immigrants escaping Communism and deemed "white," they were able to construct a narrative, and for the most part a reality, of immigrant success. See Croucher 1996.

3. Snowball sampling is a popular technique for finding research subjects. One subject gives the researcher the name of another subject, who in turn provides the name of a third, and so on. This strategy takes advantage of the social networks of identified respondents to provide a researcher with an ever-expanding set of potential contacts. Snowball sampling is particularly effective as an informal method to reach a target population. If the aim of a study is primarily explorative, qualitative, and descriptive, then snowball sampling offers practical advantages (Thomson 1997; Vogt 1999). Using this method, I conducted 106 formal, semistructured interviews: 60 in San Miguel, 28 in Ajijic/Lake Chapala, and 18 in Mexico City.

CHAPTER ONE

1. The historical discussion here draws from an important contribution to the topic by Mary Alcocer-Berriozábal. Completed in 2000, her dissertation for the University of Kansas, "The Structure and Development of the American Expatriate Community in Mexico City since World War II," provides crucial background.

2. http://www.overseasvotefoundation.org/; http://www.aaro.org/map.html; http://www.democratsabroad.org/; http://www.republicansabroad.org/.

CHAPTER FIVE

1. Although I am borrowing Okin's rhetorical strategy here, I tend to disagree with her analysis of global gender issues for the reasons articulated in a cogent reply to her article by Jane Flax (1995).

2. E-mail and telephone correspondence with Elena Zúñiga Herrera and Gustavo Nigenda of the Fundación Mexicana para la Salud (FUNSALUD), August 2007.

3. *Como todos los presidentes gringos George Bush no va a otros países a ofrecer amistad sino negocios. En el caso de México habría una muy interesante oferta para aprovechar las bondades del clima menos severo que el del norte y hospedar en centros hospitalarios, asilos y fraccionamientos de clase media a unos 100 millones de jubilados y pensionados que se retirarán en los siguientes 30 años. Una lucrativa posibilidad que implicaría grandes inversiones y fundamentalmente mínimas garantías de seguridad.*

4. *Por ejemplo, el Jardín Principal era de toda la gente, era un espacio para venir a la ciudad y hacer diversas actividades, o para descansar o encontrarse; decíamos: nos vemos en el jardín . . . Eso ya no existe, ahora ahí se habla inglés. Antes podía uno ir a comprar un refresco a cualquier tiendita alrededor del centro, ahora ya no hay tienditas y si quieres agua o café tienes que ir al restaurant y pagarlo varias veces más de su precio normal.*

5. *Esos que vieron el negocio bueno comenzaron a establecerse y apoderarse de la producción de los artesanos, de terrenos, a construir sus hoteles (sus casas disfrazadas pero que son hoteles), y comenzaron también a introducirse en la economía, en los alimentos, en todo. Actualmente tenemos hasta gringos que andan de plomeros y electricistas y que contratan a otro gringo y ese a otro, o sea que ya ni siquiera ese espacio laboral dejan a los mexicanos, están avasallando todo.*

6. *La diferencia es que con el español todavía había unos espacios donde meterse, como el de la religión, pero el gringo no tiene religión, no tiene nada, para el gringo todo es dinero, entonces ahí son ya los problemas con la tradición y la cultura, porque cómo le haces para meterte con alguien que no tiene religión y que solo le importa el juego del dinero.*

7. *Algo que me pareció, digamos raro, es que Ajijic está lleno de gringos, prácticamente la mitad de las personas que vi eran gringas. El pueblo está lleno de 5 cosas:* Dentistas (dental care), *Abogados* (attorney at law), *Galerías de artistas* (galleries), *Agencias de bienes raices* (real state agency), *Bares. Los primeros 4, son negocios que ponen los gringos viejitos que se vinieron a vivir a Ajijic, y el último a mí me parece que es para todos los hijos de los gringos viejitos. Por lo tanto, todos los letreros en el pueblo están en inglés y en español, pero no me deja de sorprender esto.*

8. The scholarship on this question is immense. One scholar known for arguing that immigration has detrimental implications for the U.S. economy is George Borjas (1999). Julian Simon (1999) makes the counterargument. Two recent articles

that summarize well the various aspects of this topic are Jacoby (2006) and Lowenstein (2006).

9. Data on gross domestic product per capita by municipality are difficult to compile, and according to an official at INEGI, the problems are not unique to Mexico. The measures I refer to here come from the 2000 human development index by municipality constructed by the Mexico office of the UNDP and from INEGI data on value added per capita by municipality.

10. Various U.S. government studies document these concerns. See Senate Special Committee on Aging 2003a, 2003b, 2003c, 2004.

BIBLIOGRAPHY

AARO (Association of Americans Resident Overseas). 2007. "6.6 Million Americans." http://www.aaro.org/index.php?option=com_content&task=view&id=34&Itemid=46 (accessed January 12, 2007).

Abdelhady, Dalia. 2006. "Beyond Home/Host Networks: Forms of Solidarity among Lebanese Immigrants in a Global Era." *Identities: Global Studies in Culture and Power* 13 (3): 427–453.

Abruzzese, Sarah. 2007. "Congress Tunes in to U.S. Voters Abroad." *International Herald Tribune,* June 22. http://www.iht.com/articles/2007/06/22/news/caucus.php (accessed July 30, 2007).

Alcocer-Berriozábal, Mary. 2000. "The Structure and Development of the American Expatriate Community in Mexico City since World War II." Ph.D. diss., University of Kansas.

American Citizens Abroad. 2007. "Republicans Abroad Agenda for Americans Overseas." http://www.aca.ch/acane97.htm (accessed February 20, 2007).

American Society of Mexico. 2007. http://www.amsoc.net/ (accessed April 14).

Amit, Vered, and Nigel Rapport, eds. 2002. *The Trouble with Community: Anthropological Reflections on Movement, Identity and Collectivity.* London: Pluto Press.

Anderson, Benedict. 1991. *Imagined Communities.* London: Verso.

Angell, Robert. 1967. "The Growth of Transnational Participation." *Journal of Social Issues* 23 (1): 108–129.

Anhalt, Diana. 2001. *A Gathering of Fugitives: American Political Expatriates in Mexico 1948–1965.* Santa Maria, Calif.: Archer Books.

Appadurai, Arjun. 1996. *Modernity at Large: Cultural Dimensions of Globalization.* Minneapolis: University of Minnesota Press.

Atención. 1975. Vol. 11, no. 7 (July 18).

———. 1991. "Pack 'n Mail Hosts July 4 Celebration." Vol. 27, no. 26 (July 19).

Atkinson, Paul, and Martyn Hammersley. 1998. "Ethnography and Participant Observation." In *Strategies of Qualitative Inquiry,* ed. N. Denzin and Y. Lincoln, pp. 110–136. Thousand Oaks, Calif.: Sage Publications.

Backer, Dorothy. 2001. "Rootless." *American Scholar* 56 (2): 269–274.

Banks, Stephen. 2004. "Identity Narratives by American and Canadian Retirees in Mexico." *Journal of Cross-Cultural Gerontology* 19 (4): 361–381.

Barber, Benjamin. 1992. "Jihad vs. McWorld." *Atlantic Monthly,* March, pp. 53–63.

Barrington, Lowell. 1997. "'Nation' and 'Nationalism': The Misuse of Key Concepts in Political Science." *PS: Political Science and Politics* 30, no. 4 (December): 712–716.

Basch, Linda, Nina Glick Schiller, and Cristina Szanton Blanc. 1994. *Nations Unbound: Transnational Projects, Postcolonial Predicaments, and Deterritorialized Nation-States.* Langhorne, Pa.: Gordon and Breach.

Bell, Vikki. 1999. "Performativity and Belonging: An Introduction." *Theory, Culture and Society* 16 (2): 1–10.

Benítez, José Luis. 2006. "Transnational Dimensions of the Digital Divide among Salvadoran Immigrants in the Washington, D.C. Metropolitan Area." *Global Networks* 6 (2): 181–199.

Bernal, Victoria. 2006. "Diaspora, Cyberspace, and Political Imagination: The Eritrean Diaspora Online." *Global Networks* 6 (2): 161–179.

Berry, John W. 1995. "Psychology of Acculturation." In *The Culture and Psychology Reader,* ed. Nancy R. Goldberger and Jody Veroff, pp. 457–488. New York: New York University Press.

Biswas, Shampa. 2005. "Globalization and the Nation Beyond: The Indian-American Diaspora and the Rethinking of Territory, Citizenship and Democracy." *New Political Science* 27 (1): 43–67.

Black, Harold. 1991. "Looking Back." *Atención* 27, no. 11 (March 22).

Blastland, Michael, and Andrew Dilnot. 2007. "How We 'Count' Migration." *Prospect,* issue 140 (November). http://www.prospect-magazine.co.uk/article_details.php?id=9858.

Bloom, Nicholas. 2006. "To Be Served and Loved: The American Sense of Place in San Miguel de Allende." In *Adventures into Mexico: American Tourism beyond the Border,* ed. N. D. Bloom, pp. 191–218. Lanham, Md.: Rowman & Littlefield.

Blue, Karen. 2000. *Midlife Mavericks: Women Reinventing Their Lives in Mexico.* Parkland, Fla.: Universal Publishers.

Bonacich, Edna. 1973. "A Theory of Middleman Minorities." *American Sociological Review* 38 (5): 583–594.

Borjas, George. 1999. *Heaven's Door: Immigration Policy and the American Economy.* Princeton, N.J.: Princeton University Press.

Bourne, Randolph. 1916. "Transnational America." *Atlantic Monthly* 118 (July): 86–97.

Bower, Doug. 2005. "Can't Afford Illness in America." *American Chronicle,* July 3. http://www.americanchronicle.com/articles/viewArticle.asp?articleID=568 (accessed February 16, 2006).

———. 2006. "The Ugly American Syndrome: Why American Expats in Mexico Deserve Some Slack." Associated Content: The People's Media Company,

December 21. http://www.associatedcontent.com/article/104434/the_ugly_
american_syndrome_why_american.html (accessed April 20, 2007).

Brouwer, Lenie. 2006. "Dutch Moroccan Websites: A Transnational Imagery?"
Journal of Ethnic and Migration Studies 32 (7): 1153–1168.

Buchanan, Patrick. 2002. *The Death of the West: How Dying Populations and Immigrant
Invasions Imperil Our Country and Civilization.* New York: St. Martin's Press.

Burns, Scott. 2001. "Mexico or Bust? Part 1." *DallasNews.com,* March 4. http://www
.dallasnews.com/s/dws/bus/scottburns/columns/archives/2001/010313TU
.htm (accessed March 1, 2007).

Butler, Kendal Dodge. 2006. "March in San Miguel Unites Ex-Pats, Locals." *Atención,* May 2.

Campo, Mike. 2006. "New Things in the City Hall." *El Charal,* December 23.

"Carlos Slim's Medical Maquiladoras." 2008. *Frontera NorteSur: On-line U.S.-Mexico
Border News,* July–September. Center for Latin American and Border Studies,
New Mexico State University, Las Cruces, New Mexico. http://www.nmsu
.edu/~frontera/hlth.html (accessed October 16, 2008).

Carvajal, Doreen. 2006. "Tax Leads Americans Abroad to Renounce U.S." *New York
Times,* December 18. http://www.nytimes.com/2006/12/18/world/18expat
.html (accessed December 18, 2006).

Cashmore, E. E. 1994. *The Dictionary of Race and Ethnic Relations.* 2nd ed. London:
Routledge.

Castañeda, Jorge. 2006. "Preparing for Mexico-Bound Baby Boomers." *Inside
Mexico* (November): 7.

CBS News. 2005. "American Dream in Mexico." *Sunday Morning,* June 26.

"Census Bureau Finds It Can't Count Americans Abroad." 2006. *The Executive,*
March 30. Washington, D.C.: The Hill. http://thehill.com/the-executive/
census-bureau-finds-it-cant-count-americans-abroad-2006-03-30.html (accessed January 12, 2007).

Chacón, Justin Akers, and Mike Davis. 2006. *No One Is Illegal: Fighting Violence and
State Repression on the U.S.-Mexico Border.* Chicago: Haymarket Books.

Chaussee, Jeanne. 2003. "Expat Support Network Keeps on Growing." *Guadalajara
Reporter,* February 22. http://www.guadalajarareporter.com/chapala.cfm (accessed February 2, 2007).

———. 2004a. "Consumer Protection Group Hopes to 'Level the Playing Field'
for Foreign Residents." *Guadalajara Reporter,* March 27. http://www.guadala
jarareporter.com/chapala.cfm (accessed February 2, 2007).

———. 2004b. "Democrats Abroad to Remember 9/11." *Guadalajara Reporter,* September 4. http://www.guadalajarareporter.com/chapala.cfm (accessed February 2, 2007).

———. 2004c. "Democrats Get On the Line." *Guadalajara Reporter,* January 17.
http://www.guadalajarareporter.com/chapala.cfm (accessed February 2,
2007).

———. 2004d. "Lakeside Republicans Buoyed." *Guadalajara Reporter,* September 4. http://www.guadalajarareporter.com/chapala.cfm (accessed February 2, 2007).

———. 2004e. "Lakesiders Talk about Election to Visiting CNN." *Guadalajara Reporter,* October 4. http://www.guadalajarareporter.com/chapala.cfm (accessed February 2, 2007).

———. 2005. "Saturday, July 2, Set for Celebrating the Fourth." *Guadalajara Reporter,* June 25. http://www.guadalajarareporter.com/chapala.cfm (accessed February 3, 2007).

———. 2006a. "Democrats Resolve against Torture." *Guadalajara Reporter,* September 2. http://www.guadalajarareporter.com/chapala.cfm (accessed February 3, 2007).

———. 2006b. "Local Democrats Vote to Investigate." *Guadalajara Reporter,* March 11. http://www.guadalajarareporter.com/chapala.cfm (accessed February 3, 2007).

———. 2006c. "Peace Rally at Lakeside." *Guadalajara Reporter,* October 14. http://www.guadalajarareporter.com/chapala.cfm (accessed February 3, 2007).

———. 2006d. "Professional Teachers Cast Worried Looks at Foreign Volunteer Impact." *Guadalajara Reporter,* July 29. http://www.guadalajarareporter.com/chapala.cfm (accessed February 3, 2007).

———. 2006e. "Thanksgiving Fare Abounds at Lakeside." *Guadalajara Reporter,* November 18. http://www.guadalajarareporter.com/chapala.cfm (accessed February 3, 2007).

———. 2006f. "US, Canadian Expats Join to Honor Veterans." *Guadalajara Reporter,* November 18. http://www.guadalajarareporter.com/chapala.cfm (accessed February 3, 2007).

———. 2007. "Canadian Official Sheila Copps Visits Lake Chapala." *Guadalajara Reporter,* January 20. http://www.guadalajarareporter.com/chapala.cfm (accessed February 3, 2007).

Cohan, Tony. 2000. *On Mexican Time: A New Life in San Miguel de Allende.* New York: Broadway Publishers.

Cohen, Erik. 1977. "Expatriate Communities." *Current Sociology* 24 (3): 5–90.

Cohen, R. 1996. "Introduction." In *Theories of Migration,* vol. 1, ed. R. Cohen, pp. xii–xvii. Cheltenham, UK: Edward Elger Publishing.

CONAPO (Consejo Nacional de Población). 2005. "Índice de Marginación a Nivel Localidad." http://www.conapo.gob.mx/publicaciones/indice2005xloc.htm (accessed April 30, 2007).

Connant, Eve. 2004. "Could Expat Voters Decide the Swing States?" *Newsweek,* October 15. http://www.msnbc.msn.com/id/6257852/site/newsweek/ (accessed March 19, 2007).

Connolly, Ceci. 2007a. "The Lifestyle Gamble." *Inside Mexico* (June): 15–20.

———. 2007b. "Press 2 for Spanish." *Inside Mexico* (June): 7.

Connor, Walker. 1978. "A Nation Is a Nation, Is a State, Is an Ethnic Group." *Ethnic and Racial Studies* 1 (4): 378–400.

"Controversy over the 'Report from Palestine.'" 2006. Center for Global Justice. http://www.globaljusticecenter.org/2006encuentro-followup/palestine_controversy.html (accessed January 24, 2007).

Corchado, Alfredo. 2007. "Former Mexican President Fox Says U.S. 'Denying Its Immigrant Soul.'" *Dallas Morning News,* October 12. http://www.dallasnews.com/sharedcontent/dws/dn/latestnews/stories/101207dnintfox.35cc8f5.html# (accessed December 18, 2007).

Corchado, Alfredo, and Laurence Iliff. 2005. "Mexico Undergoing Americanization as Retirees, Others Become Expatriates." *Bahia de Banderas News* (from *Dallas Morning News*), March. http://www.banderasnews.com/0503/nr-expatriates.htm (accessed February 16, 2006).

Cornelius, Wayne A. 1982. *America in the Era of Limits: Migrants, Nativists, and the Future of U.S.-Mexican Relations.* La Jolla: Center for U.S.-Mexican Studies, University of California, San Diego.

Cornell, Stephen, and Douglas Hartmann. 1998. *Ethnicity and Race: Making Identities in a Changing World.* Thousand Oaks, Calif.: Pine Forge Press.

"Costing More over There: Taxing Americans Abroad." 2006. *The Economist,* June 22, pp. 100–102.

Cox, Stan. 2007. "Bigfoot in Mexico." *Inside Mexico* (May): 10.

Crocombe, R. 1968. Letter to the Editor. *Australian and New Zealand Journal of Sociology* 4: 76.

Cross, Caren. 2007. *Lost and Found in Mexico* (film). http://www.lostandfoundinmexico.com.

Croucher, Sheila L. 1996. "The Success of the Cuban Success Story: Ethnicity, Power and Politics." *Identities: Global Studies in Culture and Power* 2 (4): 351–384.

———. 2003. *Globalization and Belonging: The Politics of Identity in a Changing World.* Lantham, Md.: Rowman and Littlefield.

———. 2006. "Ambivalent Attachments: Hegemonic Narratives of American Nationhood." *New Political Science* 28 (2): 181–200.

———. 2007. "'They Love Us Here': American Migrants in Mexico." *Dissent* 54, no. 1 (Winter): 69–74.

Dark, Taylor. 2003a. "Americans Abroad: The Challenge of a Globalized Electorate." *PSOnline* 36, no. 4 (October): 733–740. http://www.apsanet.org (accessed December 15, 2006).

———. 2003b. "The Rise of a Global Party: American Party Organizations Abroad." *Party Politics* 9 (2): 241–255.

Davis, John H. 1980. "Americans in Mexico: Living the Good Life South of the Border." *Town and Country,* October–November, pp. 50–86.

Dean, Archie. 2005. *Insider's Guide to San Miguel.* Self-published in Mexico, ISBN/UPC: 9709150502.

De la Garza, R., H. P. Panchon, M. Orozco, and A. D. Pantoja. 2000. "Family Ties and Ethnic Lobbies." In *Latinos and U.S. Foreign Policy: Representing the Homeland?,* ed. R. O. de la Garza and H. P. Panchon, pp. 43–101. Oxford: Rowman & Littlefield Publishers.

Del Muro, Héctor. 2006. "Sesiones de Cabildo por television." *El Charal*, December 2.

Democrats Abroad. 2008 (February 21). "Global Presidential Primary: Results Report." http://www.democratsabroad.org/sites/default/files/DA%20Global%20Primary%20Results%20FINAL%20REVISED.pdf (accessed March 1, 2008).

Denzin, Norman, and Yvonna Lincoln, eds. 1998. *Strategies of Qualitative Inquiry.* Thousand Oaks, Calif.: Sage Publications.

Deux, Kay. 2006. *To Be an Immigrant.* New York: Russell Sage Foundation.

Dickinson, Sterling. 1975. "Luxury Living in San Miguel." *Atención*, December 5.

Digeser, Peter. 1992. "The Fourth Face of Power." *Journal of Politics* 54 (4): 977–1007.

Discover Mexico Magazine. 2007. "Chapala." http://www.mexicodiscovered.com/Places/DM3%20Chapala.htm (accessed January 11, 2007).

"Dollars and Sense of Community: The American Society." 1974. NACLA's *Latin America and Empire Report* 8, no. 1 (January): 5–7.

Doran, D'Arcy. 2007. "US Presidential Candidates Head Overseas." Associated Press, October 16. http://www.boston.com/news/nation/articles/2007/10/16/us_presidential_candidates_head_overseas?mode=PF (accessed December 1, 2007).

Dulles, Foster R. 1966. "A Historical View of Americans Abroad." *Annals of the American Academy of Political and Social Science* 368 (November): 11–20.

Edelman, Murray. 1988. *Constructing the Political Spectacle.* Chicago: University of Chicago Press.

Elkins, David. 1997. "Globalization, Telecommunication, and Virtual Ethnic Communities." *International Political Science Review* 18 (2): 139–152.

eMarketer. 2005 (May 1). "U.S. Population of Older Adults and Seniors, 2005–2025 (as a percentage of total population)." http://www.emarketer.com (access restricted to paid subscribers, report available by calling 1-800-405-0844).

Emmond, Kenneth. 2008. "Across the Border, the Comforts of Home: An Inside Mexico Special Report on NAFTA." *Inside Mexico* (April): 14–19.

Esses, Victoria M., John F. Dovidio, and Gordon Hodson. 2002. "Public Attitudes toward Immigration in the United States and Canada in Response to the September 11, 2001 'Attack on America.'" *Analyses of Social Issues and Public Policy* 2, no. 1 (December): 69–85.

Faist, Thomas. 2000. "Transnationalization in International Migration: Implications for the Study of Citizenship and Culture." *Ethnic and Racial Studies* 23 (2): 189–222.

Falling in Love with San Miguel (Web site). http://www.fallinginlovewithsanmiguel.com.

Ferguson, Ian F. 2006 (October 13). "United States–Canada Trade and Economic Relationship: Prospects and Challenges." Congressional Research Service Report, order code Rl33087. http://fpc.state.gov/documents/organization/76935.pdf (accessed September 24, 2008).

Fetzer, Joel S. 2000. *Public Attitudes toward Immigration in the United States, France, and Germany.* Cambridge: Cambridge University Press.

Field, James. 1971. "Transnationalism and the New Tribe." *International Organization* 25 (3): 353–372.

Fish, Stanley. 2002. "Don't Blame Relativism." *Responsive Community* 12 (3): 27–31.

Fitzgerald, David. 2000. *Negotiating Extra-Territorial Citizenship: Mexican Migration and the Transnational Politics of Community.* Monograph Series, No. 2. San Diego: Center for Comparative Immigration Studies, University of California, San Diego.

Flax, Jane. 1995. "Race/Gender and the Ethics of Difference: A Reply to Okin's 'Gender Inequality and Cultural Differences.'" *Political Theory* 23 (3): 500–510.

Fletcher, Michael A., and Jonathan Weisman. 2006. "Bush Signs Bill Authorizing 700-Mile Fence for Border." *Washington Post,* October 27.

Flores, Nancy. 2006. "Foreigners Cast Their Ballots." *El Universal/Miami Herald,* July 3. http://www.mexiconews.com.mx/miami/vi_19088.html (accessed March 19, 2007).

Fonte, John. 2005. "Dual Allegiance: A Challenge to Immigration Reform and Patriotic Assimilation." *Backgrounder* (Center for Immigration Studies), November, pp. 1–23. http://www.cis.org/articles/2005/back1205.html.

"The Foreign Community of San Miguel de Allende." 1991. *Atención,* January 25.

Fortier, Anne-Marie. 2000. *Migrant Belonging: Memory, Space, Identity.* Oxford: Berg.

Foucault, Michel. 1980. *Power/Knowledge: Selected Interviews and Other Writings.* Edited by Colin Gordon. New York: Pantheon.

Fox, Vicente, and Rob Allyn. 2007. *Revolution of Hope: The Life, Faith, and Dreams of a Mexican President.* New York: Viking.

Fraser, Laura. 2007. "Made in Mexico." *More,* July/August, pp. 85–90.

García, María Cristina. 2006. *Seeking Refuge: Central American Migration to Mexico.* Berkeley: University of California Press.

Garcia-Navarro, Lourdes. 2006. "Rape Stirs Up Controversy over Justice in Mexico." Transcripts, National Public Radio, *Morning Edition,* March 13.

Geddes, Andres, and Adrian Favell. 1999. *The Politics of Belonging: Migrants and Minorities in Contemporary Europe.* Aldershot, England: Ashgate.

Geertz, Clifford. 1973. "Thick Description: Toward an Interpretive Theory of Cultures." In *The Interpretation of Cultures,* pp. 3–30. New York: Basic Books.

General Census of Population and Housing of Mexico XII. 2000. Instituto Nacional de Estadística, Geografía e Informática. http://www.inegi.gob.mx (accessed January 4, 2007).

Glick Schiller, Nina, Linda Basch, and Cristina Blanc-Szanton. 1992. *Towards a Transnational Perspective on Migration: Race, Class, Ethnicity and Nationalism Reconsidered.* New York: New York Academy of Science.

Golson, Barry. 2004. "La Vida Cheapo." *AARP Magazine,* March–April. http://www.aarpmagazine.org/travel/Articles/a2004-01-21-mag-mexico.html.

Gordon, Milton. 1964. *Assimilation in American Life.* New York: Oxford University Press.

"Go South, Old Man." 2005. *Economist* 377, issue 8454 (November 26): 46.

Government Accountability Office, U.S. 2004. *Counting Americans Overseas as Part of the Decennial Census Would Not Be Cost-Effective.* Report to the Subcommittee on Technology, Information Policy, Intergovernmental Relations and the Census. Washington, D.C.: Committee on Government Reform, House of Representatives.

Graham, M., and S. Khrosravi. 2002. "Reordering Public and Private in Iranian Cyberspace: Identity, Politics and Mobilization." *Identities: Global Studies in Culture and Power* 9, no. 2 (April–June): 219–246.

Grieco, Elizabeth. 2003. "The Foreign-born from Mexico in the United States." *Migration Information Source* (newsletter of Migration Policy Institute), October. http://www.migrationinformation.org/usfocus/display.cfm?ID=163 (accessed May 15, 2006).

Guadalajara Reporter. 2003 (April 5). "International Living to Open Lakeside Office." http://www.guadalajarareporter.com/chapala.cfm (accessed February 1, 2007).

Guarnizo. Luis. 1998. "The Rise of Transnational Social Formations: Mexican and Dominican State Responses to Transnational Migration." *Political Power and Social Theory* 12: 45–94.

Gutiérrez, David. 1999. "Migration, Emergent Ethnicity, and the 'Third Space': The Shifting Politics of Nationalism in Greater Mexico." *Journal of American History* 86, no. 2 (September): 481–517.

Hakimzadeh, Shirin, and D'Vera Cohn. 2007. "English Usage among Hispanics in the United States" (November 29). Washington, D.C.: Pew Hispanic Center.

Harmes, Joseph. 2004. *The Best of San Miguel de Allende.* Self-published. ISBN: 9687846720.

Hart, Rosana. 2005. "San Miguel de Allende: Conversation with a Mexican." Blog post, February 14. http://www.mexico-with-heart.com/blog/2005/02/san-miguel-de-allende-conversation.html (accessed June 26, 2007).

Harvey, David. 1990. *The Condition of Postmodernity: An Enquiry into the Origins of Cultural Change.* Cambridge, Mass.: Blackwell.

Hawley, Chris. 2007. "Seniors Head South to Mexican Nursing Homes." *USA Today,* August 15. http://www.usatoday.com/news/nation/2007-08-15-mex nursinghome_N.htm (accessed October 3, 2007).

Hegstrom, Edward. 2001. "American in Fox Cabinet Aims to Protect Mexicans Here." *Houston Chronicle,* February 22.

Hill Collins, Patricia. 2001. "Like One of the Family: Race, Ethnicity, and the Paradox of US National Identity." *Ethnic and Racial Studies* 24 (1): 3–28.

Himmelstein, David. 2005. "Illness and Medical Bills Cause Half of All Bankruptcies." News Release, February 2. Cambridge, Mass.: Harvard Medical School

Office of Public Affairs. http://www.hms.harvard.edu/news/releases/2_2Himmelstein.html (accessed October 3, 2007).

Hispanic Chamber Cincinnati USA. 2007. *From the Queen City to the Zocalo: A Pictorial View* (Private Limited Edition). Self-published. ASIN: B001BJCG4C. http://www.HispanicChamberCincinnati.com.

Hobsbawm, Eric. 1990. *Nations and Nationalism since 1780*. Cambridge: Cambridge University Press.

Hoffman, Nathaniel. 2006a. "Americans Dodging Taxes in Picturesque Mexican Town, Officials Say." DuluthNewsTribune.com, April 24. Knight Ridder Newspapers. http://www.dallasnews.com/sharedcontent/dws/dn/localnews/columnists/sjacobson/stories/DN-jacobson_08met.ARTo (accessed June 21, 2007).

———. 2006b. "Telecommuting." *Mercury News,* April 24.

Hondagneu-Sotelo, Pierrette. 1994. *Gendered Transitions: Mexican Experiences of Immigration*. Berkeley: University of California Press.

———, ed. 2003. *Gender and U.S. Immigration: Contemporary Trends*. Berkeley: University of California Press.

Horst, Heather A., and Daniel Miller. 2006. *The Cell Phone: An Anthropology of Communication*. Oxford: Berg.

Huntington, Samuel. 2004. "The Hispanic Challenge." *Foreign Policy,* issue 141 (March/April): 30–45.

Ibarra, Jesús. 2006a. "San Miguel: The End of a Journey . . . and of a Dream." *Atención,* June 23. http://www.atencionsanmiguel.org/index.php?engarchives (accessed July 1, 2006).

———. 2006b. "Up Against the Wall: Sanmiguelenses Speak Out about the Border" (A Bilingual Report). *Atención,* May 26. http://www.atencionsanmiguel.org/index.php?engarchives (accessed June 11, 2006).

———. 2007. "Residents Act to Protect City from Uncontrolled Growth." *Atención,* January 12. http://www.atencionsanmiguel.org/index.php?engarchives (accessed February 3, 2007).

Ignatieff, Michael. 1993. *Blood and Belonging: Journeys into the New Nationalism*. New York: Farrar, Straus and Giroux.

INEGI (Instituto Nacional de Estadistica, Geografia, e Información). 2006. *Anuario Estadistico de Jalisco y de Guanajuato,* Tomo 1.

Inside Mexico: The English Speaker's Guide to Living in Mexico (online journal). http://www.insidemex.com.

International Organization for Migration. 2007. "Global Estimates and Trends." http://iom.int/jahia/Jahia/pid/254#1 (accessed January 11, 2007)

Irwin, Katherine. 2006. "Into the Dark Heart of Ethnography: The Lived Ethics and Inequality of Intimate Field Relationships." *Qualitative Sociology* 29 (2): 155–175.

Itzigsohn, José. 1995. "Migrant Remittances, Labor Markets, and Household Strategies." *Social Forces* 74 (2): 633–657.

———. 2000. "Immigration and the Boundaries of Citizenship: The Institutions of Immigrants' Political Transnationalism." *International Migration Review* 34 (4): 1126–1154.

Jacoby, Tamar. 2006. "Immigration Nation." *Foreign Affairs* 85 (6): 50–65.

James, Daniel. 1960. *How to Invest and Live in Mexico.* Mexico City: Carl D. Ross.

Johnson, Georgeann. 2001. Editorial. *Atención* 27, no. 32 (August 6).

Johnson, John M. 1975. "Good Old Days." *Atención* 1, no. 11 (August 15).

Johnston, Robert. 1999. *Living Overseas: Follow Your Dreams to Affordable Living.* Vashon, Wash.: Living Overseas Books.

Jones-Correa, Michael. 2000. *Under Two Flags: Dual Nationality and Its Consequences for the United States.* Working Papers on Latin America 99/00-3. New York: David Rockefeller Center for Latin American Studies.

Jonsson, Patrick. 2006. "Backlash Emerges against Latino Culture." *Christian Science Monitor,* July 19.

Joppke, Christian, and Ewa Morawska. 2003. *Toward Assimilation and Citizenship: Immigrants in Liberal Nation-States.* New York: Palgrave Macmillan.

Jordan, Mary. 2001. "American Retirees Flock to 'Paradise' in Mexico." *Washington Post,* February 5.

Karim, K. H. 2003. *The Media of Diaspora.* New York: Routledge.

Kerber, Linda. 2006. "Toward a History of Statelessness in America." In *Legal Borderlands: Law and the Construction of American Borders,* ed. M. Dudziak and L. Volpp, pp. 135–157. Baltimore: Johns Hopkins University Press.

Kernecker, Herb. 2005. *When in Mexico, Do as the Mexicans Do: The Clued-In Guide to Mexican Life, Language, and Culture.* New York: McGraw-Hill.

Kiesling, Brady. 2007. "Civil Liberties, Privacy and the Patriot Act." Hellenic-American Democratic Association, Athens, Greece. http://www.helada.org/overseas_banking.htm (accessed March 11, 2007).

Kivisto, Peter. 2001. "Theorizing Transnational Immigration: A Critical Review of Current Efforts." *Ethnic and Racial Studies* 24 (4): 549–577.

Knight, Alan. 1986. *The Mexican Revolution.* New York: Cambridge University Press.

Krasner, S. 2001. "Think Again: Sovereignty." *Foreign Policy,* issue 121 (January/February): 20–29.

Lake Chapala Society. 2006. http://www.lakechapalasociety.org.

"Lakeside Community Raises Money for Katrina Victims." 2005. *Guadalajara Reporter,* September 17.

Lassiter, Mark. 2007. "Nation's First Baby Boomer Files for Social Security—Online." Press release from Social Security Administration, October 15. http://www.ssa.gov/pressoffice/pr/babyboomerfiles-pr.pdf (accessed December 14, 2007).

Levine, Robert M., and Moisés Asís. 2000. *Cuban Miami.* New Brunswick, N.J.: Rutgers University Press.

Levitt, Peggy. 2001a. "Transnational Migration: Taking Stock and Future Directions." *Global Networks* 1 (3): 195–216.

————. 2001b. *The Transnational Villagers.* Berkeley: University of California Press.

Lipschutz, Ronnie. 1999. "Members Only?: Citizenship and Civic Virtue in a Time of Globalization." *International Politics* 36, no. 2: 203–233.

Lipset, Seymour Martin. 1989. *Continental Divide: The Values and Institutions of the United States and Canada.* Toronto: Canadian-American Committee.

López-Guerra, Claudio. 2005. "Should Expatriates Vote?" *Journal of Political Philosophy* 13 (2): 216–234.

"Los Restaurantes Suben Sus Precios." 2006. *El Charal,* November 11.

Lowenstein, Roger. 2006. "What Is She Really Doing to American Jobs and Wages?" *New York Times Magazine,* July 9.

Luboff, Ken. 1999. *Live Well in Mexico: How to Relocate, Retire, and Increase Your Standard of Living.* Santa Fe, N.Mex.: John Muir Publications.

Maalouf, Amin. 2003. *In the Name of Identity: Violence and the Need to Belong.* New York: Penguin Books.

McIntosh, Peggy. 1988. *White Privilege and Male Privilege: A Personal Account of Coming to See Correspondences through Work in Women's Studies.* Wellesley, Mass.: Wellesley College, Center for Research on Women.

McKinley, James C. 2005. "San Miguel de Allende." *New York Times Travel Section,* May 22. http://travel2.nytimes.com/2005/05/22/travel/22goingto.html (accessed May 10, 2007).

McNeill, William. 1986. *Polyethnicity and National Unity in World History.* Toronto: University of Toronto Press.

Mahler, Sarah. 1998. "Theoretical and Empirical Contributions toward a Research Agenda for Transnationalism." In *Transnationalism from Below,* ed. Michael P. Smith and Luis E. Guarnizo, pp. 64–102. New Brunswick, N.J.: Transaction Publishers.

Maloney, Carolyn, and Joe Wilson. 2007. "Help Support American Workers and Businesses Abroad: Join the Americans Abroad Caucus." Congress of the United States, February 22. http://www.aaro.org/images/stories/Dear_Colleague_letter.pdf (accessed at above site on September 8, 2007).

Mandaville, Peter. 1999. "Territory and Translocality: Discrepant Idioms of Political Identity." *Millennium* 28 (3): 653–673.

Marchand, Marianne, and Anne S. Runyan, eds. 2000. *Gender and Global Restructuring.* New York: Routledge.

Martin, Justin, and Henry Goldblatt. 1995. "Or, If You'd Rather, Retire." *Fortune* 132, no. 2 (July 24): 94–95.

Marx, Anthony. 1998. *Making Race and Nation: A Comparison of the United States, South Africa, and Brazil.* Cambridge: Cambridge University Press.

Massey, Doreen. 2004. "Geographies of Responsibility." *Human Geography* 86 (1): 1–29.

Masterson, Bill. 2000. "Yanks Abroad: The Numbers Game. How Many Americans Really Live in Mexico? And Who Cares, Anyway?" *People's Guide to Mexico.*

http://www.peoplesguide.com/1pages/retire/work/bil-maste/%23americans
.html (accessed August 2006).

———. 2002 (February). "Question Revisited: How Many Americans Live in Mexico?" http://www.peoplesguide.com/1pages/retire/work/bil-maste/%232 americans.html (accessed January 11, 2007).

Mauss, Marcel. 1967. *The Gift: Forms and Functions of Exchange in Archaic Societies.* New York: W. W. Norton.

"Mayor Seeks to Build a Bridge." 2004. *Atención,* December 3.

Mead, Walter Russell. 2004. "Mexico and U.S. Retirement Futures." *The Globalist: The Power of Global Ideas,* September 20. http://www.theglobalist.com/DBWeb/storyId.aspx?storyId=4158 (accessed October 3, 2007).

Memmi, Albert. 1965. *The Colonizer and the Colonized.* New York: Orion Press.

Mexfiles. 2006 (July 6). "When the Going Gets Strange . . ." http://mexfiles .wordpress.com/2006/07/06/when-the-going-gets-strange-election-and-other-chicanery-update/ (accessed January 11, 2007).

Mexico Connect. http://www.mexconnect.com.

Mexico Insights: Living at Lake Chapala. http://www.Mexico-Insights.com.

Meyer, Michael, and William Sherman. 1995. *The Course of Mexican History.* New York: Oxford University Press.

Migdal, Joel S., ed. 2004. *Boundaries and Belonging: States and Societies in the Struggle to Shape Identities and Local Practices.* Cambridge and New York: Cambridge University Press.

Migration Policy Institute. 2006. *America's Emigrants: U.S. Retirement Migration to Mexico and Panama.* Washington, D.C.: Migration Policy Institute.

Mitra, A. 1997. "Virtual Community: Looking for India on the Internet." In *Virtual Culture: Identity and Communication in Cyber Society,* ed. S. G. Jones, pp. 55–79. London: Sage.

Money magazine. 2003 (May 5). "Best Places to Retire: San Miguel de Allende, Mexico." http://money.cnn.com/2002/05/01/retirement/bpretire_san_miguel/index.htm (accessed September 24, 2008).

Montague, James. 2008. "They Just Won't Mix." *New Statesman,* January 7, p. 17.

Moore, Connie. 1982. "Moore Platica." *Atención,* August 20.

Morales Castañeda, Juan Ignacio. 2007. "El gringo y el negocio." Editoriales Página 3 (7 de Marzo). *Correo Diario del Estado de GTO.* http://www.correo-gto.com .mx/notas.asp?id=17046.

Morawska, Ewa. 2004. "Exploring Diversity in Immigrant Assimilation and Transnationalism." *International Migration Review* 38 (4): 1372–1412.

Moreno, Julio. 2003. *Yankee Don't Go Home: Mexican Nationalism, American Business Culture, and the Shaping of Modern Mexico, 1920–1950.* Chapel Hill: University of North Carolina Press.

Morse, Janice. 2005. "'Speak English' Isn't So Simple." *Cincinnati Enquirer,* October 16.

Mountz, Allison, and Richard Wright. 1996. "Daily Life in the Transnational Migrant Community of San Agustin, Oaxaca and Poughkeepsie, New York." *Diaspora* 6 (3): 403–428.

Nakamura, L. 2002. *Cybertypes: Race, Ethnicity and Identity on the Internet.* New York: Routledge.

Nash, Dennison. 1970. *A Community in Limbo: An Anthropological Study of an American Community Abroad.* Bloomington: Indiana University Press.

Nevaer, Louis. 2003. "'Generation Gringo': Young Americans Moving to Mexico." Pacific News Service, New America Media, November 4. http://news.newamericamedia.org/news/view_article.html?article_id=4c6618c2588e72f4e4a877fc13301da7.

New Beginnings. http://www.newbeginningsmexico.com.

"New Mayor Meets with Foreign Community." 1991. *Atención,* December 27.

Niblo, Stephen. 1995. *War, Diplomacy and Development: The United States and Mexico 1938–1954.* Wilmington, Del.: SR Books.

Noriz, Tania. 2006. "How Much Is That Doggie in the Window?" *Atención,* June 9.

Noriz, Tania, and Jesús Ibarra. 2006. "Support and Solidarity for Mexican Workers in US." *Atención,* May 5.

Nussbaum, Martha. 1996. *For Love of Country: Debating the Limits of Patriotism.* Boston: Beacon Press.

Okin, Susan. 1994. "Gender Inequality and Cultural Differences." *Political Theory* 22 (1): 5–24.

Omhae, Kenichi. 1995. *The End of the Nation State: The Rise of Regional Economies.* New York: Free Press.

Oppenheimer, Andres. 1994a. "U.S. Citizens Live Illegally in Mexico." *Dallas Morning News,* July 17.

———. 1994b. "U.S. Job Hunters Heading South." *Miami Herald,* July 5.

O'Reilly, Karen. 2000. *The British on the Costa del Sol: Transnational Identities and Local Communities.* London and New York: Routledge.

Orozco, Manuel, and Rebecca Rouse. 2007. "Migrant Hometown Associations and Opportunities for Development: A Global Perspective." *Migration Information Source* (newsletter of Migration Policy Institute), February. http://www.migrationinformation.org/issue-feb07.cfm.

Ostergaard-Nielsen, Eva. 2003. "The Politics of Migrants' Transnational Political Practices." *International Migration Review* 37 (3): 760–786.

Otero, Lorena M. Y. 1997. "U.S. Retired Persons in Mexico." *American Behavioral Scientist* 40 (7): 914–923.

Overseas Digest. 1999 (July). "Private American Citizens Residing Abroad." http://www.overseasdigest.com/amcit_nu2.htm (accessed January 12, 2007).

Overseas Vote Foundation. 2007. "2006 Post Election Survey Results," February 8, p. 6. https://www.overseasvotefoundation.org/files/02-08-07_OVF_PR_Post_Election_Survey.doc.

Oxford English Dictionary. 2007. http://www.oed.com/.

Palfrey, Dale Hoyt. 2006a. "Chapala's Mayor-Elect Calls on Expats to Help 'Move the Rock.'" *Guadalajara Reporter,* November 18. http://www.guadalajarareporter .com/chapala.cfm (accessed February 3, 2007).

———. 2006b. "Geographer Tracks Chapala Area Expatriate Migration Trends." *Guadalajara Reporter,* December 9. http://www.guadalajarareporter.com/ chapala.cfm (accessed February 3, 2007).

———. 2006c. "Immigration Targets Wetback Realtors." *Guadalajara Reporter,* January 14. http://www.guadalajarareporter.com/chapala.cfm (accessed February 3, 2007).

———. 2007. "Chapala Government Changes Hands." *Guadalajara Reporter,* January 7. http://www.guadalajarareporter.com/ (accessed February 5, 2007).

Palma Mora, Maria Dolores Monica. 1990. *Veteranos de Guerra Norteamericanos en Guadalajara.* México, D.F.: Instituto Nacional de Antropología e Historia (INAH).

Panagakos, Anastasia, and Heather Horst. 2006. "Return to Cyberia: Technology and the Social Worlds of Transnational Migrants." *Global Networks* 6 (2): 109–124.

Park, Robert, and Ernest Burgess. 1921. *Introduction to the Science of Sociology.* Chicago: University of Chicago Press.

Paterson, Kent. 2008. "Local Dems Gear Up for 2008 U.S. Election." *Banderas News,* April. http://banderasnews.com/0804/vl-globalprimary.htm (accessed June 14, 2008).

Pedelty, Mark. 2004. *Musical Ritual in Mexico City.* Austin: University of Texas Press.

Peirano, Mariza G. S. 1998. "When Anthropology Is at Home." *Annual Review of Anthropology* 27 (October): 105–128.

Population Resource Center. 2002. "Executive Summary: A Demographic Profile of Hispanics in the U.S." http://www.prcdc.org/files/Demographicprofile ofhispanics.pdf (accessed January 11, 2007).

Portal San Miguel. http://www.portalsanmiguel.com.

Portes, Alejandro. 1999. "Conclusion: Towards a New World—The Origins and Effects of Transnational Activities." *Ethnic and Racial Studies* 22 (2): 463–477.

Portes, Alejandro, Carlos Dore-Cabral, and Patricia Landolt, eds. 1997. *The Urban Caribbean: Transition to the New Global Economy.* Baltimore: Johns Hopkins University Press.

Portes, Alejandro, Luis E. Guarnizo, and W. J. Haller. 2002. "Transnational Entrepreneurs: An Alternative Form of Immigrant Economic Adaptation." *American Sociological Review* 67 (April): 278–298.

Portes, Alejandro, Luis E. Guarnizo, and Patricia Landolt. 1999. "The Study of Transnationalism: Pitfalls and Promise of an Emergent Research Field." *Ethnic and Racial Studies* 22 (2): 217–237.

PR *Newswire.* 2004. "Expatriate Vote Could Play Role in Determining Next President." New York (August 31): National Political News Section.

Puente, Theresa. 2001. "8 Million Votes Too Alluring: Mexico Considers Expatriate Rights." *Chicago Tribune,* July 13.

Putnam, Robert D. 2000. *Bowling Alone: The Collapse and Revival of American Community.* New York: Simon & Schuster.

Quinlan, Adriane. 2008. "The Expat Factor." *New Republic,* February 12. http://www.tnr.com/politics/story.html?id=9578d579-4df4-4cf9-bc2b-55f531e73cb1 (accessed April 10, 2008).

Quiñones, Sam. 1996. "The Immigration Debate: Turned Upside Down." *El Andar Magazine,* June. http://www.elandar.com/back/www-june96/andar/feature/feature.htm (accessed July 25, 2005).

———. 2002. "Web Sites Keep Immigrants in Touch." *Houston Chronicle,* August 26. http://www.chron.com/cs/CDA/story.hts/front/1548473 (accessed June 11, 2007).

Rapport, Nigel, and Andrew Dawson. 1998. "Home and Movement: A Polemic." In *Migrants of Identity: Perceptions of Home in a World of Movement,* ed. N. Rapport and A. Dawson, pp. 19–38. Oxford: Berg.

Reeder, R. J. 1998. "Retiree-Attraction Policies for Rural Development." *Agriculture Information Bulletin,* Bulletin AIB741. Washington, D.C.: U.S. Department of Agriculture.

Rehm, Diane. 2007. "U.S. Expatriates in Mexico and Beyond." Transcripts of *The Diane Rehm Show,* American University Radio, WAMU 88.5 FM, November 6.

"Remembering Sept 11, 2001." 2005. *Guadalajara Reporter,* September 17.

"Remittances from U.S. Rise 3.4 Percent." 2007. *The Herald Mexico,* May 2.

Renshon, Stanley A. 2005. *The 50% American: Immigration and National Identity in an Age of Terror.* Washington, D.C.: Georgetown University Press.

Republicans Abroad. http://www.republicansabroad.org.

Richman, Karen. 2005. *Migration and Vodou.* Gainesville: University of Florida Press.

Rieff, David. 1993. *The Exile: Cuba in the Heart of Miami.* New York: Touchstone.

Ritchie, Greg. 2007. "The American Society: We Want You!" *Inside Mexico,* September 28. Retrieved at Inside_Mexico@mail.vresp.com.

Rivage-Seul, Mike. 2006 (August 25). "Report from Palestine." http://www.globaljusticecenter.org/articles/betterworld_palestine.htm (accessed June 4, 2007).

Robertson, Roland. 1990. "Mapping the Global Condition: Globalization as the Central Concept." In *Global Culture: Nation, Globalization, and Modernity,* ed. M. Featherstone, pp. 15–30. Thousand Oaks, Calif.: Sage.

Rodriguez, V., G. Fernandez-Mayoralas, and F. Rojo. 1998. "European Retirees on the Costa del Sol: A Cross-National Comparison." *International Journal of Population Geography* 4 (2): 91–111.

Rose, Jennifer. 1996. "Moving to Mexico's a Breeze." *Mexico Connect.* http://www.mexconnect.com/mex/jrrimmig.html (accessed August 2007).

Rosenau, James. 1990. *Turbulence in World Politics: A Theory of Change and Continuity.* Princeton, N.J.: Princeton University Press.

Rosow, I. 1967. *Social Integration of the Aged.* New York: Free Press.

Roundup (Monthly newsletter of Democrats Abroad Mexico; now titled *Action/Acción*). October 2007. http://www.mexicodemocrats.org (accessed October 17, 2007).

Rowles, G. D., and J. F. Watkinaas. 1993. "Elderly Migration and Development in Small Communities." *Growth and Change* 24 (4): 509–538.

Rubin, Ernest. 1966. "A Statistical Overview of Americans Abroad." *Annals of the American Academy of Political and Social Science* 368 (November): 1–10.

Ruggie, James. 1993. "Territoriality and Beyond: Problematizing Modernity in International Relations." *International Organization* 47 (1): 139–174.

Rumbaut, Rubén. 2003. "Conceptual and Methodological Problems in the Study of the 'Immigrant Second Generation' in the U.S." Paper presented at the Conference on Conceptual and Methodological Developments in the Study of International Migration, Princeton University, May 23–24.

Russell, David W. 2002. "A Banker's Overview of the USA Patriot Act." *The Bullet"iln"* (newsletter of the International Lawyers Network) 2, no. 2 (December 18). http://www.ag-internet.com/bullet_iln_two_two/bose_mckinney .htm (accessed July 1, 2007).

Russell, Ron. 2005. "Ajijic and Lake Chapala: Reply to Post" (January 7). "All Experts" Web site, Mexico Section. http://en.allexperts.com/q/Mexico-82/Ajijic-Lake-Chapala-1.htm.

Salazar Anaya, Delia. 1996. *La Población Extranjera en México,* pp. 99–106. México, D.F.: Instituto Nacional de Antropología e Historia.

"San Miguel Police Learn English." 1991. *Atención,* August 16.

Santos, Diego A. 2007. "Mexico's Fox Blames Racism for Holding Up Immigration Accord." *Houston Chronicle,* October 8. http://www.chron.com/disp/story.mpl/world/5198027.html (accessed October 20, 2007).

SAR (Sons of the American Revolution). 2003. "New Spain Eligibility Guidelines." Mexico Society. http://www.sar.org/mxssar/mxssar-e.htm (accessed July 11, 2007).

Saunders, Robert. 2006. "Denationalized Digerati in the Virtual Near Abroad." *Global Media and Communication* 2 (1): 43–69.

Schachter, Jason. 2006 (November). "Estimation of Emigration from the United States Using International Data Sources." United Nations Secretariat, Department of Economic and Social Affairs. http://unstats.un.org/UNSD/demographic/meetings/egm/migrationegm06/DOC%2019%20ILO.pdf (accessed January 12, 2007).

Schiavo, Fran. 2006a. "See You Later." July 24. http://franschiavo.com/sma/ (accessed January 6, 2007).

———. 2006b. "Too L.A." September 4. http://franschiavo.com/sma/ (accessed January 6, 2007).

Schmidt, Carol. 2006a. "Count of Expats in Town Increases." *Atención,* June 23.

———. 2006b. "Sentencing Not Yet Set in Serial Rape Cases." *Atención,* July 21.

———. 2007a. "Carol's Blog: The 8 New Movie Theaters Opened (Feb 3)." http://www.fallinginlovewithsanmiguel.com/gpage.html (accessed April 4, 2007).

———. 2007b. "Carol's Blog (Feb 15)." http://www.fallinginlovewithsanmiguel.com/gpage.html (accessed July 2007).

———. 2007c. "Carol's Blog (June 22)." http://www.fallinginlovewithsanmiguel.com/gpage.html (accessed July 2007).

Schmidt, Carol, and Norma Hair. 2006. *Falling in Love with San Miguel: Retiring to Mexico on Social Security.* Laredo, Tex.: SalsaVerde Press.

Schnapper, Dominique. 1999. "From the Nation-State to the Transnational World: On the Meaning and Usefulness of Diaspora as a Concept." *Diaspora* 8 (3): 225–254.

Scholte, Jan Arte. 2000. *Critical Introduction to Globalization.* New York: St. Martin's Press.

Schonfeldt-Aultman, Scott Michael. 2004. "White Rhetorics: South African Expatriate Discourse in the United States." Ph.D. diss., Department of Cultural Studies, University of California, Davis.

Scott, James. 1985. *Weapons of the Weak: Everyday Forms of Peasant Resistance.* New Haven, Conn.: Yale University Press.

Secretaría de Hacienda y Crédito Público. 2008. "Resultados Preeliminares de la Encuesta de Percepción entre Ciudadanos Estadounidenses y Canadienses Residentes en México." March 26. México, D.F.: Unidad de Seguros, Pensiones y Seguridad Social.

Senate Special Committee on Aging. 2003a. *America's Pensions: The Next Savings and Loan Crisis?* 108th Cong., 1st sess., October 14.

———. 2003b. *Analyzing Social Security: GAO Weighs the President's Commission's Proposals.* 108th Cong., 1st sess., January 15.

———. 2003c. *In Critical Condition: America's Ailing Health Care System.* 108th Cong., 1st sess., March 10.

———. 2004. *Retirement Planning: Do We Have a Crisis in America?* 108th Cong., 2nd sess., January 27.

Shain, Yossi. 1999. *Marketing the American Creed Abroad: Diasporas in the U.S. and Their Homelands.* Cambridge: Cambridge University Press.

Sheridan, Laura. 2007. "The World's Top Retirement Havens in 2007." *International Living,* September 1. http://www.internationalliving.com/retire/paid/09-01-07-top-heavens.html (accessed October 2, 2007).

Shetterly, Margot. 2006. "Who Are We?" *Inside Mexico,* November, pp. 17–22.

Simmen, Edward T. 1988. *Gringos in Mexico.* Fort Worth: Texas Christian University Press.

Simon, Julian. 1999. *The Economic Consequences of Immigration.* 2nd ed. Ann Arbor: University of Michigan Press.

Smith, Anthony. 1991. *National Identity.* Reno: University of Nevada Press.

Smith, Michael Peter. 2007. "The Two Faces of Transnational Citizenship." *Ethnic and Racial Studies* 30 (6): 1096–1116.

Smith, Michael P., and Luis E. Guarnizo, eds. 1998. *Transnationalism from Below.* New Brunswick, N.J.: Transaction Publishers.

Smith, Robert. C. 1998. "Reflections on the State, Migration, and the Durability and Newness of Transnational Life: Comparative Insights from the Mexican and Italian Cases." In *Soziale Welt: Transnationale Migration,* ed. L. Pries, pp. 198–217. Baden-Baden: Verglagsgesellschaft.

———. 2003. "Migrant Membership as an Instituted Process: Transnationalization, the State and the Extra-territorial Conduct of Mexican Politics." *International Migration Review* 37 (2): 297–343.

———. 2006. *Mexican New York: Transnational Lives of New Migrants.* Berkeley: University of California Press.

"Sobre el articulo en inglés del 23 de diciembre." 2007. *El Charal,* January 6.

Solutions Abroad. http://www.solutionsabroad.com.

Soysal, Yasemin. 1994. *Limits to Citizenship.* Chicago: University of Chicago Press.

———. 2000. "Citizenship and Identity: Living in Diasporas in Post-War Europe." *Ethnic and Racial Studies* 23 (1): 1–15.

Spivak, Gaytri. 1988. "Can the Subaltern Speak?" In *Marxism and the Interpretation of Culture,* ed. Cary Nelson and Larry Grossberg, pp. 271–313. Chicago: University of Illinois Press.

Steger, Manfred B. 2003. *Globalization: A Very Short Introduction.* Oxford: Oxford University Press.

Stephens, Angela. 2006. "Americans, Mexicans Reject Border Fence." World Public Opinion Web site (posted March 28). http://www.worldpublicopinion.org/pipa/articles/brlatinamericara/184.php?nid=&id=&pnt=184&1b=brla (accessed November 12, 2006).

Stepick, Alex, Guillermo Grenier, Max Castro, and Marvin Dunn. 2003. *This Is Our Land: Immigrants and Power in Miami.* Gainesville: University of Florida Press.

Stokes, Eleanore M. 1981. "La Colonia Extranjera." Ph.D. diss., State University of New York at Stony Brook.

———. 1990. "Ethnography of a Social Border: The Case of an American Retirement Community in Mexico." *Journal of Cross Cultural Gerontology* 5, no. 2 (April): 169–182.

Strange, Susan. 1996. *The Retreat of the State.* Cambridge: Cambridge University Press.

Summers, June Nay. 1998. "A Brief History of Ajijic." *Ojo del Lago* (Guadalajara-Lakeside) 14, no. 12 (August). http://www.chapala.com/chapala/ojo/back issues/august_1998.html (accessed January 20, 2007).

Sunil, T. S., Viviana Rojas, and Don Bradley. 2007. "United States' International Retirement Migration: Reasons for Retiring to the Environs of Lake Chapala, Mexico." *Aging and Society* 27, no. 4 (July): 489–510.

"Suppressing the Overseas Vote." 2004. *Guardian Unlimited,* October 25. http://

www.guardian.co.uk/uselections2004/salon/0,14779,1335573,00.html (accessed March 10, 2007).

Suro, Roberto, and Gabriel Escobar. 2006. "Pew Hispanic Center Survey of Mexicans Living in the U.S. on Absentee Voting in Mexican Elections." http://pewhispanic.org/reports/report.php?ReportID=60 (accessed March 11, 2007).

"Surreal Estate." 1981. *Atención,* March 3.

Swarns, Rachel. 2006. "Congressman Criticizes Election of Muslim." *New York Times,* December 21. http://www.nytimes.com/2006/12/21/us/21koran.html?ex=1324357200&en=aaacb563abfea4f2&ei=5088 (accessed August 19, 2007).

Tanner, R. E. S. 1966. "European Leadership in Small Communities in Tanganyika prior to Independence." *Race* 7 (3): 289–302.

Thompson, Kenneth. 2002. "Border Crossings and Diasporic Identities: Media Use and Leisure Practices of an Ethnic Minority." *Qualitative Sociology* 25 (3): 409–418.

Thomson, S. 1997. "Adaptive Sampling in Behavioural Surveys." NIDA *Research Monograph,* 296–319. Rockville, Md.: National Institute of Drug Abuse.

Tilly, Charles. 2007. "Trust Networks in Transnational Migration." *Sociological Forum* 22 (1): 3–24.

Toll, Roger. 2006. "The Mexico They Never Left." *Sky Magazine,* February, pp. 75–77.

Tölölyan, Kachig. 1991. "The Nation-State and Its Others: In Lieu of a Preface." *Diaspora* 1: 3–7.

———. 1996. "Rethinking Diaspora(s): Stateless Power in the Transnational Moment." *Diaspora* 5: 3–36.

Truly, David. 2002. "International Retirement Migration and Tourism along the Lake Chapala Riviera: Developing a Matrix of Retirement Migration Behavior." *Tourism Geographies* 4 (3): 261–281.

———. 2006. "The Lake Chapala Riviera: The Evolution of a Not So American Foreign Community." In *Adventures into Mexico: American Tourism beyond the Border,* ed. Nicholas Bloom, pp. 167–217. Lanham, Md.: Rowman & Littlefield.

Turkle, S. 1996. *Life on the Screen: Identity in the Age of the Internet.* London: Weidenfeld & Nicolson.

UNDP (United Nations Development Program). 2000. "Índice de Desarrollo Humano en México por Municipio." Oficina del Informe sobre Desarrollo Humano en México. http://saul.nueve.com.mx/disco/index.html (accessed April–May 2007).

United Nations Population Division. 2005. World Migration Stock: The 2005 Revision, Population Database. http://esa.un.org/migration/p2k0data.asp (accessed July 1, 2007).

Useem, J., R. H. Useem, and J. Donoghue. 1963. "Men in the Middle of the Third Culture: The Roles of American and Non-Western People in Cross Cultural Administration." *Human Organization* 22 (3): 167–179.

Veblen, Thorstein. 1914. *The Instinct of Workmanship and the State of the Industrial Arts.* New York: Macmillan.

Velázquez Benavides, Eliazar. 2007. "San Miguel de Allende 'For Sale.'" Cuaderno del cronista (29 de Marzo), *Correo Diario del Estado de GTO.* http://www .correo-gto.com.mx/notas.asp?id=19477 (accessed May 1, 2007).

Vertovec, Steven. 2004. "Cheap Calls: The Social Glue of Migrant Transnationalism." *Global Networks* 4 (2): 219–224.

Viruell-Fuentes, Edna. 2006. "'My Heart Is Always There': The Transnational Practices of First-Generation Mexican Immigrant and Second-Generation Mexican American Women." *Identities: Global Studies in Culture and Power* 13 (3): 335–362.

Vogt, W. P. 1999. *Dictionary of Statistics and Methodology: A Nontechnical Guide for the Social Sciences.* London: Sage.

Waldinger, Roger. 2007. "Between Here and There: How Attached Are Latino Immigrants to Their Native Country?" (October 25). Washington, D.C.: Pew Hispanic Center.

Waldinger, Roger, and David Fitzgerald. 2004. "Transnationalism in Question." *American Journal of Sociology* 109 (5): 1177–1195.

Walker, S. Lynne. 2004. "Expatriate Vote a Hot Commodity This Year." *San Diego Union Tribune,* September 13. http://www.signonsandiego.com/news/ mexico/20040913-9999-1n13expat.html (accessed March 4, 2007).

Warner, David C. 1999. *Getting What You Paid For: Extending Medicare to Eligible Beneficiaries in Mexico.* U.S.-Mexican Policy Report No. 10. Lyndon B. Johnson School of Public Affairs. Austin: University of Texas.

Warnes, A. M. 1991. "Migration to and Seasonal Residence in Spain of Northern European Elderly People." *European Journal of Gerontology* 1: 53–60.

"War on Terror: Perspectives." 2001. *Newsweek,* November 5, p. 25.

Weber, Max. 1948. *Essays in Sociology.* Translated by H. H. Gerth and C. Wright Mills. London: Routledge.

"We Have Made Too Many Mistakes in Washington, D.C." 2007. *El Charal* (English Section), January 20.

Weintraub, Sidney. 1993. "The Interplay between Economic and Political Opening in Mexico." *Proceedings of the American Philosophical Society* 137 (1): 64–78.

Welch, Matt. 2007. "Illegal Gringos: An Army of Gray-Hairs, Some of Them Undocumented, Are Changing This Central Mexican Town." *Los Angeles Times* (Opinion Daily), February 20. http://www.latimes.com/news/opinion/la-oew-welch20feb20,0,4125353.story?coll=la-opinion-center (accessed June 10, 2007).

West, Marvin. 2007. "Here and There." *Mexico Connect,* July 7. http://www.mex connect.com/mex_/travel/mwest/westwords0707.html (accessed August 4, 2007).

Wilkins, Mira. 1970. *The Emergence of Multinational Enterprise: American Business Abroad from the Colonial Era to 1914.* Cambridge, Mass.: Harvard University Press.

Wiseman, R. F., and C. C. Roseman. 1979. "A Typology of Elderly Migration Based on the Decision-Making Process." *Economic Geography* 55 (4): 324–337.

"Workers' Remittances to Mexico." 2004. *Business Frontier,* Issue 1. Federal Reserve Bank of Dallas, El Paso Branch. http://www.dallasfed.org/research/busfront/bus0401.html (accessed September 4, 2008).

Wu, Wei. 1999. "Cyberspace and Cultural Identity: A Case Study of Cybercommunity of Chinese Students in the United States." In *Civic Discourse: Intercultural, International, and Global Media,* ed. M. H. Prosser and K. S. Sitaram, pp. 75–90. Stamford, Conn.: Ablex Publishing Corp.

Yasui, Holly. 2005. "Fifty Years of Foreigners in San Miguel de Allende." Historical Project, Center for Global Justice. http://www.globaljusticecenter.org/articles/project_50years.htm (accessed September 28, 2008).

Yelvington, Kevin, ed. 1992. *Trinidad Ethnicity.* Knoxville: University of Tennessee Press.

Zeller, Shawn. 2006. "Journalists Debate Blurry Border." CQ *Weekly: Vantage Point,* April 10, p. 951. http://library.cqpress.com.proxy.lib.muohio.edu/cqweekly/weeklyreport109-000002104477 (accessed March 19, 2007).

INDEX

and host nation, 111, 112–113; and
Mexican immigrants to the United
States, 113, 178–180; and political
parties, 111, 112; and power, 135; and
state, 111–112
Portal San Miguel, 89
Porter, Katherine Anne, 33
postal service. *See* technology
postnationalism, 83–84, 139
power: American immigrants to Mexico
and, 8, 137, 170, 181; exercise of, 8; and
fieldwork, 15; and identity, 170; and
immigration, 7, 22; and political
transnationalism, 135; and privilege,
181; and state, 179; and terminology,
23; and transnationalism, 132–133
privilege: American immigrants to
Mexico and, 8, 73, 134, 136–138, 170,
173, 178–183; exercise of, 8; and identity, 170; and immigration, 22; and
power, 181; and terminology, 23
Protestant church, 31
push/pull framework, 52–53

race: racial makeup of American immigrants to Mexico, 24–25; racial tensions in Mexico, 165
rape, in San Miguel de Allende, 61–62
Red Scare. *See* McCarthyism
remittances, 132, 137, 179
Republicans Abroad: 116–117; and
American immigrants to Mexico, 2;
and American policy, 118–119; and
global primary, 109; and health care,
197; and liberals, 121; lobbying efforts
for census, 47; media coverage of,
122; as representation, 129; and 2004
election, 115, and 2008 election, 120,
143, 144
retirement migration, and American immigrants to Mexico, 29–30, 34, 103,
182, 195–198, 201

Revolution of 1910, 32
Reyes, Silvestre, 204
Rockefeller, Nelson, 150–151
Rotary Club, 10
Rubin, Larry, 115

Salazar, Ana Maria, 115, 118
San Miguel de Allende, Mexico: as
Americanized, 190; American population of, vii–viii, 9, 28, 35–36, 49,
50, 172; American seniors in, 29–30;
biblioteca of, 40; Centro in, 164–165;
community security advisory committee of, 10; and CONAPO index of
marginalization, 194; GDP of, 194–
195; "Golden Age" of, 39–40; history
of settlement of, 39–43; *el jardín,* 187;
and Lake Chapala, 149–150; local reaction to American immigrants, 131,
183–184, 186–188; map of, *4;* media
coverage of, 42; mock election in,
129; Office of International Relations,
127; quality of life in, 194–195; rapes
in, 61–62; real estate in, 41, 193; and
UNDP's human development index,
193–194
Save a Mexican Mutt (SAMM), 68
Schmidt, Carol, 52, 55, 89, 93, 152
Sears and Roebuck, 33
Secretary of Housing and Public Credit
(SHCP), 185
Secure Fence Act of 2006, 204
September 11th, 105, 125, 139, 160–161
Siqueiros, David Alfaro, 39
Slim, Carlos, 185
Smith, Michael Peter, 112–113
snowball sampling, 209n3
"SOB" (south of the border), 148–149
Social Security, 152, 196
Society for the Prevention of Cruelty to
Animals (SPCA), 126
Society for the Protection of Animals, 68

U.S. Census Bureau, 43, 45, 46–47, 103, 198; Census Bureau Overseas Test, 46

U.S. Congress: Americans Abroad Caucus, 119; and representation for American immigrants in Mexico, 130

U.S. Department of Commerce, 45, 46

U.S. Department of Defense, Foreign Voter Assistance Program, 117

U.S. Department of Homeland Security, 105, 106

U.S. Department of the Treasury, 45

U.S. Embassy in Mexico, 43, 45, 117

U.S. Justice Department, 45, 46

U.S.-Mexican border. *See* Mexican-U.S. border

U.S.-Mexican relations. *See* Mexican-U.S. relations

U.S. Senate, Special Committee on Aging, 57

U.S. State Department, 43, 45, 46; Bureau of Consular affairs, 48

Villarreal García, Luis Alberto, 128, 184

Voice over Internet Protocol (VOIP). *See* technology

Waldinger, Roger, 81, 131, 202

Wal-Mart, in Mexico, 35, 38, 41, 56

Warner, David, 104

Western Hemisphere Travel Initiative (WHTI), 46

"white man's burden," 151

Williams, Tennessee, 33

Wilson, Joe, 119

Wright, Sam Bollings, 150

Young Democrats Abroad, 10, 16

Zavala, Carlos Lorenzo, 181–182